# SLOW TRAVEL IN EUROPE

## THE ROUGH GUIDE

First edition

**ROUGH GUIDES**

# Publishing information

This first edition was published in 2024 by Apa Publications Ltd.
7 Bell Yard, London, WC2A 2JR

**Distribution**

*UK, Ireland and Europe*
Apa Publications (UK) Ltd; sales@roughguides.com

*United States and Canada*
Ingram Publisher Services; ips@ingramcontent.com

*Australia and New Zealand*
Booktopia; retailer@booktopia.com.au

*Worldwide*
Apa Publications (UK) Ltd; sales@roughguides.com

**Special Sales, Content Licensing and CoPublishing**
Rough Guides can be purchased in bulk quantities at discounted prices. We can create special editions,
personalised jackets and corporate imprints tailored to your needs. sales@roughguides.com.

roughguides.com

Printed in Czech Republic

A catalogue record for this book is available from the British Library

The publishers and authors have done their best to ensure the accuracy and currency of all the information in
**The Rough Guide to Slow Travel in Europe**, however, they can accept no responsibility for any loss, injury,
or inconvenience sustained by any traveller as a result of information or advice contained in the guide.

# Credits and acknowledgements

**Original concept:** Joanna Reeves
**Editor**: Joanna Reeves
**Head of Publishing**: Sarah Clark
**Picture Editor**: Piotr Kala
**Picture Manager:** Tom Smyth
**Layout**: Pradeep Thapliyal
**Head of DTP and Pre-Press:** Rebeka Davies
**Cartography**: Katie Bennett
**Proofreader:** Siobhan Warwicker
**Indexer:** Penny Phenix
Thanks to all our writers and photographers, credited at the back of the book, for their great ideas,
fine writing and beautiful pictures.

# CONTENTS

# INTRODUCTION

For anyone keen to see the world, there are few more romantic experiences than crossing a continent by rail, as ever-shifting landscapes slip past the windows and new cultures await beyond every station. From traversing the Swiss Alps via the dizzying heights of the Bernina Express, to a stuck-in-time passage from Bucharest to Chişinău on board the last Soviet-era train in service – the journey often is the destination.

And with the climate crisis escalating, trains have become an ever-more attractive option for those wanting to reduce their carbon footprint. It is not only easier than ever to explore Western and Central Europe's capital cities but also to access Eastern Europe and beyond. A flurry of investment has opened up new corners of the continent. Berlin and Stockholm are now connected by sleeper train, and in 2025, the fabled Orient Express returns to the tracks – nearly four decades since the original ceased serving Istanbul in 1977.

It's not, however, just about cutting down on flights. It's about exploring lesser-visited destinations as a driving force for sustainable tourism. It's about travelling outside of peak season to ease pressure on infrastructure. It's about favouring small, independent businesses over big corporations. This is the time of the slow travel resurgence. From a road trip across the Faroe Islands to an Azores-hopping escapade and a nostalgic night train from Belgrade to Bar, our Rough Guides experts have shared their most memorable no-fly adventures in Europe.

Whether you choose to hike through the heart of Transylvania, cycle along disused train tracks from Mostar to Dubrovnik or journey from Albania to North Macedonia through the mystical Accursed Mountains, we have the essential transport details and the best places to stay, eat and shop along the way. Please tag us with any of your own journeys using the hashtag #RGSlowTravel; we'd love to hear from you.

Joanna Reeves
Editor

# YOUR TAILOR-MADE TRIP
## STARTS HERE

**Tailor-made trips and unique adventures crafted by local experts**

Rough Guides has been inspiring travellers with lively and thought-provoking guidebooks for more than 35 years. Now we're linking you up with selected local experts to craft your dream trip. They will put together your perfect itinerary and book it at local rates.

Don't follow the crowd – find your own path.

## HOW ROUGHGUIDES.COM/TRIPS WORKS

**STEP 1**

Pick your dream destination, tell us what you want and submit an enquiry.

**STEP 2**

Fill in a short form to tell your local expert about your dream trip and preferences.

**STEP 3**

Our local expert will craft your tailor-made itinerary. You'll be able to tweak and refine it until you're completely satisfied.

**STEP 4**

Book online with ease, pack your bags and enjoy the trip! Our local expert will be on hand 24/7 while you're on the road.

# BENEFITS OF PLANNING AND BOOKING AT ROUGHGUIDES.COM/TRIPS

## PLAN YOUR ADVENTURE WITH LOCAL EXPERTS

Rough Guides' English-speaking local experts are hand-picked, based on their experience in the travel industry and their impeccable standards of customer service.

## SAVE TIME AND GET ACCESS TO LOCAL KNOWLEDGE

When a local expert plans your trip, you save time and money when you book, even during high season. You won't be charged for using a credit card either.

## MAKE TRAVEL A BREEZE: BOOK WITH PEACE OF MIND

Enjoy stress-free travel when you use Rough Guides' secure online booking platform. All bookings come with a money-back guarantee.

## WHAT DO OTHER TRAVELLERS THINK ABOUT ROUGH GUIDES TRIPS?

# PLAN AND BOOK YOUR TRIP AT ROUGHGUIDES.COM/TRIPS

# UNDER FIVE DAYS

Scenic switchbacks in the Faroes

# FIERY FAROES

## A road trip at the ends of the Earth

There are slow roads, and then there are the buttercup routes of the Faroe Islands. Named after the country's national flower, these often-unpaved stretches meander through mountain valleys, skirting waterfalls and flocks of sheep. A total of thirteen buttercup routes thread through five of the Faroes' eighteen volcanic islands – Vágar, Streymoy, Eysturoy, Borðoy and Suðuroy – taking in abandoned villages, black sand beaches, and views of sea stacks wreathed in mist and myth. Explore this Mid-Atlantic archipelago between Scotland and Iceland on an exhilarating road trip that navigates bridges, undersea roundabouts and wormhole-like mountain tunnels.

# THE JOURNEY

Years-long eruptions from undersea volcanoes spawned this astonishing island group over 55 million years ago. Perhaps that is why they can feel prehistoric, mythical and timeless. Angular moss-covered mountains reach high into the sky, with clouds sitting on their shoulders like a fluffy ermine stole, while sheep graze their treeless slopes. Foam-tipped waves wash the black sand beaches, leaving lacy patterns in their wake. Wherever you go, a sense of awe follows. Though your eyes need to concentrate on winding roads, the powerful views keep trying to steal them away.

Some things to know about the Faroe Islands: there are more sheep living here than people, and there are few trees. It is illegal to use your phone while driving. Many roads are single track only and can be impassable in bad weather. Service stations are stocked with Cadbury chocolate bars – a legacy of the British troops who lived here in World War II – and you should stop and fill up your petrol tank whenever you see one, so you don't get caught without fuel. Oh, and driving here is like nowhere else on Earth.

Fifty years ago, the islands' wool industry was so strong that it was nicknamed 'Faroese gold', and the Tarmac roads were unpaved tracks traversed by haystack-laden wagons. Today, life is changing fast; great hooped rings in glassy fjords give away the location of underwater fish farms – the country's key source of income – and there's a growing openness to inviting international travellers to experience this hidden corner of Europe. Visitors are rewarded with the improbable setting of a tiny village cradled in an ancient caldera, giant boulders larger than houses peppering the slopes of volcanoes, and epic waterfalls pouring down sheer-sided mountains. The

Risin og Kellingin (The Giant and the Witch) sea stacks and Kalsoy island

best souvenir to take home is a humbled appreciation of nature. Typically, visitors fly to Vágar Airport and rent a car, or sail into Tórshavn – the capital of the Faroes on Streymoy – from Denmark or Iceland on a car ferry with their own vehicle. Distances are short so where you base yourself doesn't matter much in terms of itinerary; many choose Tórshavn for its choice of hotels, but you could just as well opt for Gjógv on Eysturoy, Bøur on Vágar or any of the other villages filled with characterful B&Bs across the islands.

## FLOATING LAKES AND REMOTE WATERFALLS

Starting in Vágar, home to the country's airport, the first buttercup route (9.4km) is one of its finest: the road from Sørvágur to Gásadalur and the Múlafossur waterfall. Until 2004, the only way to reach this little village was to hike over the mountain, a sheer wedge of cliff traversed by a hardy postman three times a week on a cairn-marked path. These days, it's far easier via the paved road. En route, stop at the village of Bøur where you can see the sea arch of Drangarnir and the uninhabited island of Tindhólmur, then continue until the road runs out.

Park in Gásadalur and walk to the waterfall for views of frantically flapping puffins, and dark and mysterious offshore islands. As you drive back along the same road past the airport, trace the shores of Sørvágsvatn, also known as the Floating Lake – a nod to the optical illusion that makes it look like the pool of water is hovering above the sea.

A quick drive through the 5km-long Vágatunnilin undersea tunnel takes you to Streymoy for a further three routes. The first is the high road into the capital, Tórshavn, a winding 21km route that skirts Norðradalur village and descends through the mountains to the town. Prepare to encounter something unusual for the Faroe Islands: the humble traffic light. There are just five sets of traffic lights in the entire archipelago, and only one exists outside the capital, on the island of Borðoy. The tiny capital city is all about the harbour: be sure to walk down Gongin, a history-steeped alleyway between *Mikkeller Bar* and *ROKS* restaurant, and swing

## PRACTICAL INFORMATION
**Distance covered:** 150km
**Recommended journey time:** 4–5 days
**Transport details:**
- Smyril Line (www.smyrilline.fo) runs ferries to Tórshavn from Iceland (19hr; Oct–May 1 weekly, June–Sept 2 weekly; one-way from €112 w/bike, €212 w/electric car) and Denmark (36hr; Oct–May 1 weekly, June–Sept 2 weekly; one-way from €156 w/bike, €296 w/electric car).
- Atlantic Airways (www.atlanticairways.com), Scandinavian Airlines (www.sas.com) and Widerøe (www.wideroe.no) offer direct flights to Vágar Airport from Edinburgh, Reykjavík, Paris, Oslo, New York, London and Copenhagen.
- The Faroes' buttercup routes are only accessible by car; rental companies include 62N (www.62n.fo) and Arctic (www.arctic.fo), with offices at Vágar Airport and Tórshavn.

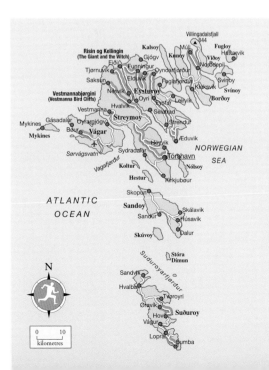

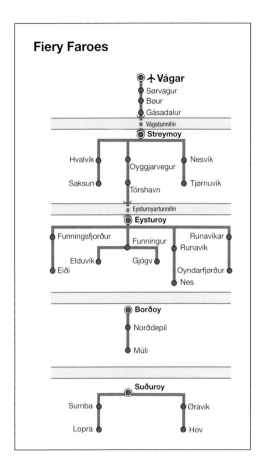

## Fiery Faroes

◎ ✈ **Vágar**
● Sørvagur
● Bøur
● Gásadalur
▪ Vágatunnilin
◎ **Streymoy**
Hvalvík ● ● Nesvík
● Oyggjarvegur
Saksun ● ● Tjørnuvík
● Tórshavn
▪ Eysturoyartunnilin
◎ **Eysturoy**
● Funningsfjørður ● Runavíkar
● Funningur ● Runavík
Elduvík ● ● Gjógv
● Eiði ● Oyndarfjørður
● Nes
◎ **Borðoy**
● Norðdepil
● Múli
◎ **Suðuroy**
Sumba ● ● Øravík
Lopra ● ● Hov

by the former home of the Faroese Parliament, a string of red buildings on a sea-facing promontory.

Streymoy's two other buttercup routes are also captivating. First, from Hvalvík to Saksun, a scenic 11km drive through the long Saksunardalur valley on a single-track road, leading to a cluster of turf-roofed cottages, a church and a sea lagoon. You can walk down to the beach at low tide; as with many hiking routes in the Faroes, fees are often charged (pay by card at the gate) and it's important to keep to the path. In this nation, where sheep roam free all over the mountains, stepping on their pastures is ruinous for local farmers.

The other drive is the 13km route from Nesvík to Tjørnuvík, a village with a renowned surf beach and views of the sea stacks Risin og Kellingin (The Giant and the Witch). According to legend, the giant and his wife were tasked with pulling the Faroe Islands closer to Iceland, but failed to do so in the allotted time, and so were turned to stone as the sun rose. It is also possible to walk to Tjørnuvík from Saksun via a three-hour route along the old mountain trail guided by cairns. Viking graves have been found in the hinterland behind Tjørnuvík, where today sheep graze on the slopes and a population of around fifty people live. The mountains here are so steep that in winter the low-lying sun doesn't manage to rise above them at all.

## THE WORLD'S FIRST UNDERSEA ROUNDABOUT

Six buttercup routes are located on Eysturoy, reached by bridge or from Streymoy via Eysturoyartunnilin, a 11km tunnel burrowed beneath the Tangafjørður strait. Navigating the world's first underwater roundabout is an unique experience, scented with rock and diesel, and illuminated by artistic multicoloured lighting. There's a piece of public art here under the sea, a central installation depicting Faroese people holding hands in a traditional chain dance. Once back on land at Strendur, some of the best driving awaits in the four buttercup routes wiggling across the north of the island. This tangle of roads leads to various destinations: to Eiði, a dinky village draped across a promontory with views of the sea on both sides; to Gjógv, a 200m-long sea-filled gorge flanked by trailheads and cliffs where seabirds wheel in the air; to Elduvík, which also has a beautiful gorge and an alternative view of The Giant and the Witch sea stacks; and finally, via an extraordinary switchback road, to Funningur, a huddle of coloured houses in the cleft of a valley.

Another route wends its way from Eystur to Oyndarfjørður, one of the island's oldest villages. It's possible to hike over the mountains on an old 3km village path to Elduvík from here, which takes around an hour. The view from the summit is expansive: this is where locals stood to watch for pirates in the old days. Look out for the jagged outline of Kalsoy, the island where James Bond was buried in *No Time to Die*. Eysturoy's final route is in the south, a short drive around Lake Toftir on Runt Agnið, ending at Æðuvík's unassuming campsite where pitches overlook the sea.

## THE FAROES' REMOTE REACHES

To complete the set of buttercup routes, head to the far-flung island of Borðoy for perhaps the most romantic of them all. Start in the fjordside village of Norðdepil (note the archipelago's sole traffic light outside Tórshavn), before you dodge the many daft sheep that stand in the middle of the road, taking it slow and steady over the sheep grids and along the gravel tracks, until you reach Múli. This deserted hamlet dates to the fourteenth century and is now a ghost town, last inhabited in 1992. An ageing population and urbanisation are just two of the reasons behind its abandonment.

The final two routes, on Suðuroy, are the remotest of all. To reach them, take the Skopun ferry from Tórshavn to Sandoy and then drive to Suðuroy via the archipelago's newest underwater tunnel, Suðuroyartunnilin, which opened at the end of 2023. While driving around this lesser-visited island, look out for black sand beaches, the sharp cliffs near Lopranseiði – the site of an epic shipwreck rescue in the 1700s – and traditional farming villages tucked into the folds of emerald hills, including the northern settlement of Hvalba. Then it's back to Tórshavn for the ferry home, or Vágar for flights, and back to a reality that doesn't include jaw-dropping mountains, scene-shifting weather, and errant sheep.

There are more sheep than people in the Faroes

Heima í Stovu, an eclectic boutique hotel on Suðuroy

# LIKE A LOCAL

## STAY

**Æduvík Camping** Æduvík, Eysturoy, Faroe Islands 645; www.visiteysturoy.fo. This simple campsite at the southern tip of Eysturoy offers serene sea views and has space for fifteen campervans and five tents. Open April to September or by request. Guest facilities include a kitchen, washing machine and tumble dryer, and a hot tub for rent.

**Gjáargarður Guesthouse** Dalavegur 20, Gjógv, Eysturoy, Faroe Islands 476; www.gjaargardur.fo. Located in the village of Gjógv, with its sheer gorge and network of hiking trails just metres away, this guesthouse has options to suit solo travellers, couples and families, and has a restaurant (useful as tiny Gjógv has few dining options). While it's in a quiet village at the northeastern tip of Eysturoy, it is just an hour's drive from capital city Tórshavn on Streymoy.

**Heima í Stovu** Bíarvegur 89–91, Hvalba, Suðuroy, Faroe Islands 850; www.heimaistovu.fo. This five-bedroom boutique hotel on Suðuroy occupies a 1912-built house and focuses on making guests feel at home. Hike in the mountains, dive into the vintage book collection or sign up for the owners' supper club for an insight into local food and culture.

**The View** Bíggjarvegur 13, Bøur, Faroe Islands 45; www.theview.fo. A collection of four grass-roofed cottages with astonishing vistas in the tiny village of Bøur on Vágar. Mullioned windows frame views of sea stacks and wheeling seabirds. Scandi-chic interiors lend a modern twist to this historical home-style rental.

## EAT

**Fiskastykkið** 12 Úti á Bakka, Sandavágur 360, Vágar; www.fiskastykkid.fo. A century-old former fish-drying terrace sits outside this fish factory-turned-café in Sandavágur, on Vágar. Its accompanying museum tells the story of *klippfisk* (dried salted cod), once a large export product from the islands. On the menu: local fish, soup and home-made cakes. There's also a small handicrafts area and a little museum.

**Heimablíðni** Various; see www.eatlocal.fo for a full and updated list of options. Supper clubs are the order of the day in the Faroe Islands and beat self-catering hands down. For approximately 400–1250kr (£45–145) you can join a blend of islanders and other visitors eating at a traditional farm or Faroese home. Menus vary; expect local lamb or fish, perhaps with a rhubarb-based dessert or cake, plus the chance to find out what it's really like to live here.

**ROKS** Gongin 5, 100 Tórshavn, Streymoy; www.roks.fo. Head chef Poul Andrias Ziska's other restaurant is the remote Michelin-starred *KOKS* in Greenland. Here, at *ROKS* in Tórshavn, you'll find a more relaxed but still exceptional menu including the likes of snow crab, razor clams, sea urchin, blue mussels and, for dessert, rhubarb sorbet, served in stylish surroundings.

## DRINK

**Mikkeller Bar** Gongin 2, 100 Tórshavn, Streymoy; www.mikkeller.com. Danish craft brewery Mikkeller has one of the most welcoming bars in town, with sixteen taps of its own beers set in a 400-year-old turf-roofed house in the heart of Tórshavn. It's simple and welcoming, even to those in hiking boots and windcheaters, and an oasis on a stormy day.

## SHOP

**Guðrun & Guðrun** Niels Finsens Gøta 13, 100 Tórshavn, Streymoy; www.gudrungudrun.com. Nobody goes to the Faroe Islands to shop – although you'd make an exception for Guðrun & Guðrun. Beautiful, eye-wateringly pricey fashion-forward knits of all descriptions can be found in this Tórshavn boutique – take your own piece of 'Faroese gold' home with you.

*Mikkeller Bar*

*Saaremaa Veski*, a windmill restaurant in Kuressaare on Saaremaa island

# ESTONIAN ADVENTURE
## Exploring the west coast by EV

Nobody can challenge Estonia's winning
formula: the symbiosis of clean air,
scant development, dense forest that
cloaks half the country, and fewer
locals than in Leeds. There's hardly a
leafier, quieter, purer playground on the
continent. When Euromonitor brings out
its annual ranking of green destinations,
naturally, Estonia hovers near the top.
This Baltic trip begins in Tallinn, the
2023 European Green Capital, with the
hire of an electric vehicle (EV) or hybrid
car at the ferry terminal, before looping
around old oak forests, solar-powered
communities, wind farms and a dozen
charging stations – all while hugging the
limestone coast. Just four days will do
the trick.

Along Estonia's west coast, long, flat vistas stretch toward island homesteads. Migrating storks and white-tailed eagles nest in the birch trees. Lighthouses offer sweeping Baltic Sea views. The region's potential to soothe is greater than the sum of its parts.

Tallinn, the country's capital, is connected by ferry to Finland and Sweden (to be replaced by zero-emissions craft in 2026). The city's sawtooth coastline lures anyone with a spare hour to its nautical museums and curious Russian relics. Arriving in town by boat, you get a sense of the city's weird and wonderful sensibility right away. To the east is the Russalka Memorial paying homage to the sunken Russian warship *Rusalka*, and beside the port itself: the monolithic stepped amphitheatre, built for the Moscow 1980 Summer Olympics. Before you set off to explore Estonia's limestone coastline, make a pit stop at the Noblessner marina, where preppies in yachting

---

**PRACTICAL INFORMATION**

**Distance covered:** 250km
**Recommended journey time:** 4 days
**Transport details:**

- Tallink Silja (www.tallink.com) runs regular ferries from Helsinki to Tallinn (2hr; daily 7.30am–10.30pm; from €15).
- Finnair (www.finnair.com) offers regular flights between London Heathrow and Helsinki (2hr 50min; from £167).
- Car-hire companies at Helsinki-Vantaan Airport include Green Motion (www.greenmotion.com) and Europcar (www.europcar.co.uk), while Avis (www.avis.com) and Sixt (www.sixt.co.uk) have outlets based at Tallinn's ferry terminal.
- Praamid (www.praamid.ee) ferries connect Virtsu, on the Estonian mainland, and Kuivastu on Muhu island (27min; daily 7.20am–midnight; from €4.20).

---

Sörve Lighthouse on Saaremaa

shoes drink pints of dark Valmiermuiža lager outside *Wambola Surf & Bar*.

## MUD BATHS AND MEDIEVAL CASTLES

The smooth, spartan road leaving Tallinn is impeccably kept, with a shoulder of close-cropped grass and an occasional shiny sign announcing a village centre or a crossing for elk. Even the spruce and aspen forests seem to have arranged themselves in tidy rows, their skinny, towering trunks radiating out from the single carriageway. On the coast around Haapsalu, the roads become narrower, the paving fritters away. The slow, serene town is a far cry from its heyday, two centuries ago, when the busy seaside resort was popular with the Russian aristocracy for its therapeutic mud baths. Today, residents live in clapboard houses on cobbled streets orbiting a medieval turreted castle and the Kultuurimaja, a huge cultural centre built in the 1970s by

0
20
kilometres

N

NAISSAARE
looduspark
Naissaar
Aegna

*Tallinna laht*

**Tallinn**

Väike-
Pakri
Paldiski
Keila
8

LÄÄNEMERI
(BALTIC SEA)

Suur-
Pakri
*Kurkse väin*
Keila
Saue
E67
4

Osmussaar
Rummu

Nova

Riisipere

**Silma**
**looduskaitseala**
9
Turba

4
E67

Tahkuna
looduskaitseala
Lehtma

**Vormsi**
Risti
Palivere
**Märimetsa**
**looduskaitseala**

Kärdla
Sviby

Hari kurk

**Kõpu tuletorn**
(Kõpu Lighthouse)
*Kõpu*
*poolsar*
**Pihla-Kaibaldi**
**looduskaitseala**
Suuremõisa
Rohuküla
**Haapsalu**
Silla
Märjamaa

**Leigri**
**looduskaitseala**
Kalana
Käina
Heltermaa
**Kloostri**
**observation**
**tower**
Laiküla
Valgu
Valgu

**Hiiumaa**
*Väinameri*
**Matsalu**
**rahvuspark**
(Matsalu National Park)
*Matsalu laht*
Vana-
Vigala

Kassari
10
Penijõe
**Lihula**

Emmaste
*Soela väin*
**Muhu**
**Ostrich**
**Farm**
**Muhu**
Virtsu

Koguva
Liiva
Kuivastu
Pärnu-
Jaagupi

Panga
Pank
Leisi
Orissaare

Panga
Angla
Lavassaare
4
E67

Veere
Valjala
5

**Vilsandi**
**rahvuspark**
Mustjala
**Lindi**
**looduskaitseala**
Sindi

Kihelkonna
Putla
**Pärnu**
**Vilsandi**
Kaarma
Tõstamaa
*Pärnu*
*laht*
6

**Papissaare**
Kuusnõmme
Kärla
10
Püha
Uulu
4

Karala
**Kuressaare**
**Saaremaa**
Pöötsi
4

Salme
*Suur*
*katel*
Manilaid
**Luitemaa lka**
**rahvuspark**
Häädemeeste
E67

**Sõrve**
**poolsar**
Abruka
*Liivi laht*
(Gulf of Riga)
**Kihnu**
**Nigula**
**looduskaitseala**

**Viierristi**
**looduskaitseala**
*Kihnu väin*

Sääre

*Kura kurk*
Ainaži
*Salaca*

*Irbes šaurums*
**Ruhnu**
Salacgrīva
**Pāle**

Kolkasrags
4

Mazirbe
**LATVIA**

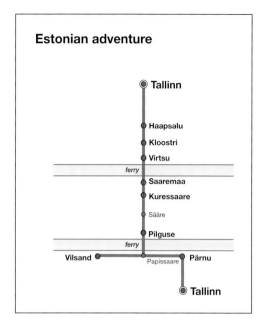

## Estonian adventure

Tallinn
Haapsalu
Kloostri
Virtsu
*ferry*
Saaremaa
Kuressaare
Sääre
Pilguse
*ferry*
Vilsand
Papissaare
Pärnu
Tallinn

modernist master Ado Eigi (1938–2008) and is fit for a great metropolis. Arranged as a series of concrete blocks interspersed with banks of glass, the hub was recently restored and renovated to accommodate galleries of big, bold contemporary art, a rambling hall for live music, a theatre and a cinema with showings every night.

Yet the sea mud is still the thing in Haapsalu. You can take to the waters and sign up for a time-honoured mud wrap at Fra Mare (www.framare.ee), a thalassotherapy centre set back from the surfing beach. The only spa in these parts open continuously since the days when the Romanovs came to be packed in the stuff, it still harvests thick, salty mud from the shore. If there's no time to immerse yourself over a weekend, the facility offers a day pass for treatments and use of the steam bath and saltwater pools, drawn from the surrounding sea and springs.

## A DESOLATE LAND

You can't ignore geography on Estonia's west coast, where rivers flood the grasslands with each tide. Between country roads, raised boardwalks cross the marshlands to ancient bogs so vast they cover a fifth

of the country. Leaving Haapsalu, the road wraps around the Kasari river plain, with the bogs to one side and the Väinameri Sea to the other. Pull over at the Kloostri observation tower and climb the 16m-high structure to take in the scene – and the silence – of nature taking over. Watching the inky water consume the countryside, with only nesting storks for company, makes for a surreal scene.

The ferry terminal is thirty minutes away in Virtsu, and the crossing to Muhu island is barely that – just long enough to snag an open sandwich or sugar-dusted pancake in the canteen-style café. Drive off onto Muhu's open road, beneath open skies, following the trajectory of the sun. Skirting the popular EuroVelo 10 bike route, you'll doubtless spot a cyclist from Scandinavia or Latvia, come to partake of the clean air and clear trails.

Signs of human habitation are scarce here – just the odd farm shop, or a chalky-white church concealed behind a field of tall grass. In the barely there hamlet of Nautse, a dirt track leads to Muhu Ostrich Farm, a thatch-roofed working farm that, in summer, welcomes visitors into its menagerie of ostrich, alpaca, zebra and kangaroo. The animals frolic over the acreage, coming up close to feed from your hand.

## ESTONIA'S WESTERNMOST POINT

A few minutes beyond the appropriately named Eemu windmill, the road reaches the causeway connecting Muhu to Saaremaa. Once on Estonia's largest island, the easy drive to the country's westernmost point belies the epic history of the island, a refuge for Vikings, pirates, shipwreck survivors and, more recently, the Soviets, who marched through during World War II and stayed until the 1980s. Islanders who didn't escape to Sweden were sent to Siberia, drafted or forced to farm vast fields that still supply the area with organic produce, berries and chicken. The fields nudge right up to the restored Old Town of Kuressaare and a scattering of crumbling Soviet-style blocks.

In town, a medieval moated castle gives onto a pretty sailing bay. Summer residents meander from the church gardens to a town square hemmed in by gabled townhouses, now with terraces for wine and local Pihtla beer. *Saaremaa Veski*, a historic windmill restaurant beloved for its seafood salads and smoked-fish sides, is an obvious stop for a festive lunch indoors or out. As far as hotels, go, though, the smart set bypasses Kuressaare's quaint heritage B&Bs in favour of *Pilguse*, a countryside creative residency with artists' studios and family rooms dotted around a restaurant and wild swimming pond.

Before checking in, first make a diversion to beachy Sääre, a spit of land crowned by an iconic lighthouse and home to a makeshift history museum in a whitewashed villa. Pleasure boats tether offshore to either side, and the remnants of wartime bunkers crumble on the pebbly beach. At the weekend, families gather to pick shells from the surf and listen

to live music outside *Sääre Paargu*. Hike around the sandy point, then continue along the secluded coast.

Back at *Pilguse*, an off-grid hideaway restored from a sixteenth-century manor and hospital, mingle with an interesting, mostly Estonian crowd eager to switch off, unplug and gather around organic delicacies sprinkled with foraged herbs. Some come for a writing retreat, others simply for a sauna and a swim. In the warmer months, when the sun barely dips beneath the miles-out horizon, *Pilguse* feels like the end of the Earth. Canoeing into the marshes or reading in a deck chair, you are more likely to be approached by a family of swans or a hairy local pony than other people – though at night you can join the fellow wine-swilling guests, or else hide inside by the fire. If you care to venture out, there's a family berry farm over the road

Elk crossings are ubiquitous in Estonia

Kuressaare Castle on Saaremaa

that makes home-made juniper syrup over an open fire, and conducts tastings in the garage for its small-batch gins.

## A PROTECTED ISLET

The one trip you must make is the crossing to Vilsandi, a speck of land just off Saaremaa's western shore. At low tide you could very well wade across from the grassy point at Kuusnõmme village, or else blag a ride from one of *Pilguse*'s illustrious guests who happen to have a boat at their disposal. Ring ahead (+372 509 2932), however, and you can arrange a lift from the boatman at Papissaare harbour. Either way, you'll arrive at an unspoiled national park pealing with birdsong, swarmed by butterflies and honking with grey seals. Left to flourish by the island's three permanent residents, 32 species of orchid form streaks of purple between the windswept pines.

You can walk across Vilsandi in around an hour – or circle its perimeter via beaches and teetering rocks to the island's lighthouse and lookout tower, both of which you can climb for views across the Baltic Sea towards Gotland. The pair were built to serve passing ships, many of which ran aground, or worse, in the shallow waters. A rescue station perched on the beach nearby was kept busy for a century before its boat was lost, too. Today, it's preserved by a private owner. Plans, now underway, will convert Vilsand's old schoolhouse to an art gallery and hotel with glamping ground (summer only).

Drive the next leg in stages, or power through in a morning. The four-hour route doubles back to the island causeway, over Muhu and back to the mainland, with a break on the ferry for a traditional snack or cup of coffee. The final hour slices off the ragged coast, which makes a detour to the sea all the more exciting.

Veering off-course to the tiny village of Tõstamaa offers the reward of a lonely green forest road and a hiking trail around a hobby farm.

Further along, on a finger of land pointing down into the waves, is the Meremaa marina, a harbour for three or four bobbing sailboats. A modest café punches above its weight serving the likes of sea urchin pasta and wood-fired pizzas – but only in summer, when you can sit on the wooden deck beneath strings of glittering fairy lights.

## A BREEZY SUMMER PLAYGROUND

Now round the bay, past a coastal meadow grazed by cows, to Pärnu, a youthful city on Estonia's western fringes. The medieval stronghold caught on more than a hundred years ago as the nation's summer capital. Its wide, half-empty protected beach is its main calling card – particularly after a long stint of driving. Yet the affluent community at its centre and the knot of commercial streets with their timber-sided storefronts are as charming as old Helsinki or Stockholm. No hotel is more atmospheric than palatial merchant's mansion *Villa Ammende*, its cosy common rooms festooned with painted Art Nouveau detail in elegant colour.

A hub of civilisation in the hinterland of western Estonia, Pärnu is the place to dine out on lobster, listen to jazz (try *Bum-Bum pubi*), or both at once. And then there's the flour-soft beach, minutes from the hotel across acres of green punctuated by quirky outdoor sculptures. Of Estonia's 3780km of coastline, Pärnu has a solid ten: pristine and underused, with jetties on which you can walk out to the depths. The bay isn't known for its restlessness – or its warmth. Normally, kayakers explore the reedy inlets flanking the strand.

The clapboard houses of Haapsalu

But on rockier days, teens drag their rented surfboards and kites to and from the swell, and a scene amasses around the Surf Centre.

The E67 is the route back to Tallinn, a fairly straight shot to the turreted skyline. If there's time, dip into the ancient centre to gaze upon the magnificent onion domes of Alexander Nevsky Cathedral. It's barely ten minutes from the basilica to the capital's ferry terminal, where you can catch one of the frequent crossings to Helsinki. The slow, meditative journey offers a last glimpse of island life and the deep blue vistas that are still relatively unknown.

## LIKE A LOCAL

### STAY

**Pilguse** Jõgela-Pussa, Jõgela, Saaremaa, 93312 Saare maakond; www.pilguse.com. For a slice of pared-back luxury, *Pilguse* is a rural residency hugging the western coastline of Saaremaa. The 90-hectare estate wraps around a 1558-built manor house filled with elegant rooms, a season-led restaurant, and a handful of artist studios, mirror-clad cabins and wooden pods. The wild swimming pond is a treat in summer.

**Villa Ammende** Mere pst 7, Pärnu, 80010 Pärnu maakond; www.ammende.ee. This palatial mansion in Pärnu is an Art Nouveau masterpiece. A room here is more like a suite at a heritage hotel in London, large enough to cartwheel through, and swathed in expensive upholsteries and silk rugs. Beds are hung with diaphanous canopies opening to the wood fire.

### EAT

**Meremaa Resto** Värati küla, 88120 Pärnu maakond; +372 5353 8117. This unassuming little café packs a culinary punch, serving excellent seafood pasta and cheese-blistered wood-fired pizzas. Open only in the

Pilguse, Saaremaa

summer months, when tables are set across a breeze-cooled wooden deck strung with fairy lights.

**Saaremaa Veski** Pärna 19, Kuressaare, 93814 Saare maakond; www.saaremaaveski.ee. Set in an architectural monument of national importance, this windmill restaurant is famed for its seafood and smoked fish. Pick a table inside the rustic dining space or outside in the courtyard.

**Sääre Paargu** Sääre, 93249 Saare County. A beachfront restaurant on the Sääre promontory poking out of Saaremaa's southwestern tip. The menu unsurprisingly is seafood-heavy, with catch of the day and grilled fish a favourite. Tables spill outside onto the lawns, where diners can eat overlooking the sea, often to a soundtrack of live music in summer.

## DRINK

**Bum-Bum pubi** Kuninga 1, Pärnu, 80011 Pärnu maakond; +372 608 0588. A popular jazz bar in Pärnu hosting local musicians and bands. Also offers a menu of traditional food and has a smattering of tables outside.

**Wambola Surf & Bar** Allveelaeva T4, 10415 Tallinn; www.wambola.surf. A watersports centre and bar for sporty types at pier no. 44 and on the minesweeper *Wambola M311*. Tables are scattered across the boat's deck and onto the cobblestoned waterfront. Street food and music after dark, with a buzzy vibe.

## SHOP

**Muhu Ostrich Farm** Nautse, 94728 Saare County, Muhu; www.jaanalind.ee. Muhu Ostrich Farm has a small shop where you can buy all manner of curiosities associated with the world's largest bird: an ostrich feather-duster, giant eggs and all-natural skin products infused with ostrich oil.

**Saaremaa Kadakasiirup** Kadakakoda, Leedri, 93316 Saare maakond; www.saaremaakadakasiirup.ee. Opposite *Pilguse*, this family-run berry farm sells home-made juniper syrup and small-batch gins.

Church of Saint Sava, Belgrade

# MONTENEGRO EXPRESS
## A nostalgic Belgrade-to-Bar trip

Jump aboard the train in Belgrade, fall asleep with the moon casting its glow on the hillside villages and wake up to the sun peeking above the mountains as the train rumbles towards the Adriatic coast. Despite traversing one of Europe's most scenic rail routes, the Montenegro Express is not overtly popular: you're likely to be able to reserve a seat even for a same-day departure, especially in low season. But why hurry? Allow a couple of days to explore the Serbian capital before embarking on the 500km journey through the Balkan heartlands. Enjoy the coastal charms of Bar before heading to capital city Podgorica, an ideal base for exploring the region.

# THE JOURNEY

From the vibrant streets of Belgrade to the coastal charm of Bar, leaving hillside villages, verdant fields, winding rivers, craggy mountains and bird sanctuaries in between, the Montenegro Express captures the essence of the Balkans. The best way to experience the Belgrade-to-Bar route is to take the night train and resist the urge to disembark in the Montenegrin capital, Podgorica. This way, you will also see Lake Skadar, Dalmatia's largest lake, gliding past from the comfort of your berth, moments before the train reaches the Adriatic coastline.

Apart from a scenic feast, this nocturnal voyage offers a nostalgic touch of yesteryear's travel as tickets must be bought in person at the station – no apps or QR codes here.

## SERBIA'S STORIED CAPITAL

Opened in 1976 by the former president of Yugoslavia, Tito, the tracks didn't only serve as a means of transport but also as a symbolic connection between Serbia and Montenegro. The Serbian capital, Belgrade, isn't just an entryway to explore Serbia and the broader Balkans but a fascinating city with a long history. Rooted in antiquity, Belgrade boasts the legacy of the Vinča culture, a prehistoric civilisation that flourished here in the sixth millennium BC. Over the centuries, the city has witnessed the ebb and flow of Roman, Ottoman and Habsburg rule, leaving an indelible mark on its character. Today, Belgrade is an awe-inspiring mix of ancient history, medieval charm and stark concrete architecture from its era as the capital of Yugoslavia.

Travelling through the Balkan heartlands

The main sights include the Church of Saint Sava, Serbia's largest Orthodox church, with a construction span covering much of the twentieth century. Resembling Istanbul's Hagia Sophia, the church's golden domes and exuberant mosaics emanate a sacred aura. Another must-see is the Belgrade Fortress, dating back to 279 BC. Perched at the confluence of the Sava and Danube rivers, the ancient stronghold offers fine views while immersing visitors in centuries of Serbian heritage through its well-preserved fortifications and a military museum. From here, stroll down Knez Mihailova, a bustling pedestrian thoroughfare and protected historic landmark. As one of the city's oldest parts, the street is adorned with beautiful buildings from the late nineteenth and early twentieth centuries.

Yet, perhaps the true magic lies in the simple act of wandering to stumble across everything from traditional tavernas to edgy clubs – a nod to the city's varied restaurant scene. For a taste of Belgrade's bohemian soul, venture to Skadarlija, affectionately dubbed Belgrade's Montmartre. The district pulsates with energy, brimming with bars, art galleries and antique shops. Pull up a chair in one of the area's many restaurants, enjoy a feast of traditional Serbian food – washed down with *rakı* – and soak in the ambience. But when you are ready to leave, make sure you have secured a ticket for the Montenegro Express.

## A NOSTALGIC JOURNEY

For those seeking a touch of retro charm, the Montenegro Express offers more than just a mode of transport. Tickets, starting at €21 for the seasonal day train Tara (running from mid-June to mid-September), must be purchased at the station, adding a nostalgic flair to your travel experience.

Other times, the only option is to take the night train named Lovćen after a Montenegrin mountain. This is the best way to experience the scenery, as the most breathtaking stretch of the route lies towards the end of the line, between Bijelo Polje and Bar in Montenegro. For the overnight option, add around €6 to €20 on top of the basic fare for different sleeping

accommodation, from a shared six-bed couchette to a one-, two- or three-bed sleeper.

The departure point is the newly opened Belgrade Centre Station, also known as Prokop. Don't mistake it for the now-closed Belgrade Main Railway Station, a grand relic near the Sava River. This historic station was built in the 1880s by the Oriental Railway Company as part of the Istanbul–Vienna railway but is now left crumbling in the city centre, its former grandeur still palpable in the facade.

To get to the new train station, take bus number 36, for example, at the central Savski Trg–Slavija stop. The bus runs every forty minutes (daily 4.20am–11.40pm; 50RSD/€0.45). The night train sets off at 8.20pm. For those seeking a peaceful night's rest, book a private sleeper cabin. Use the retro-style handle to roll down the window and let the soft evening breeze flow in as the train embarks on its slow journey through the Serbian countryside.

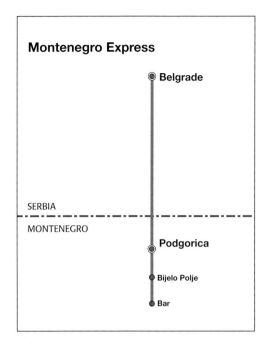

**Montenegro Express**

◉ Belgrade

SERBIA
- - - - - - - - - - - - - - - - - - - - -
MONTENEGRO

◎ Podgorica

● Bijelo Polje

● Bar

As the train rumbles on, passengers are treated to vistas of rolling hills and quaint villages that have witnessed centuries of cultural crossroads. Soon after departure, the sky starts to darken and the air becomes brisk. Fog envelops the landscape, veiling both the moon and the quaint villages that dot the route. Roll up the window, snack on your packed dinner (not all trains on this route have a restaurant car), tuck yourself into bed and let the rhythmic clatter of the train lull you to sleep, only to be briefly interrupted by passport controls at the border.

## BUCOLIC SCENES
As dawn breaks, travellers awaken to a pastel sunrise, revealing the rugged and mountainous terrain of Montenegro. Windows frame awe-inspiring views of the Dinaric Alps and the Tara River Canyon, Europe's deepest gorge. Here, the train slows its pace – perhaps to give passengers time to enjoy the vistas, but probably more likely due to the driver needing to navigate one of the 254 tunnels and 435 bridges, ranging from 200 to 1700 metres in height.

## PRACTICAL INFORMATION
**Distance covered:** 476km
**Recommended journey time:** 4–5 days
**Transport details:**

- Belgrade is accessible by train from a number of European cities, including Vienna and Budapest (from 2025, a new high-speed train will connect the Serbian and Hungarian capitals in 3hr 30min). The Serbian capital is also connected to Budapest by bus services, including FlixBus (6hr; 2 daily; from €21; www.flixbus.com) and Terra Travels (6hr 45min; 1 daily; from €24; www.terratravels.rs); and to Vienna by Lukic Tours (8hr 30min; 1 daily; from €30; www.lukictours.com), Naisturs (6hr 23min; 3 weekly; from €65; www.naisturs.com) and FlixBus (8hr 45min–12hr 25min; 1 daily; from €35).

- Bar is linked to Podgorica by frequent bus services; be sure to print tickets beforehand (1hr 20min; 5–9 daily; €4.50; www.busticket4.me). Trains depart every few hours daily (1hr; from €2.60).

- Airlines such as Lufthansa (www.lufthansa.com), Air Serbia (www.airserbia.com), British Airways (www.britishairways.com), and Wizz Air (www.wizzair.com) operate flights from the likes of Munich, Paris, London and Rome to Belgrade's Nikola Tesla Airport.

- The Belgrade-to-Bar train is Železnice prevoz Crne Gore (ŽPCG); tickets can only be bought at the train station, no online booking (from €24). The Lovcen night service is 10hr (add €6 for a couchette, €15 for a bed in a 3-bed sleeper, €20 for a bed in a 2-bed sleeper); the Tara daytime service is 11hr (mid-June to mid-September; add €3). Whichever train you plan to take, be prepared for delays.

Knez Mihailova, Belgrade

This is a stretch that provides an adrenaline-inducing experience for thrill-seekers and a feast for the eyes for slow-travel enthusiasts. From lofty vantage points, the Morača and Mala Rijeka rivers meander below, while striking viaducts connect the barren, craggy peaks. A standout is the Mala Rijeka Viaduct, located twenty kilometres north of Podgorica. Spanning an impressive 4988 metres, it is also the longest bridge on the Belgrade–Bar railway line.

As the Montenegro Express nudges towards Podgorica, the train begins its descent, offering glimpses of early-rising fishermen casting their lines along the riverbanks. At times, the train stops at small stations with very few passengers hopping on or off. Podgorica, Montenegro's capital, is the country's main transport hub and makes a good base for day-trips. For example, you can visit the beach resort Budva, with its 2000-year-old Old Town, or Kotor and its walled Venetian historic core.

Yet, resist the urge to disembark in Podgorica. Instead, ride the train to its final destination, Bar, for an unforgettable highlight: Lake Skadar, its stunningly blue surface lined with conical hills. The lake's reed canals shelter a multitude of wildlife, making it one of the largest bird reserves in Europe (and also a great day-trip option from Podgorica). The lake is the largest in the Dalmatian Peninsula and home to several endangered species, such as Dalmatian pelicans and pigmy cormorants.

## FINAL DESTINATION

After the train has slowly passed the lake, occasionally clattering over iron bridges, the journey continues through gently undulating coastal hills before reaching its grand finale, the Adriatic coastline. Disembarking at Bar railway station, you'll be struck by the beauty and calmness of the journey. Curiously, the night train doesn't leave passengers drowsy. Quite the opposite: you will emerge revived and ready for adventure.

The pleasant town of Bar is edged by a rocky beach and home to the magnificent ruins of Stari Bar, five kilometres up the hill. The natural drama of its setting is quite staggering – sheer cliffs surround this Old Town on all sides, and tiny farming communities dot the valleys below. For some of the finest views, head to the eleventh-century fortress, from where isolated expanses of mountains and olive groves ripple into the distance. Fragments of pottery found in the area date it as far back as 800 BC, though it wasn't until the sixth century that the Byzantine Empire created what you see today; the destruction also in evidence was caused during the Ottoman resistance battles of the 1870s.

Look out for the thirteenth-century St Nicholas' Franciscan Monastery, splashed with time-faded Byzantine-style frescoes; it was converted to a mosque in 1595. Ottoman additions include a well-preserved Turkish bathhouse possibly dating as far back as the seventeenth century, the 1752-built clock tower and the seventeenth-century aqueduct that was used to transport water from a natural spring three kilometres away (rebuilt after an earthquake in 1979).

From here, it is just an hour's train journey to Podgorica, a city that's well-connected to scenic towns and major travel hubs across the region. However, it's worth lingering in the Montenegrin capital – the newest in Europe, one of the smallest, and quite possibly the least visited. Also, it's quite possibly the only European capital in which the river water looks positively tasty – the city centres on the canyon-like Morača, a fast-flowing turquoise river edged by parkland and spanned by a couple of pedestrian bridges. One of these, the Gazela, dives down below street level, and there are some interesting fortress ruins a little further south at the confluence with the Morača's tributary, the Ribnica. Also worth noting is Gorica Forest Park, which has some scenic walking trails.

Ruins of Stari Bar

# LIKE A LOCAL

## STAY

**Cermeniza Eco Resort & Winery** Boljevići, Virpazar, Montenegro; www.cermeniza.me. A fabulous family-owned base from which to explore Lake Skadar. After kayaking or biking, visit the resort's winery (the family has almost four hundred years of viticultural experience), take a plunge in the scenic swimming pool and savour a dinner prepared from locally sourced ingredients.

**Hayal Boutique Hotel** Ulica Zalazak Sunca, Bar 85000. A 15min drive from central Bar, the seaside spot Utjeha offers a calmer sanctuary to enjoy the Montenegrin seaside. This second-generation family-run hotel has a newly built villa on its private beach, with impeccable views of the Adriatic coast.

**Savamala B&B** Kraljevića Marka 6, Topolica III, Belgrade 11000; www.savamalahotel.rs. Located in the quiet part of Belgrade's popular Savamala district, this eleven-room B&B occupies an early-twentieth-century building decorated with mid-century furniture given a modern spin by local designers. Belgrade's bus station and dozens of bars, cafés and restaurants are within a 10min walk.

**Villa Kovacevic** Ulica Šćepana malog, 85000 Bar; www.villakovacevic.com. A night in this charming Bar-based villa is a homey stay – if your home happens to be located 600m from a string of Mediterranean beaches. A budget-friendly option with a couple of rooms and communal cooking facilities.

Cermeniza Eco Resort & Winery

*Rakija Bar & Shop*, Belgrade

## EAT

**Knjaževa bašta** 55 Ulica Jovana Tomasevica Knjazeva Basta, 85000 Bar. Located next to the botanical garden of King Nikola's Palace, this restaurant pairs international dishes with carefully selected wines sourced from Montenegro, Bosnia and Herzegovina and Croatia.

**Kod Feta** Avda Međedovica 48, Stari Aerodrom, Podgorica; +382 67 444 074. Fetah Mahmutović is a local legend in Podgorica, and his restaurant serves the best *burek* in town, from traditional recipes with meat fillings to sweet varieties topped with chocolate and dusted with sugar.

**Splav Taverna Jakovljević** Ušće 1a, Belgrade 11070; www.splav-tavernajakovljevic.com. Set on an island in the Danube, this family-owned taverna rustles up Serbian feasts loved by locals and visitors alike. Apart from the home-made sausages and local cheeses, the menu includes other Balkan delicacies, such as *ćevapi* (grilled dish of minced meat) and cabbage rolls; all served with a side of serene river views.

## DRINK

**Bajloni** Džordža Vašingtona 55, Belgrade 11000. By day, Belgrade's farmers' markets are the place to pick up local foods, crafts and art. Once or twice a month, after dark they moonlight as open-air clubs. The pick of the bunch, Bajloni is the liveliest and open till midnight.

**Rakija Bar & Shop** Dobračina 5, Belgrade; www. rakiabar.rs. If you've got into the taste of *rakija* (fruit brandy), don't pass by this little Belgrade shop and bar filled with the national spirit. Located near the National Museum of Serbia and the National Theatre, it's a great pit stop for a tipple.

## SHOP

**Makadam** Kosančićev venac 20, Belgrade 11000; www.facebook.com/makadambelgrade. Shop locally made clothes, kitchenware and foodie treats, or sit outside on the terrace and sip on Serbian wine, at this boutique-cum-bistro. Dresses, rugs, candles and cosmetics are all made by Serbian artisans and make great mementos from Belgrade.

# BRITAIN'S REMOTE TIP
## A hike to a lonely Cape Wrath bothy

Bothies hold a near-mythic status for the hiker-traveller adventuring in isolated corners of Scotland. The word originates from the Gaelic *bothán*, which means hut or cabin. Originally used by estate workers, these primitive shelters are typically remote and difficult to reach, often requiring a long stint on foot or even, sometimes, a kayak trip. Bothies dot the land in England and Wales, too, but are predominantly associated with the Scottish Highlands. Shepherds' huts; a free Airbnb; an old pile of bricks — however you view them, they could offer a practical stop on your journey. They could even become the destination, like this one on Britain's northwestern tip.

Cape Wrath, the British mainland's most northwesterly point

# THE JOURNEY

The oldest bothy in Scotland – Corrour, on the National Trust-owned Mar Lodge Estate in Aberdeenshire – dates back to 1877. Today, over one hundred bothies are scattered across the country. These primitive shelters dot the shores of lonely lochs, are tucked into the folds of snow-dusted peaks and sit quietly on deserted beaches. Kearvaig, Scotland's remotest bothy, can be found in the far clutches of Cape Wrath – one of the most inaccessible (and darkly named) corners of the UK. Closer to Iceland than to London, the headland takes its moniker not from stormy seas but from the Norse word *hvarf* ("turning place"), a throwback to the days when Viking warships passed en route to raid the Scottish coast. The British mainland's most northwesterly point – and one of only two capes in the country – is tipped by a Stevenson lighthouse and stands above Clò Mòr, the highest sea cliffs (280m) in Britain and a prime breeding site for guillemots, razorbills, kittiwakes and puffins. On a clear day you'll gaze out to Orkney and the Outer Hebrides. To reach the bothy itself demands a 13km hike. But you've got to get to Cape Wrath first.

## A SCENIC TRAIN RIDE

This journey begins at King's Cross railway station in London. It takes around eight and a half hours to travel to Inverness, and usually involves changing trains at Edinburgh Waverley. The route from Edinburgh to Inverness is characterised by beautiful scenery, best taken in from a window seat (make sure to nap in the first leg of this long trip so as not to miss out). It's a good idea to stay the night in Inverness and catch the bus to Durness the next day. Book a room at *Drumdevan Country House*, which dates back to 1790 and is tucked quietly in the southern fringes of Inverness city centre.

While here, it would be remiss of you not to take in Loch Ness and the thirteenth-century ruined lochside Castle Urquhart, built as a strategic base to guard the Great Glen. The castle was taken by Edward I of England

and later held by Robert the Bruce against Edward III, only to be blown up in 1692 to prevent it from falling to the Jacobites. Alternatively, swing by the Inverness Museum and Art Gallery, filled with treasures from the times of the Picts and Vikings, taxidermy exhibits such as "Felicity" the puma, caught in Cannich in 1980, and an interactive introduction to the Gaelic language. Elsewhere, keen readers shouldn't miss a spell in Leakey's – Scotland's largest secondhand bookshop.

## ON TO DURNESS

The next day, make your way to the Inverness Bus Station to catch the no. 805 bus to Durness. As is the way in these remote parts, services are few and far between. From May until October there is a bus three times a week – Monday, Tuesday and Thursday – all leaving at 2.45pm. Scattered over sheltered sandy coves and grassy clifftops, Durness is the most northwesterly village on the British mainland, straddling the point where the road swings from peat bogs to the fertile limestone machair of the north coast. The village sits above Sango Sands, whose fine beach has made it a modest resort. Beatle John Lennon came here as a teenager on family holidays to stay with his Aunt Lizzie (Elizabeth Parkes) – his memories later went into the song *In My Life*, and he revisited in 1969 with Yoko Ono.

A kilometre east of Durness is Smoo Cave, a gaping hole in a limestone cliff created by the sea and a small burn. Tucked at the end of a narrow cove, the main chamber is accessible via steps from the car park. The much-hyped rock formations are quite impressive and, between April and September, twenty-minute guided tours take visitors into two further caverns; note that advance bookings are not possible and if it has been raining, tours may not run so check in advance (www. smoocavetours.com).

If dark spaces aren't your thing, head to Balnakeil Bay instead, which is stunning in any weather, but especially spectacular when sunny days turn the sea a brilliant Mediterranean turquoise. Despite its remote position, Durness has plenty of accommodation options, such as the elegant *Mackay's Rooms* or no-frills *Aiden House*. After a good night's sleep, it's on to Keoldale via the no.

## PRACTICAL INFORMATION

**Distance covered:** 843km
**Recommended journey time:** 3–4 days
**Transport details:**

- Trains run from London King's Cross to Inverness (8.5hr; 1 hourly; from £110; www.trainline.com). The Caledonian Sleeper leaves London Euston Mon–Fri at 9.15pm (Sun 9am) and arrives at Inverness at 8.45am (seat from £55, classic twin-bunk room from £195; www.sleeper.scot).
- The #805 bus connects Inverness and Durness (2hr 45min; May–Oct 3 weekly; £20 one-way; www.thedurnessbus.com).
- The ferry to Cape Wrath departs from the East Keoldale Pier (10min; May–Oct daily 11am, plus June–Aug 9am; £10 return; 07719 678729, call to confirm sailings).

## Britain's remote tip

◉ London

● Edinburgh

● Inverness

○ Durness

○ Achiemore

○ Cearbhag

○ Cape Wrath

● Kearvaig

806 bus, which departs from the post office. From the East Keoldale Pier, a foot-passenger ferry chugs across the Kyle of Durness estuary. The boat, as described by the employee on the other end of the Durness Bus phone line, is a "law unto itself". In theory, from May until October, two sailings are scheduled every day, one at 9.15am, the other at 12.30pm. But, in reality, the ferryman decides if and when the ferry runs, and it all very much depends on the weather.

## A WIND-WHIPPED HIKE

If you catch the earlier ferry, you'll have the whole morning to tackle the 13km hike to Kearvaig, and the rest of the day to enjoy the stunning surroundings. From the jetty, join the Cape Wrath Trail, a 320km walking trail from Fort William. This section of the long-distance route hugs the coast and offers dramatic views of the cliffs and towering sea stacks lashed into jagged sculptures by the North Atlantic. Seabirds swoop and screech above.

Pack binoculars for the chance to spot golden eagles. Glance down onto the shores below to sight basking seals. If you're lucky, you may glimpse a dolphin or a whale slipping through the foam-tipped waves. Beware, though, the trail is unmarked and the terrain is challenging in places: there are bogs, steep hills and loose rocks. Expect rough, steep climbs at times and uneven stone causeways.

## THE PARPH

When you hit Achiemore, a former crofting community, the trail winds inland. Welcome to the Parph, 277 square kilometres of barren moorland wilderness. The path is studded with chequered sentry boxes, a reminder that the Ministry of Defence (MoD) maintains Garvie Island (An Garbh-eilean) as an air bombing range. When the firing range is in use, access to and use of the bothy is prohibited. To find out when the MoD is in operation (and the bothy therefore out of bounds), check the Mountain Bothies Association website (www.mountainbothies.org.uk).

However, most days you are more likely to only stumble across deer and perhaps a shy pine marten in these parts. After you pass the dinky town of Cearbhag, Kearvaig will spring into sight, a squat whitewashed cottage just steps from a cerulean bay laced by pristine sands. The name Kearvaig derives from the Gaelic "Cearbhaig", a Norse word meaning "bay for galleys", and nods to the bothy's position in a former safe spot for a viking galley to pull ashore.

At first glimpse, the blue-green water and white sand suggest you might be 4000km southwest in the British Virgin Islands. Dramatic cliffs, nearly 300m high, peer down imperiously over the deserted beach. Puffins and great skuas jostle for space on the rocks. Walk away from Kearvaig and gaze back towards the bay for a soul-calming view: a great expanse of wilderness framing the bothy.

## THE BOTHY

Bothies, typically left unlocked and available for anyone to use free of charge, aren't places to come unprepared. The Mountain Bothies Association states: "Bothies are used entirely at users' own risk". Kearvaig has no supplies or sleeping accoutrements and no running water or heating, but there is a river nearby from which you can drink.

Around five kilometres to the west is the headland's 1828-built, 20m-high lighthouse, which shelters a café serving tea and cakes. It looks out onto nothing but the wild surf and, beyond, the Faroe Islands. Other historic sites nearby include the Lloyd's of London

*Mackay's Rooms, Durness*

signal station built in 1894 to track shipping around the cape, and the abandoned crofting settlement of Achiemore. But perhaps the best thing to do is nothing at all. Switch off your phone (there is no signal anyway) and appreciate the isolation. Wake to the sound of the crashing ocean. Pluck up the courage for a dip in the sea. No swimming suit, naturally. There's no one around to see you.

# LIKE A LOCAL

## STAY

**Aiden House** 5 Balvoolich, Durness, Lairg IV27 4PW; www.aidenhouse.co.uk. A lovely croft in the village of Durness, a place where mountains meet sea. This family-run B&B is helmed by Alexandra and Kenny, who love to share their favourite spots with guests.

**Drumdevan Country House** Torbreck Dores, Inverness IV2 6DJ; www.drumdevan.net. Dating back to 1790, this protected Georgian abode offers a slice of country living just 3km from Inverness city centre. The rooms exude faded charm, the pick of the bunch with four-poster beds.

**Mackay's Rooms** A383, Durness, Lairg IV27 4PN; 01971 511202. A seven-room Durness-based B&B in an 1800s stone building, with friendly owners Robbie and Fiona Mackay more than happy to share local tips or prepare picnic lunches.

**Sango Sands Oasis** Sangomore, Durness IV27 4PZ; www.sangosands.com. This flat, spacious campsite spreads over cliffs above the turquoise waters of its namesake, offering the most spectacular views; try and bag a cliff-edge pitch if you can. There's also an on-site breakfast bar selling hot bacon rolls, coffee and the like.

## SHOP

**Leakey's Bookshop** Church St, Inverness IV1 1EY; www.leakeysbookshop.com. A welcoming fire-warmed secondhand bookshop – Scotland's largest – spread across two floors in a converted church. Opened in 1979 by Charles Leakey and later moved into its current location in Greyfriars Free Church, this temple to reading is packed to the rafters with glorious books.

The Ćiro trail weaves through the Bosnian countryside

# CYCLING ČIRO

## Mostar to Dubrovnik in the saddle

There are several ways to travel from the pretty river-threaded town of Mostar in Bosnia and Herzegovina to Dubrovnik on Croatia's southern Dalmatian coast: the 150km journey would take two and a half hours by car and slightly longer via coach. But adventurous cyclists can now test their mettle on the 160km Čiro route, Europe's latest rails-to-trails biking path. It follows a disused Austro-Hungarian railway line and passes through a beautiful swathe of southern Bosnia that travellers rarely see. You can start the route in either Mostar or Dubrovnik, but it's best to strike out from the former, as there are fewer calf-busting upward climbs on the north–south journey.

# THE JOURNEY

On 15 July 1901 a train pulled out of the station in Ragusa, a town on the southern Dalmatian coast that was, at the time, in the domain of the Austro-Hungarian Empire. This was a significant moment in the history of the region: it was the first train in this part of the Balkans, a transport that would shuttle people and goods between Ragusa and the Bosnian town of Mostar, famous for its arched medieval bridge.

Fast forward 116 years and a lot has changed: the seaside city of Ragusa is now called Dubrovnik, changed after the Austro-Hungarian Empire crumbled in the wake of World War I and when Yugoslavia (1918–1992) was created, a country made up of the socialist republics of Bosnia and Herzegovina, Croatia,

Macedonia, Montenegro, Serbia and Slovenia. And the once-celebrated Austro-Hungarian railway line was abandoned in 1976 because communist revolutionary Josip Broz Tito, the Yugoslav strongman and uniter-in-chief deemed it impractical.

## ON THE ROAD

If you're tackling the Ćiro trail from north to south, consider fuelling up with a hearty meal in Mostar before setting off, perhaps some classic Bosnian grilled meat will provide much-needed energy. The beginning of the route is the least remarkable as bikers initially have to share the streets with cars. But after a few kilometres, the road narrows to a single path, flanked by clusters of houses and shops, and eventually sidles up to the emerald-green Neretva River. In the village of Žitomislići, around twenty kilometres south of Mostar, you may want to take a breather at *Neretvanski Gusar*, a bar owned by a charming fellow who likes to go by the name Svabo – Bosnian slang for "The German". Svabo may or may not be able to replenish your water supply but he's a very good enabler and soon enough you'll more than likely be sitting by the river sipping an ice-cold beer.

Back on the bike, the paved pathway continues to follow the slow, meandering Neretva as it flows southward and eventually takes a westward turn toward the Adriatic Sea. The Ćiro trail, however, bids farewell to the river and passes through the village of Šurmanci. In the town square you're likely to find about a dozen tables, babushka-clad women behind them, displaying religious knickknacks, a reminder that the Ćiro trail is a few kilometres from the famed religious pilgrimage site Međugorje, where six children claimed to have seen an apparition of the Virgin in 1981.

The small town of Čapljina, across the river, is a good place to bed down for the night. You may want to take some time to visit Mogorjelo – or what remains of the ruins of the Roman-era villa rustica and fortress. A few kilometres up the opposite side of the Neretva is the picturesque town of Počitelj, which is dominated by a sixteenth-century mosque and minaret, a remnant

Stari Most, Mostar's iconic bridge

**PRACTICAL INFORMATION**

**Distance covered:** 160km
**Recommended journey time:** 3–4 days
**Transport details:**

- There are daily buses between Dubrovnik and Mostar via FlixBus (3hr; www.global. flixbus.com), but they don't have bicycle transport so are only suitable for those hiring bikes. The best option is to use Epic Croatia, which offers bike rentals and transport to Mostar, so that you can cycle the route one-way to Dubrovnik (€20 per mountain bike per day/€30 per e-bike per day, plus €200 for the van which can accommodate up to five people and five bikes; www.epiccroatia.com).

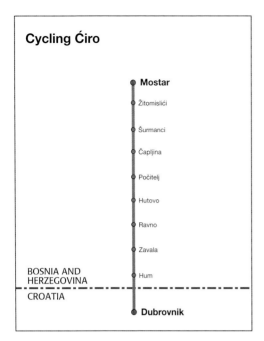

**Cycling Ćiro**

- Mostar
- Žitomislići
- Šurmanci
- Čapljina
- Počitelj
- Hutovo
- Ravno
- Zavala
- Hum

BOSNIA AND HERZEGOVINA

CROATIA

- Dubrovnik

---

ranging from twenty metres in length to five hundred metres. It takes a minute for your eyes to acclimatise to the gloom, and only another for the sudden high-pitched twangs above you: bats. They might be annoyed because your presence has roused them out of their sleep, but they are harmless.

After pushing through all ten tunnels, the trail heads refreshingly downhill for a while, as the now-paved path winds through the village of Hutovo and Hutovo Blato Nature Park, the largest ornithological reserve in Europe. The majestic mountains in the distance, part of the long Dinaric Alps that stretch down the Balkan Peninsula, are pyramid-shaped. Finally, around twenty kilometres later, you'll arrive in the village of Ravno. Stay overnight at *Stanica Ravno*, a train station that's been transformed into a boutique hotel, with a handful of rooms and suites and a tempting wine bar serving up local bottles and grilled steak.

## A COMPLEX HISTORY

In the morning, back in the saddle, stop in the village of Zavala, six kilometres south of Ravno, for a coffee at *Gostinica* – another erstwhile train station that's been reimagined as a restaurant. Inside the dining room, take a look at the framed black-and-white photograph from 1901 of the first train passing through the village; the railway was flanked by hundreds of cheering onlookers. A few kilometres beyond Zavala, you might want to take an hour or so to explore Vjetrenica, a vast network of underground chambers and corridors that is home to over two hundred species of animals and insects, making it one of the most biodiverse caves on the planet.

As you ride along an elevated ridge, Popovo Polje – one of Bosnia's largest valleys – studded with conical mountains, looks majestic in the distance. After a few kilometres, the road signs change from the Roman alphabet to Cyrillic script, and a sign informs you that you're now in Republika Srpska, one of the many quasi-autonomous Bosnian Serb-dominated bubbles sprinkled throughout Bosnia and Herzegovina – a result of the 1995 Dayton Accords that ended the Bosnian War.

---

from the time when this part of Europe belonged to the Ottoman Empire.

## BEWARE OF BLOODY VAMPIRES

The first part of the journey on day two takes cyclists over a string of old iron bridges. Around ten kilometres into the ride, it's time for a choose-your-own-adventure option: turn left on the trail and you'll be able to ride on relatively flat and paved roads until you reach your destination, the village of Ravno. Turn right and you'll be making a climb up a dirt track littered by fist-sized limestone rocks.

The high road may not seem like fun but the views of Svitavsko Lake and the leafy Bosnian countryside are worth the exertion. On this route, note the graffiti sprayed across a limestone cliff on the right-hand side: written in Bosnian, it says, "Beware of bloody vampires". This is more than just random street art, as you'll find out about twenty or so minutes later, when you pedal around a long bend and are faced with a dark tunnel, a nod once again to the fact that you're following an old railway. This is the first of ten tunnels,

About thirty kilometres down the trail, you'll pass through Hum, which was heavily damaged in the Bosnian War of the 1990s. The village looks abandoned but there are still apparently around ten people living here. The last stretch of Bosnia and Herzegovina before the border with Croatia is a gradual, steady uphill climb where you'll pass a deserted and near-ruined train station where cows have moved in. Push on or pause to take a photo. The bovine residents will remain unimpressed either way. You'll also see plenty of signs along the trail warning of landmines – another reminder of the war that took place here – so wander off the path at your own peril.

At the Bosnia–Croatia border, flash your passport at the guard and then it's smooth sailing down a steep paved road where you'll cruise past the original train station in Dubrovnik that saw the first Čiro train make its inaugural journey.

## LIKE A LOCAL

### STAY

**Karmen Apartments** Bandureva ul. 1, 20000, Dubrovnik; www.karmendu.com. Located in the Old Town of Dubrovnik, *Karmen Apartments* is run by a friendly Brit who's lived in town most his adult life.

**Motel Jelčić** Pocitelj bb, 88300, Bosnia and Herzegovina; 387 36 826-165. A basic, no-frills hotel in the town of Čapljina.

**Stanica Ravno** Ravno 88370, Bosnia and Herzegovina; www.stanica-ravno.com. This comfortable, sleek boutique hotel in a converted train station is a fitting place to stay while cycling the Čiro trail.

### EAT & DRINK

**Konoba Hercegovac** Gojka Suska bb, Čapljina 88300, Bosnia and Herzegovina; 387 36 806-849. Strung along the Neretva River in Čapljina, this rustic tavern serves up hearty grilled meat and a decent wine list.

**Neretvanski Gusar** Žitomislići, Mostar, Bosnia and Herzegovina. A good pit stop for liquid refreshments.

**Stanica Ravno** Ravno 88370, Bosnia and Herzegovina; www.stanica-ravno.com. In Ravno, this train station-turned-hotel shelters a lovely wine bar and restaurant dishing up Bosnian and Balkan specialities, such as meat grilled under a *peka*, a bell-like lid that traps heat.

The train crosses the Landwasser Viaduct before disappearing inside a sheer rock face

# FROM PEAK TO PALM
## On board the lofty Bernina Express

The highest railway line in the Alps transports passengers from the glaciers and snow-swept peaks of Switzerland to the historic sights and swaying palms of northern Italy. Look at a map of this region and you'll see a land of high mountains pressed in together, riven with deep gorges and fast-moving little tributaries that flow into major rivers. It appears like an impossible place for a railway line and yet here it is: the cloud-raking Bernina Express, reaching vertiginous heights of almost 2255 metres. This awe-inspiring journey trundles from Chur, Switzerland's oldest town, to quietly charming Tirano, climbing the steepest train tracks in the world en route.

# THE JOURNEY

The Bernina Express is all about the views. Wiggling 144km through pine forests and along ravines, the train climbs to dizzying heights of 2253m where glaciers encrust the peaks. The route links Chur in the Graubünden canton of the Swiss Alps to Tirano, a quiet town in northern Lombardy, rumbling through 55 tunnels and crossing 196 bridges along the way. For the exercises in engineering it took to make this happen, the railway has held UNESCO World Heritage Site status since 2008.

Though it's named the 'Express', this train is by no means speedy. Its sibling service, the Glacier Express, which takes eight hours to travel between Zermatt and St Moritz, has jokingly been referred to as the "slowest express train in the world". Both are fitted with panoramic windows curving up to the ceiling.

But, then again, this is a journey that truly isn't about speed. The beauty of the experience is travelling through – and taking in – those translucent sparkling heights. That said, Tirano is a charming Italian town, Chur is well worth spending a day in, and there are many more opportunities along the way.

## SWISS CHARM

The journey can be taken in either direction, or twinned with the Glacier Express by transferring at the hyper-

The Bernina Express crosses a whopping 196 bridges

## PRACTICAL INFORMATION

**Distance covered:** 144km

**Recommended journey time:** 3–4 days

**Transport details:**

- Zürich connects directly with several mainline European cities, including Berlin, Vienna, Paris and Milan either by high-speed rail or by sleeper. TGV-Lyria operates high-speed trains to Zürich from France (4hr; daily; one-way from €49; www.tgv-lyria.com). From Germany, Deutsche Bahn runs high-speed rail services (9hr; July, Aug & Sept–Dec daily; from €40; www.int.bahn.de) and sleeper trains (12hr; from €50) to Zürich. Visit www.raileurope.com for full options.

- FlixBus (www.flixbus.co.uk) is a low-cost operator with routes to Chur from Milan, Munich, London and Rome.

- SWISS (www.swiss.com), British Airways (www.britishairways.com) and easyJet (www.easyjet.com) offer direct flights to Flughafen Zürich from London, Milan, Amsterdam, Stockholm, Budapest, Madrid, Seoul, Dubai and New York.

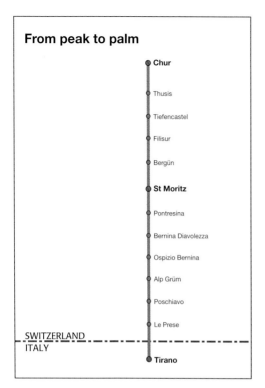

## From peak to palm

- Chur
- Thusis
- Tiefencastel
- Filisur
- Bergün
- **St Moritz**
- Pontresina
- Bernina Diavolezza
- Ospizio Bernina
- Alp Grüm
- Poschiavo
- Le Prese

SWITZERLAND
ITALY

- **Tirano**

luxury resort town of St Moritz. Chur, at the Swiss end of the link, is reputedly the oldest town in the country, with artefacts dating back 5000 years. Its Old Town is wonderfully preserved, with cobbled streets lined by characterful buildings and fluttering flags.

Look out for the little red signs directing visitors to historic sights. The 800-year-old Cathedral of the Assumption of Mary is one of the town's most important buildings and much more Gothically ornate inside than the exterior might lead you to believe. But the independent shops and local restaurants are alluring too. If you stay for the night before a departure, as many do, sample a glass of the locally brewed Calanda beer, named for the massif that looms ever-present over the town.

### SNOWY SCENES

At 8.28am precisely (and additionally at 1.34pm between May and October), the Bernina Express departs Chur for its expedition over the pass. The train trundles west, along the flat and fertile Rhine Valley, with the bare cliffs and forested slopes of the 2805m-high Calanda mountain rising to the north. This part of the journey is gentle and scenic, skirting woodland and tiny villages, slipping between fields and alpine meadows, carpeted in wildflowers come spring.

After Thusis, the topography changes. The route twists south, and the train slips into the narrow Albula gorge. Here, it rattles along the mountainside, crossing bridges with plummeting drops, plunging into the darkness of a tunnel mouth and then emerging in a dazzle of daylight among the treetops. It hugs the escarpment, climbing along crags and passing terraces of fields again. The railway line traces the contours of the Albula river for almost its entire length, from its confluence with the Rhine to its source.

Though the service doesn't stop at Alvaneu, the station is a good landmark to note because not long after it, the train approaches the Landwasser Viaduct. The 142m-long and 65m-high six-arched bridge follows a pronounced curve before disappearing inside a tunnel burrowed into the vertical face of a sheer rock wall. You don't have to fear heights to feel breathless by the experience. The scenery on the other side – rugged ridgelines, rivers opaque with snowmelt, untamed meadows – never gets any less captivating. Caught in the ruck between mountains, are more distant snowy peaks – creeping closer all the time.

Soon, signs of this frosty world start to unfurl beyond the window: flanks of mountains streaked with snow, and thin trails of ice that catch the light. The train pushes into the 6km-long Albula Tunnel at around 1820m and emerges in the Engadin valley. Those boarding at St Moritz, the priciest of the high-end resort towns, will join the journey at this point.

### DIZZYING HEIGHTS

As the train ascends, the landscape becomes more barren, greens mute in hue and then give way to the silver-grey of bare rock. Sharply angled peaks and sweeping ridgelines crowd outside the window.

At Ospizio Bernina, the train reaches its highest point, also the most beautifully stark, as it passes a string of mountain lakes, Lago Bianco the largest among them. In winter, the water's glittering surface might be invisible beneath a thick blanket of snow; in summer, it reflects the deep blue of the sky. Then it's downhill to Alp Grüm, where there's a ten- to twenty-minute stop and a decent little station café. But you might be too busy turning in circles on the platform to take in all angles of the panorama wrapping around you. Fill your lungs with the fresh alpine air and imprint the sight in your memory, as it's back on board for a swooping descent down tight switchbacks with 180-degree curves.

This section of the tracks, poised above the secluded waters of dinky Lago Palü, is enchanting. As the train nudges towards Poschiavo, the view over the valley to the lake gleaming between two hulking massifs seems almost mythic.

## CROSSING BORDERS

Poschiavo is another good option for an overnight stay. This tiny Swiss town, so close to the border, has a distinctly Italian feel and a stay here allows you to immerse yourself in the landscape you've just watched pass by the train window. Disembark at Poschiavo's station, or, for a more adventurous option, hop off at Ospizio Bernina and hike down the historic pack-mule track via Alp Grüm (15km; July–Sept). Icy plunge in glacier-fed Lago Bianco? Optional.

Down the line, at Brusio, the rail zigzags, crosses a bridge, and then descends in a full circle to pass directly beneath that same bridge it just traversed. Shortly after, the line crosses into Italy and then arrives at Tirano. This quiet town is worth spending time in for its restaurants and historic churches.

The Santuario della Madonna di Tirano, crowned by its ornate white bell tower, is believed to have

Snow-carpeted landscapes abound

been built on the instruction of the Virgin Mary, who appeared before a townsperson during a time of plague and advised that doing so would rid the town of the disease.

If you bought a one-way ticket, your options now are to continue on to Lake Como or Milan. Those with a return ticket have a little time to explore before taking the train back into those giddy, glinting heights.

# LIKE A LOCAL

### STAY

**Berggasthaus Battagliahütte** Ambrieschweg 1, 7074 Malix. Ride the gondola from Chur up to this rustic mountain cabin with four simple, cosy guest rooms, then sit beneath the stars on the outdoor terrace with a fondue.

**Bogentrakt** Sennhofstrasse 19a, 7000 Chur; www.bogentrakt.ch. Allegedly once Switzerland's toughest prison but now a contemporary, comfortable and friendly hostel with private rooms, women-only dorms and curtained bunks for privacy and cosiness.

**Ostello del Castello** Via dei Castelli 17, 23037 Tirano SO; www.ostellotirano.it. Set in a restored farmhouse with soul-soothing views of the mountains, this charming family-run hostel has eight guest rooms, all with private bathrooms, and is only 10min from the centre of Tirano.

**Le Stanze del Trenino Rosso** Via S. Carlo, 3, 23037 Tirano SO; www.lestanzedeltreninorosso.it. Inviting family-run B&B in the historic centre of Tirano, with four simple, clean and warm rooms and a spread of local breads, fruit and jams for breakfast.

**Zunfthaus zur Rebleuten** Pfisterpl. 1, 7000 Chur; www.rebleutenchur.ch. In the centre of the Old Town, this quaint, characterful hotel in a 1464 building is small with no lift, but its dinners are renowned.

### EAT & DRINK

**Buendner Stube** Reichsgasse 11, 7000 Chur; www.stern-chur.ch. Sheltered within the *Hotel Stern Chur*, this upscale pine-clad restaurant offers a seasonal menu of regional specialities such as barley soup or *maluns*: grated fried potato with apple compote and alpine cheese.

**Osteria Roncaiola** Via S. Stefano 3, 23037 Tirano SO; www.osteriaroncaiola.it. It's a steep and winding road up, but the views from the *Osteria Roncaiola*'s mountainside perch are astonishing. Food, too, is local and delicious.

**Parravicini Restaurant & Wine Bar** Piazza Parravicini 1, 23037 Tirano SO; www.ristoranteparravicini.it. Behind the rustic exterior is a classy restaurant with vaulted ceilings serving regional Valtellina cuisine. Try the *sciatt*, crisp round buckwheat fritters filled with local cheese.

**Restaurant Drei Bünde** Rabengasse 2, 7000 Chur; www.dreibuende.ch. A friendly tavern tucked away in Chur's Old Town. The food is superb and reasonably priced: the house specialty is steak, the region specialty is *capuns* (meat-filled dumplings wrapped in a chard leaf).

**El Trigo** Viale Italia 51, 23037 Tirano SO. Arrive early for just-baked pastries or breeze in at lunch for fresh pasta handmade by a family team headed by chef Maurizio. Steps from the train station and reasonable prices, too.

### SHOP

**Churer Wochenmarkt** Obere Gasse & Untere Gasse, Chur; www.churer-wochenmarkt.ch. Every Saturday morning from May to October, Chur's weekly farmers' market springs up in the Old Town, colourful stalls groaning beneath the weight of fresh produce from all over Graubünden.

**Muja Glass Design** u. Gasse 28, 7000 Chur; www.muja.ch. Local glassblower Muja works stones picked up on his walks along the Rhine into bottles, which are then filled with local liqueurs, like cherry liqueur.

**Teeladen Chur** Storchengasse 7, 7000 Chur; www.teeladen-chur.ch. Sleek tea shop showcasing Swiss herbal teas among a selection of black and green varieties. The owner is happy to advise, and you can even devise your own unique blend.

Chișinău's grand railway station

# A ride on the last Soviet-era train

Every evening, as dusk sets over Bucharest, a Soviet train is wheeled out of its ramshackle depot. Its passengers board carriages that have changed little over the past half-century, before the train slowly begins its long journey through the night across the outskirts of the former Eastern Bloc. Welcome aboard the Prietenia: the last Soviet-era train still in service, a famous (and somewhat infamous) sleeper connecting the Romanian capital to its Moldovan counterpart Chişinău, one of Europe's least-visited cities. Its journey is 358km in total, taking around thirteen and a half hours – when it arrives on time.

# THE JOURNEY

The Prietenia is slow travel for those who want to experience it as it was decades ago – for better or worse. Riding the ancient rails across countries once firmly behind the Iron Curtain, on an era-appropriate train that makes you forget which century you're in. The train rattles through historic towns, villages and the twilight mountains of these once-brutalised landscapes. The route starts in Bucharest. Like its cognate-named, fellow capital Budapest, the heart of Romania has been greatly revitalised since the collapse of the Soviet Union all those decades ago. One can't so easily say the same for some of its neighbours, including the city you'll wake up in tomorrow morning – so before you start your trip through the past, it's worth exploring this thriving hub for a day or two.

From the immense Palace of Parliament over to the enthralling National Village Museum, across the uneven cobblestones of the Old Town, through historic passages and down into basement bars, Bucharest is ripe for exploration. And when night starts to settle over the city, make your way to the Gara de Nord railway station.

## SUSPENDED IN TIME

The Prietenia (translates to 'Friendship' in Romanian) departs Bucharest at 7.08pm every evening – and as soon as you board, it feels like the clocks have rolled back fifty years. Narrow train corridors clad in fake pine are yellowed by years of stray cigarette smoke. Shuffle your bag to your cabin, before flipping its heavy light switch. Two types of passenger car await, depending on your budget: first-class two-bed sleepers (which can be booked for single occupancy) or second-class four-bed couchettes (which must be shared). The former offers a slice more comfort to those with

Chișinău flea market is packed with Soviet-era trinkets

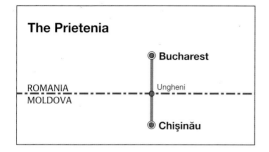

## The Prietenia

Bucharest

ROMANIA
MOLDOVA — Ungheni

Chişinău

**PRACTICAL INFORMATION**
**Distance covered:** 358km
**Recommended journey time:** 4–5 days
**Transport details:**

- The Prietenia runs from Bucharest to Chişinău (12hr; daily 7.08pm; from €25 for bed in four-berth sleeper, €34 in two-berth sleeper, €61 for single-bed sleeper).
- CFR Calatori runs direct trains daily to Bucharest from Budapest (16hr; from €39), Vienna (19hr; from €59) and Sofia (10hr; from €35), plus a direct daily train from Istanbul in the summer months (21hr; from €26). From Chişinău, the only direct international train is back to Bucharest on the Prietenia, but multiple local trains run throughout Moldova.
- Daily buses run to Bucharest from Belgrade (15hr; €50), Sofia (7hr; from €13), Istanbul (11hr; from €38) and Chişinău (10hr; from €30). From Chişinău, daily buses connect to Warsaw (40hr; from €100) and Bucharest (10hr; from €30).
- Multiple airlines fly direct to Bucharest and Chişinău from major European hubs like Istanbul, London, Milan, Vienna, Amsterdam, Paris, Berlin, Prague and Budapest among others.

deeper pockets, though some would argue the latter's cramped quarters are more authentic.

Whichever you choose, it's a veritable time-warp: throwbacks to the height of 1970s Eastern Europe design, no doubt once the era's chicest styles, but now retro-gaudy blends of red faux-velvet and brown leatherette seats, all framed by garish gold curtains. In fact, it's all seen better days, but that's a large part of its charm and you'll become more than familiar with this cinematic colour palette come morning.

As the train rumbles into life, Bucharest's well-preserved skyline slowly gives way to more rural landscapes. In the distance, Romania's saw-toothed Carpathian mountains slip into shadowy silhouettes as the last glimmers of light flicker out.

Night sets in, but it's still too early to sleep – and the rickety seat-bed isn't promising a particularly comfortable one. There's hardly a soul on board this mechanical beast, even though at every turn you expect to bump into a George Smiley-type character from John le Carré's spy stories. The contrast is surreal: eerily quiet and yet deafeningly rattling, especially in the open vestibules that connect each car.

At least people can usually be found in the buffet car. Nothing more than a stark carriage with standing tables, here locals swill cheap Moldovan beers and gorge on plates of hot food. Barrel-voiced chef-servers pop your beer with bread knives, before handing over plates of sausage, eggs and fresh vegetables – all for a few euros.

Once satiated, return to your compartment for the night and out comes the bedding, well worn but clean: flowery bedsheets and pillowcases, accented with a deep-red blanket to complement the room's colour palette. Even though the seat-bed is unsurprisingly uncomfortable, there's something soothing about hunkering down on a sleeper train. The clanking tracks soundtrack your slumber like a metronome, compartments rocking gently as the train nudges into the unknown.

## A RUDE AWAKENING

Sometime in the dark depths of the early morning, expect to be abruptly awoken by the train grinding to a halt at Ungheni, on the Moldovan border. Doors are

slammed open, lights switched on with nary a word of warning. Officials barrel in and, curiously, lift carpets, as if searching for contraband. Immense beams are levered from beneath the train.

Outside, railway workers drag gargantuan tools across the cold metal tracks. Then, a large jolt – upwards rather than forwards – like the train is being lifted. It is being lifted. It's time for the switching of the train's trucks – wheels, base, axles and all – to broader gauges that match Moldova's antiquated, Soviet-era tracks.

This happens on every single Prietenia journey, without fail – simply because it must. The train couldn't move without this changing of the guard rails. And considering the sizeable expense night after night – railway workers, train conductors, replacement trucks – it feels like it would be more economical to just buy a new converting train or possibly replace Moldova's

track network entirely. But that would be half as fun for passengers. The whole shebang takes around an hour. Then the customs officer makes their way around the compartments – searching bags, asking perfunctory questions, stamping passports – before you can finally close the door and switch off the lights. The early morning sun is now creeping through chinks in the curtains, but there is the possibility of a few more hours' shuteye before arriving at your destination.

As dawn breaks, the Moldovan topography starts to reveals itself. It's an ever-shifting land of contrasts: an arid flat expanse peppered with bare vegetation giving way to a gorgeous lake reflecting the rising sun; charming houses climbing neatly up hillsides, followed by blocks of bleak communist-era buildings enclosed within graffiti-covered walls. The view speaks largely to the country's shifting and often-turbulent history over the past century.

## A COLD MORNING IN CHIŞINĂU

Chişinău isn't a particularly pretty city, but its railway station is. Despite its grand Russian-style interiors, it's a remarkably quiet transport hub. Travel across Moldova and beyond is largely by bus, including to the breakaway state of Transnistria.

There's no sugar-coating the fact that Moldova is one of the poorest nations in Europe, and once you leave the opulent train station that becomes obvious. Chişinău still retains its Soviet past's brutalism in its oppressive architecture and rundown streets, but there's a charm to the city, too – from parks to cathedrals, Tsarist houses to modern street art and a bustling café culture. The capital is surrounded by pristine countryside; a mosaic of vineyards nodding to the country's surprising viticultural credentials.

And isn't this the point of slow travel? To experience the best, the worst and the most curious parts of a country – the ones that define a culture far more than any guided tour ever could. To really experience a destination, you must be willing to journey as a local would. Like, say, slipping through time on a lumbering beast of a relic from an era long extinct, where the journey truly is the destination.

# LIKE A LOCAL

### STAY

**Chişinău Hotel** Bulevardul Constantin Negruzzi 7, Chişinău 2001; www.chisinauhotelmoldavia.com. Self-proclaimed as one of the few 'Stalin-style hotels' remaining in Chişinău, this Brutalist building is home to a cluster of basic, affordable rooms.

Cârtureşti Carusel, an opulent bookshop in Bucharest

**Grand Hotel Bucharest** Bulevardul Nicolae Bălcescu 4, Bucureşti 010051; www.grandhotelbucharest.ro. Built during the height of the communist era, this was Bucharest's first skyscraper, though its retro aesthetic has been slightly updated for modern travellers.

**Gregory Hotel** Strada Alexei Şciusev 83/1, Chişinău 2012; www.gregoryhotel.md. Harking back to Chişinău's imperial Russian roots, this family-run boutique hotel has regal rooms, many opening onto grand balconies overlooking the centre.

**Scala Boutique Hotel** Strada C. A. Rosetti 19, Bucureşti 020011; www.scalaboutiquehotel.ro. A former nineteenth-century Romanian physician's house turned boutique hotel in the heart of Bucharest. Rooms have an old-world Parisian style; service is discreet but attentive.

### EAT

**Abel's Wine Bar** Str. Nicolae Tonitza 10, Bucureşti 030113; www.abelswinebar.ro. This independently owned bar serves a careful curation of Romania's finest underrated wines, paired with charcuterie boards showcasing local cheeses and meats.

**Beca's Kitchen** Strada Mihai Eminescu 80, Bucureşti 020081; www.becaskitchen.ro. A small, family-run restaurant located north of Bucharest's city centre. Food is simple, home-made and affordable, with each night's offerings chalked on a blackboard and served by Beca herself.

**La Şezătoare** Strada Alexei Şciusev 51, Chişinău 2012; www.facebook.com/restaurant.lasezatoare. The service might be slow, but the food is authentic and delicious at this old-fashioned, family-owned restaurant in Chişinău. Dishes are simple, hearty Moldovan and Russian fare, served in unassuming traditional surroundings.

## DRINK

**Carpe Diem** Strada Columna 136, Chişinău 2004; www.carpediem.md. Moldova grows more wine grapes per capita than anywhere in the world, and this bar-shop of a family-owned winery is the perfect place to indulge.

## SHOP

**Cărturești Carusel** Strada Lipscani 55, Bucureşti 030033; www.carturesticarusel.ro. The former grand residence of a nineteenth-century banker, this

stunning Bucharest bookshop offers a huge selection of books, including a large variety of Eastern European authors translated into English.

**Dizainăr** Strada Puţul cu Plopi 17, Bucureşti 010177; www.dizainar.com. A collaborative design shop where over fifty Romanian designers exhibit their wares, from arts and crafts through to furniture.

**Moldeco** Bulevardul Moscova 14/1, Chişinău; www.moldeco.md. Originally a humble frame shop, Moldeco evolved first into the best place to discover Moldovan painters and artists, and then into a store selling locally made ceramics, bronze figures, candles, T-shirts and more.

**Vintage Room** Stefan cel Mare si Sfant Boulevard 64, Chişinău 2001; www.instagram.com/vintageroom.md. A hidden, women-owned, Lenin-themed vintage store packed with some of the coolest retro fashion sourced across Eastern Europe. The selection is predominantly women-centric, but they have something for everyone.

# 5-7 DAYS

Olavinlinna, a medieval castle in Savonlinna

# FINNISH LAKELAND
## Kayaking Finland's Lake District

Finland is ten percent water. Every summer, the cities empty and urban-dwellers disappear to one of the country's 188,000 lakes for rest and respite. This adventure starts in Mikkeli, a town in the heart of Finland's Lake District, just three hours from Helsinki by train. From here, hop on a bus to tiny Puumala – the kayaking capital of Lakeland – strung along the shores of glassy Saimaa. Spend a few days paddling around forested islands, swimming in secluded bays and camping in deserted coves. Visit this remote and relatively undiscovered corner of Northern Europe in May, and you're more likely to encounter a Saimaa ringed seal than another person.

Finnish Lakeland is best explored by kayak

## PRACTICAL INFORMATION

**Distance covered:** 140km by canoe

**Recommended journey time:** 7 days

**Transport details:**

- Vr train services run from Helsinki to Mikkeli (2hr 15min; 3–4 daily; £20 one-way; www. vr.fi), and from Jyväskylä to Helsinki (3hr 35min; 38 daily; around £15); buy tickets in advance via the app or at the train station.
- Himanem bus services connect Mikkeli and Puumala (£14; www.tilausliikenne himanen.fi), and Puumala and Jyväskylä (3hr; 3–4 daily; £14); tickets can be purchased by app or at the bus station.
- Soisalon Liikenne Oy connects Mikkeli and Jyväskylä (1hr 20min; 2 daily; £12; www. soisalonliikenne.fi).

# THE JOURNEY

Sipping an espresso on a train served in a little porcelain cup is one of life's small joys. Finns take their coffee seriously, and nowhere is that more evident than on one of the country's long-distance trains pulling out of Helsinki. The server jabs drink orders into the till while chatting with regulars: they're used to travelling on this double-decker red train that meanders into Finland's wild frontier, skirting Russia's far western border.

Finland is a long, narrow country, peppered with an estimated 188,000 lakes. Journeying from north to south can take the whole day and the restaurant car is prepared for hungry passengers: creamy servings of mashed potato, rosti, roast vegetable tarts and lingonberry jam are dished up, filling the carriage with a sweet berry scent. In summer, rain often slashes against the window. Finland's weather can't easily be outrun, even by a streaking cherry-hued train.

And yet come June, urban-dwelling Finns flee to their *mökki*, lakeside cabins typically built from local wood, extended over time and passed down from generation to generation. A couple of uncluttered weeks is spent with friends and family, waking with refreshing morning swims before the sun creeps above the bottle-green conifers.

## FINLAND'S LAKES BY KAYAK

A slow sojourn around Finland's labyrinth of islands, inlets and bays might not replicate the raucous nights of a Finnish family get-together, but a break in nature is sure to reset your buttons.

The air is noticeably cleaner when you step off the train in Mikkeli. It becomes fresher the deeper you travel into the Lake District as trees outnumber people and lakes replace houses. Strung along the shores of Saimaa – Finland's largest lake – Puumala is the unofficial kayak capital of Lakeland, though you could easily start your journey in any one of the other waterside towns: Savonlinna, Joensuu or Koli.

Visit in the summer (June to early August) when fewer hours of darkness means more time to peacefully drift through the water in an ethereal half-light.

There are more kayak-rental places in Lakeland than you can shake an oar at. Saimaa Canoeing (www.saimaacanoeing.fi) can help plan self-guided excursions and provide the gear and route maps to make it happen. Plus, the team's recipe for the only four ingredients you need in life is compelling: "Suomi, Saimaa, Saari and Sauna" (Finland, Saimaa, Islands and Sauna). The archipelago is blessed with *jokaisenoikeudet*, or the freedom to roam, which grants visitors permission to pitch a tent anywhere. The rules are simple: no fires are allowed outside of designated areas and be sure to take home anything you bring.

It's time to pack the kayak with tents and a stash of food to last a couple of days, but first, a Finnish breakfast of strong black coffee and *karjalanpiirakka*. Karelian pies are the dream endurance food: rice porridge wrapped in rye pastry and then baked, served with an egg whipped into butter, which melts over the pie.

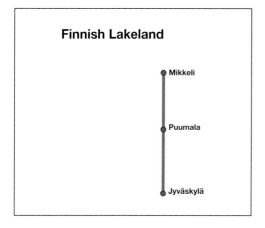

**Finnish Lakeland**

● Mikkeli

● Puumala

● Jyväskylä

## KAYAKING KATOSSELKÄ

The Katosselkä route traces the rocky contours of Viljakansaari, a large tree-cloaked island adrift in the east of Lake Saimaa. The first day is an arm-strengthening 19km paddle towards Sopalan kämppä, a remote no-frills hut with bunk beds, a drinking water well and a sauna. For a back-to-nature experience, simply pull up on the shore and pitch a tent. After a day gliding through cragged inlets and calling at islets ground down by glacial ice, a sweat in the sauna followed by plunging off the wooden jetty into the cool water is the perfect tonic for aching limbs.

Dinners of freshly caught fish and garlic-laden chanterelles (mushrooms), mopped up with a tranche of bread, are eaten on the little beach overlooking the pink-streaked sky. The natural larder of the archipelago's forests and lakes is ripe for foraging. In August, blueberries can be plucked from the shrubs to fuel day hikes into the hills. Look out, too, for clumps of white fungi in moist ground. Finns love to eat chanterelles cooked in dill-spiked cream and served with pancakes. However, when you're lakeside with limited tools, they're also delicious cooked gently in butter over a fire.

## SEALS AND SAUNAS

The second day of the Katosselkä trail is the longest in distance (29km), but it's such a slow, serene paddle around the lake to Latukan kämppä, an unassuming log cabin and sauna peeking out from a spruce grove, that the biggest challenge is deciding which cove to take a dip in. You might encounter some traffic: a lone kayaker or perhaps an endangered Saimaa ringed seal endemic to these waters, but otherwise, you're off the beaten track. Back in Puumala, reward your exertions with a cold glass of *lonkero,* a traditional Finnish drink of gin and sparkling grapefruit soda. If you have a few extra days, hike into the backcountry. If you didn't spot any on the water, then the 13km ringed seal trail takes you close to these elusive creatures, as well as a few secret swimming spots.

## WANHA WITONEN

A final kayaking adventure awaits. This time it's along the 75km Wanha Witonen canoe trail, a few miles north of the city of Jyväskylä, a short bus ride from Puumala. The route isn't as off-grid as around Lake Saimaa, but its sights are no less epic. An eleven-hour paddle passes the UNESCO-protected Petäjävesi Old Church and steep grey cliffs that plunge into the water. No stockpiling food here: lunch awaits at the rest stop of *Kievari Rantapirtti.* The trip makes time for a restorative dinner and an overnight stay at the *Jämsän Lomamökit.* It's an out-and-back route, and the second leg is best fuelled by a hearty breakfast of cep (porcini) pancakes. Back in Jyväskylä, it's time to board the train back to Helsinki.

# LIKE A LOCAL

## STAY & EAT

**Jämsän Lomamökit** Asemakatu 2, 42100 Jämsä; www.jamsangasthaus.fi. A cosy hotel hugging Lake Toivasjärvi, with a sauna, fire-warmed lounge and comfortable rooms; also the option to rent a cabin.

**Kievari Rantapirtti** Petäjävedentie 448, 42440 Koskenpää; www.kievarirantapirtti.com. On the shores of Salosvesi, *Kievari Rantapirtti* is a no-frills lodge and restaurant serving Finnish food, with a focus on local game. There's a campsite plus rooms and cabins.

The Wanha Witonen canoe trail passes the Petäjävesi Old Church

Explore the Wachau Valley by riverboat

# DANUBE RIVER CRUISE
## Austria's Wachau Valley by boat

The fabled Danube, which meanders into Lower Austria from the west near Ybbs and wiggles east into Slovakia near the capital Bratislava, carves a picturesque path through the province's vine-combed hills and neat fields. Austria's most spectacular section of the river is between Krems an der Donau and Melk, known as the Wachau Valley – a UNESCO World Heritage Site for its harmonious blend of natural and cultural beauty. From glorious Vienna, travel through the river-threaded valley past a mosaic of vineyards, forested slopes, time-worn villages and imposing fortresses; disembarking at gilded abbeys, medieval castles and wine cellars along the way.

Views from Melk's Benedictine abbey

## THE JOURNEY

This Danube adventure begins in Vienna. From awe-inspiring architecture to classical music and rich chocolate torte, Austria's capital is steeped in decadence. One of the city's most iconic buildings is the vast Rococo Schönbrunn Palace, with over 1400 lavishly decorated rooms and huge gardens sheltering a maze, an orangery, a huge greenhouse and even a zoo. If you're short on time, the Hofburg palace is more central but just as immense: a highly ornate edifice packed with imperial importance. Skip the rather dull Kaiserappartements in favour of Schatzkammer, where you'll see some of the finest medieval craftsmanship

and jewellery in Europe, including relics of the Holy Roman Empire and the Habsburg crown jewels. On the north side of the Hofburg, the imperial stables shelter the Lipizzaner horses of the Spanish Riding School, known for their extraordinary dressage performances. Catch a morning exercise session or join a guided tour for a glimpse of these majestic creatures in action; alternatively, peek in at the horses in their stalls through the glass windows on Reitschulgasse.

Of all Vienna's cultural riches, the Kunsthistorisches Museum steals the limelight. One of the world's greatest collections of Old Masters, it is filled with an unrivalled curation of sixteenth-century paintings by Brueghel the Elder; other standouts include the Peter Paul Rubens collection and works by Vermeer and Caravaggio. And of course you can't visit Vienna without soaking up its historic café culture; one of the city's finest coffeehouses is the nineteenth-century *Demel*, where you can see chefs whipping up *Kaiserschmarrn* (fluffy shredded pancakes).

It is then time to board the *Riverside Mozart*, a beautifully designed vessel with the feel of a luxury hotel. As the boat slips away from the dock, the hum of the city is whipped away on the river breeze, its crowded skyline giving way to uncluttered riverbanks. Austrian specialities made with local, seasonal ingredients are served in the glass-sided restaurant as the sky darkens beyond. Each of the 124 elegant suites is fitted with sliding glass doors, best nudged open for a serene soundtrack of water slooshing against the hull.

Wake to breakfast served with soul-soothing views of the riverbanks slipping by as the boat slowly nudges towards Bratislava, the pace as unhurried as the tide that shapes the ever-shifting Danube.

## PRACTICAL INFORMATION

**Distance covered:** 150km

**Recommended journey time:** 5 days

**Transport details:**

- The Köln–Vienna sleeper (13hr; from £30; www.bahn.de) is the easiest way to reach Austria by train; pick from cabins or couchettes. From London, connect via Brussels on the Eurostar (www.eurostar.com); the entire trip, from London to Vienna, takes around 20hr.

- The Eurail Austria Pass allows unlimited travel on Austrian Railways; available for 3–8 days travel within one month (www.eurail.com).

- For a similar cruise along the Danube, one option is the Highlights of the Wachau: Vienna to Vienna, with prices from £2126 per person (www.riverside-cruises.com). Riverside Cruises also offers other European cruises; check the website for details.

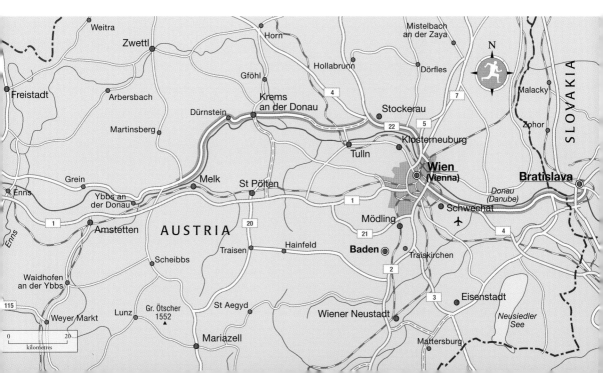

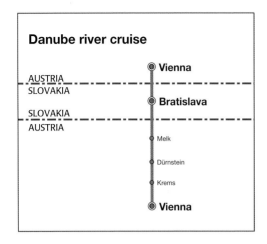

## Danube river cruise

| AUSTRIA | ◉ **Vienna** |
|---------|------|
| SLOVAKIA | |
| SLOVAKIA | ◉ **Bratislava** |
| AUSTRIA | |
| | ◉ Melk |
| | ◉ Dürnstein |
| | ◉ Krems |
| | ◉ **Vienna** |

Most SNP in Bratislava

## BRATISLAVA: A STORIED PAST

Slovakia's capital since the country gained independence in 1993, Bratislava wears its history on its sleeve: its storied past etched across the old stones of its medieval and Gothic core and written into the bleak facades of its communist-era blocks. Pick up a *Bratislavský rožok* (walnut-filled croissant) to fuel wanderings around Baroque palaces masterminded by Hungarian nobles, before a visit to the city's hilltop castle to revel in its Renaissance glory. For art, Nedbalka gallery showcases nineteenth- and twentieth-century works by Slovak artists across five floors. If time allows, grab a pint of *Bratislavský meštiansky pivovar* at one of the many pavement bars dotting the centre. Before returning to the boat, pick up a sweet reminder of your trip at Cera Mel, an independent shop dedicated to local, handmade honey-related products.

Back on board the *Mozart*, make a swift diversion to the laidback lounge for an expertly mixed cocktail. Huge swathes of glass frame fine views of Bratislava's retreating back. Overnight, the vessel weaves its way towards the Wachau Valley, a tapestry of tiny hamlets, vineyards and ancient fortresses stitched together by old stone walls. Austria's most dramatic stretch of the Danube greets passengers through the ship's windows when morning announces itself with its golden embrace.

## MARVELLOUS MELK

There are few finer sights than Melk's Benedictine abbey, teetering atop a rocky outcrop. Disembarking from the *Mozart*, a short walk brings you to the fairy-tale monastery church. Even closer, it's a feast for the eyes: a butter-yellow beauty framed by twin spires and crowned by a high octagonal dome. The interior is a riot of Baroque extravagance: plump cherubs, elaborate twirls and acres of gleaming faux marble. The high-altar painting depicting St Peter and St Paul is by Peter Widerin, while the ceiling frescoes are mostly by Johann Michael Rottmayr. Originally, the Babenbergs built a castle on the grounds, which was gifted to Benedictine monks in 1089, who converted

it into a fortified abbey. Though fire destroyed the original, the Baroque beauty seen today was built between 1702 and 1738. There is a stunning *bibliothek* (library) and *marmorsaal* (marble hall), both adorned with showstopping *trompe-l'œ* ceilings by Paul Troger.

After a morning wandering the complex, amble through the small town. If the weather is warm, a barbecued lunch is served on the *Mozart*'s deck. The boat remains moored until midnight before continuing onto Dürnstein, so the afternoon is free to pass as you please – a swim in the pool, a massage treatment or perhaps just reading on a lounger as a gentle breeze dances across your shoulders.

## DÜRNSTEIN

Early in the morning, the sun creeping above the vine-striped slopes pressed tightly in on the Danube, the boat noses towards its next stop: Dürnstein, a dinky town hooked around a bend in the river. Pretty sixteenth-century houses line the narrow streets, sitting in the shadow of the carefully restored Chorherrenstift. A landmark blue tower spirals from the former Augustinian monastery dating to 1410; the Baroque masterpiece before you today is the result of an eighteenth-century makeover helmed by Josef Munggenast. Look up to see ceiling frescoes and altar paintings by Kremser Schmidt.

A short calf-busting hike leads to the ruins of Kuenringerburg, a hilltop castle where Richard the Lionheart was imprisoned during the Third Crusade. His crime? Throwing shade at the duke of Austria, Leopold V, who did not take kindly to being insulted. Richard tried to avoid punishment by travelling in disguise through Austria en route home from the Holy Lands, but was caught. His freedom came at a price: payment of an enormous ransom of 35,000kg of silver

The foliage-filled *Palmenhaus* in Vienna

(which partly funded the building of Wiener Neustadt). As you return to the cruise liner, expect to be caught up in a sea of hikers and cyclists sweeping along the riverside path. Many fit types walk or bike the Wachau Valley, picnicking like a local along the way.

## KREMS

The final stop on the river cruise before returning to Vienna is Krems. The gateway town to the Wachau is the place to try the bounty of the vines that climb the slopes of the riverbanks. Try glasses of excellent Grüner Veltliner and Riesling in quaint wine cellars or bustling outdoor bars, before feasting on regional delicacies that are making a name for Krems as an emerging foodie destination. There's one fruit that's been grown in the valley for over 4000 years: apricots. They are blended into everything from brandies to sweet treats, and you can even spend a day with farmers in a local orchard learning about cultivation and harvesting methods.

Elsewhere are cultural museums, cool churches and leafy parks, plus plenty of restaurants and bars to while away the days. Don't miss Landesgalerie NÖ, the latest addition to the Kunstmeile or Art Mile. This statement edifice in grey aluminium tiles looms over the Museumsplatz like a futuristic spacecraft. Inside, ever-changing exhibitions showcase ahead-of-the-curve modern art and large-scale installations. Another must-see is Forum Frohner, housed in a former Minorite monastery and named after the artist Adolf Frohner. It has an impressive programme of conceptual work, both Austrian and international.

From Krems, the *Mozart* wends its way back to Vienna, offering passengers a final chance to embrace the dreamiest aspect of river cruising: watching the scenery sweep by as you drift along the water.

## LIKE A LOCAL

### STAY

**Benediktushaus im Schottenstift** Freyung 6A, 1010 Wien; www.benediktushaus.at. A tranquil Benedictine abbey guesthouse free from the noise of modern life (no TVs, though wi-fi is available). Excellent location on Freyung square, near *Café Central*.

**Hotel KUNSThof** Mühlfeldgasse 13, 1020 Wien; www.hotelkunsthof.at. Close to the retro Prater fairground, the family-run *Kunsthof* is a traditionally styled bolthole hung with eye-catching contemporary art. The vine-entwined courtyard is a peaceful spot.

**Magdas** Ungargasse 38, 1030 Wien; www.magdas-hotel.at. Located between the Stadtpark and Belvedere Palace (home to Klimt's *The Kiss*), this budget hotel is for travellers with a conscience — the former priest's residence is staffed by refugees; rooms are filled with vintage finds; and the café serves local, organic cuisine.

### EAT & DRINK

**Bratislava Flagship** Námestie SNP 8. A theatre turned restaurant-brewpub serving traditional Slovak fare and house-brewed beers.

**Palmenhaus** Burggarten 1, 1010 Wien. Grab a bite to eat at Vienna's *Palmenhaus*, a greenhouse-turned-restaurant filled with foliage; in summer people throng the outside terrace overlooking Burggarten park.

**Reštaurácia Divný Janko** Jozefská 2991/2. A beautiful Bratislava restaurant with flaking plaster walls and original stone arches, serving Slovakian specialities in a convivial environment.

### SHOP

**Café L'Aura & Antik art shop** Rudnayovo námestie 4552/4. A cosy Bratislava café set in a string of exposed-brick cavernous spaces illuminated by chandeliers and scattered with one-off antiques, which you can take home with you (at a price).

**Dobrý trh** Panenská, 811 03 Bratislava; www.facebook.com/DobryTrh. Outdoor market held only a few times a year, but a great opportunity to try home-made food from Slovakian producers and buy artisanal goods from local makers. The city's cultural centres, galleries and bookstores open their doors and run fun events as part of the occasion.

# SUSTAINABLE SLOVENIA
## An Alps-to-Adriatic sojourn

Within compact Slovenia, journeys can be both short and slow. Famously, this is where you can ski on the alpine slopes in the morning and swim in the Adriatic after lunch. This week-long itinerary takes in the best of the country: the riverside city of Maribor, lively capital Ljubljana, fairy-tale Lake Bled, snow-dusted Triglav and, finally, the Adriatic coast. Everything can be reached by train or bike – the transport of choice for sustainable travellers and local adventure outfit GoodTrail. This Slovenia-based trailblazer in two-wheeled travel is the driving force behind the Trans Dinarica cycle route that runs through former Yugoslavia to Albania.

# THE JOURNEY

Slovenia, wedged between the Alps and the Adriatic, might be tiny but what it lacks in size, it makes up for in diversity. Imperious limestone mountains cradle sparkling lakes, historic coastal resorts stud a craggy coastline. Add to the mix handsome Baroque towns, sweeping vineyards, theatrical castles and enchanting wayside villages, and it's clear to see why this nation of just two million people packs a mighty punch. But it is Slovenia's status as one of Europe's most environmentally sound countries that really sets it apart, something that becomes startlingly obvious the further you explore. Slovenia's eco-credentials are impeccable, its pristine landscapes perfectly in keeping with a strong commitment to sustainable tourism. The 2016 European Green Capital, Ljubljana was the first city in Europe to pioneer a zero-waste programme, while large parts are now pedestrianised. Look out for the Slovenia Green mark at accommodations, parks, attractions, restaurants and beaches.

## SLOVENIA'S SECOND CITY

Verdant parks and car-free streets typify Slovenia's second city, Maribor. An hour by train from Graz, the capital of Lower Styria feels very close to Central Europe. Its Baroque castle, Renaissance town hall and predominantly Gothic cathedral date back to medieval times – even the Plague Column, centrepiecing the pretty main square of Glavni trg, is stunningly Baroque, crafted from white marble in the 1740s. Other sights are more hidden. On the river, by the Judgement Tower associated with witch trials, the Woman's Bench was created by home-grown contemporary sculptor Metka Kavčič to tell the story of the Inquisition against "witches" in Maribor in the Late Middle Ages. It's part of a city-wide series of public benches created by artists, designers, authors and other creatives to examine elements of urban history, installed in quiet spots for a relaxed ponder. The renovated promenade is one of several recommended cycle routes around

View over red-roofed Ljubljana

## PRACTICAL INFORMATION

**Distance covered:** 355km

**Recommended journey time:** 4–5 days

**Transport details:**

- Slovenian Railways runs a network of national train services, including from Maribor to Ljubljana (2hr; 8 daily; from €12; www.eshop.sz.si); Ljubljana to Lesce-Bled (45min–1hr; every 30–90 min; from €6.50); Bled-Jezero to Bohinjska Bistrica (20min; 7 daily; from €2.40); Bohinjska Bistrica to Nova Gorica (1hr 20min; 8 daily; from €6).
- Ljubljana train station faces a concourse of buses, nominally Ljubljana bus station; buy an Urbana chargecard (€2 fee set against fares) to use the city's trams and buses. Bus services connect Ljubljana and Bled (1hr–hr 20min; every 30–90 min; from €6; www.ap-ljubljana.si).
- The Slovenian section of the EuroVelo 9, a 1930km-long cycle route from Gdańsk, Poland, to Pula, Croatia, runs from Maribor to Ljubljana (www.en.eurovelo.com/ev9).
- The Trans Dinarica is a 2024-opened cycle route traversing eight countries – Slovenia, Croatia, Bosnia and Herzegovina, Serbia, Kosovo, North Macedonia, Albania, Montenegro – and it wiggles across the Soča Valley from Triglav to Nova Gorica (www.transdinarica.com).
- Nearly all Bled travel agencies offer cycling tours to Triglav, of varying distances and challenges; reliable operators include 3glav Adventures (Ljubljanska cesta 1, Bled; www.3glav.com) and Bled Tours (Jelovška cesta 25, Bled; bledtours.si).

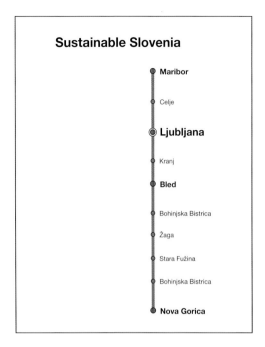

## Sustainable Slovenia

- Maribor
- Celje
- **Ljubljana**
- Kranj
- **Bled**
- Bohinjska Bistrica
- Žaga
- Stara Fužina
- Bohinjska Bistrica
- **Nova Gorica**

Maribor, well-served for bike-rental outlets. Cycling to Ljubljana follows EuroVelo 9, and is challenging in places. You can break the journey at bustling Celje (58km from Maribor), whose historic castle dominates the skyline, before continuing to the capital (76km) – or jump on the train (2hr). Twenty-five kilometres on from Celje, Zidani Most is worth a stop for the namesake stone bridge reflected in the water at the point where the Sava and Savinja rivers meet.

### LOVELY LJUBLJANA

Ljubljana is one of Europe's brightest and most engaging cities, retaining its low-key charm despite an increase in its profile. From the station, a tangle of cobblestoned streets leads down to the showcase square of Prešernov trg, backdropped by the pinkish-red Baroque facade of the Franciscan Church of the Annunciation. Free walking tours in English depart from here at 11am daily or you can stroll along the narrow Ljubljanica, past the main bar hub, until you reach the Dragon Bridge, sporting four examples of the city's fiery symbol. The other notable river crossing

is the Triple Bridge, redesigned by the city's keynote architect, Jože Plečnik. Opposite, Pogačarjev trg hosts a Friday *Odprta Kuhna* (Open Kitchen), where notable chefs prepare dishes, and an organic market on Saturday, with themed culinary events. This is the continuation of the busy Central Market, partly laid out in a Plečnik-designed colonnade, near the southern foot of the Dragon Bridge.

Following a bend in the river towards Cobblers' Bridge, you'll find an antique flea market on Sunday mornings, a treasure trove of Yugoslavia-era paraphernalia. Overlooking all this activity, Ljubljanski Grad atop Castle Hill offers striking views of the capital and can be reached by funicular.

Once you've had your fill of the city's charms, it's on to Lake Bled. Trains from Ljubljana take around an hour to reach Lesce-Bled railway station, which is 4km from Slovenia's fairy-tale lake (10min by bus or taxi or a 50min walk). Cyclists might like to break up the surprisingly plain, 60km-long journey along the D2 with an overnight stay in Kranj, with its pretty medieval core.

### A FAIRY-TALE LAKE

Slovenia doesn't need to sell Lake Bled. One look at the pictures – the stark-white exquisite Cerkev Sv Marija Božja (Church of the Assumption) set on a tiny verdant island in an expanse of pure blue glacial waters – and you're hooked.

You're not alone, of course, which is why winter is a great time to visit, when the surrounding slopes are Christmas-card white. Icy waters may mean that the traditional *pletna* boats won't be gliding over to Bled Island, the only way to reach the seventeenth-century church and its richly carved altar. If winter is severe enough, locals don skates.

In summer, swimming is allowed at designated spots, notably Grajsko kopališče, a grassy area on the north shore beneath Bled's other key landmark: Blejski Grad, a clifftop medieval castle enclosed by a Romanesque wall and studded with stout-looking parapets, towers and ramparts. Inside, an extensive museum tells its story. At the western tip of the lake,

Ojstrica looms above the lake, with fine views (and a welcome bench) the reward for a steep twenty-minute scramble up the 2350m-high mountain.

## MIGHTY TRIGLAV

Thirty kilometres west, within touching distance of the Austrian and Italian borders, is Ojstrica's taller, better-known sibling: Triglav. Bled is connected to Triglav National Park by one of Europe's most scenic train journeys, the Bohinjska proga (Bohinj railway) or Transalpina. Built 1900–1906 by the Habsburgs, the 129km line starts in Jesenice, near the Austrian border, crosses the Julian Alps through the Bohinj Tunnel, stretches to Nova Gorica on the border with Italy before reaching Trieste. This section connects Bled Jezero, near the northwest corner of the lake, with bucolic Bohinjska Bistrica (20min). From here, it's a ten-minute taxi or bus ride or a 1hr 15min walk to Stara Fužina, home to an information centre for Triglav National Park – the only one in Slovenia.

Occupying nearly 900 square kilometres of the Julian Alps, this dramatic idyll attracts climbers,

hikers, mountain bikers and botanists. Protected medicinal plants number among the 59 species of rare flora found here. Most visitors, though, come to admire the glacial lakes, notably Bohinj – the quietly confident alter-ego of glamorous Bled – and cascading waterfalls, particularly Boka.

Only electric-powered boats may cross Bohinj's clean waters, regularly replenished by karst streams and springs. Kayaking and wild swimming are popular in summer, when the lake's temperature clears 20 degrees Celsius, though be aware that there are no lifeguards. The shoreline nearest Stara Fužina suits competent swimmers, with a wooden jetty from which divers plunge into Bohinj's depths, while the lake's north bank is more secluded.

Access to the Boka waterfall is from the small Alpine village of Žaga (where much of 2008 Disney film *The Chronicles of Narnia: Prince Caspian* was shot), halfway between the larger towns of Kobarid and Bovec, each a gateway to the beautiful Soča Valley. Slap Boka, 106m high and 30m wide, is a thundering curtain of water pouring from a mountainside around

Whitewater rafting down the Soča River

two kilometres northeast of Žaga, with a secured climbing path by the falls.

## THE SUBLIME SOČA VALLEY

Returning to Bohinjska Bistrica via Stara Fužina, train travellers can again pick up the Bohinj Railway for the most dramatic stretch of its journey west, through the Soča Valley. More than six kilometres of the route is taken up by the Bohinj Tunnel, an incredible feat of Habsburg engineering. Leaving the Alps behind, tracing the turquoise Soča and pushing between steep green slopes, the line crosses the river over Solkan Bridge, the world's longest stone-arch railway bridge. Just ahead is Nova Gorica, gateway to the coast.

# LIKE A LOCAL

### STAY

**BE:CYCLE** Pipuševa ulica 4, Maribor; www.becycle-maribor.com. A four-apartment complex in a heritage building in Maribor, geared to sustainable travel, with upcycled furniture and energy-saving policies.

**Fani&Rozi** Pristan 6, 2000 Maribor; www.fani-rozi.si. Named after much-loved members of the family that's run the B&B since 1925, this atmospheric Maribor abode serves organic breakfasts overlooking the river.

**Hostel Celica** Metelkova ulica 10, 1000 Ljubljana; www.hostelcelica.com. A former prison-turned-hostel, offering singles, doubles and dorm beds. Part of the same complex as the Metelkova cultural centre, long at the forefront of Ljubljana's alternative scene and the stage for art exhibitions and music gigs (www.metelkovamesto.org), with bars aplenty.

**Hotel CUBO** Slovenska cesta 15, 1000 Ljubljana; www.cubogroup.si. Set in a Ljubljana heritage building, this boutique hotel offers package deals for urban cyclists.

**Old Bled House** Zagoriška cesta 12, 4260 Bled; www.charming-bled.com/en/accommodation/old-bled-house. Just 300m from Lake Bled, this 300-year-old farmhouse has been reimagined as a cosy guesthouse with thirteen rustic-chic rooms (including four family suites) adorned with handmade furniture.

**Penzion Rožić** Ribčev laz 42, 4265 Bohinjsko jezero; www.pensionrozic-bohinj.com. Tucked away in woodland 100m from Bohinj, this year-round hotel-restaurant rents rowing boats and canoes, and has an eco-shop proffering the likes of fresh local honey.

**Rikli Balance Hotel** Cankarjeva cesta 4, 4260 Bled; www.sava-hotels-resorts.com. Named after Swiss holistic therapist Arnold Rikli who founded the Natural Healing Institute – and wellness tourism – in Bled in the nineteenth century, this four-star offers thermal relaxation in a pool complex overlooking the lake.

## EAT

**Fudo** Poštna ulica 1, 2000 Maribor; www.fudo.si. Helmed by colourful soul Fudo, this laidback urban eatery in Maribor shines a light on home-made food made from seasonal, organic ingredients, mostly sourced from local markets and farms.

**Green One** Mestni trg 19, 1000 Ljubljana; www.greenone.si. Locally sourced vegan dishes dominate the concise menu at this central Ljubljana eatery, with soups and stews echoing Slovenian tradition.

**Oštarija Peglez'n** Cesta svoboda 19a, 4260 Bled; +386 4 574 42 18. Cosy defines this authentic Slovenian eatery, the perfect place to sample Bled's famed *kremšnita*, a cream cake crammed with vanilla and whipped cream and topped with flaky pastry.

**Pod Skalco** Ribčev laz 58, 4265 Bohinjsko jezero; www.pod-skalco-bohinj.com. This rustic terrace restaurant and guesthouse specialises in grilled meat and trout from Lake Bohinj barely five minutes away. It also organises cycling, fishing and rafting activities.

**Špica** Cesta svoboda 9, 4260 Bled; www.restavracija-spica.si. Local producers supply this smart restaurant with the likes of *pršut* (dry-cured ham) and Bled cheese; its rowing theme a nod to local tradition.

## DRINK

**Devil Bar** Cesta svobode 15, 4260 Bled; www.facebook.com/devillounge. For lake-view coffees in the morning and imaginative cocktails after dark, this is a rare lively hangout in Bled.

**Isabella** Poštna ulica 3, 2000 Maribor; www.isabella-maribor.si. From superb coffee to fine cocktails, this funky day-to-night spot can be found on Maribor's liveliest street for dining and drinking.

**Pivnica Union** Celovška cesta 22, 1000 Ljubljana; www.union-experience.si. Ljubljana's symbolic red-labelled beer is produced at this brewhouse, also a courtyard bar and restaurant.

## SHOP

**Smile Concept Store** Mestni trg 6, Ljubljana 1000; www.smileconceptstore.eu. Three Ljubljana women are behind this local design hub, be it Yugo-nostalgia, cool notebooks or zero-waste make-up remover pads.

**Zelena japka** Dominkuševa ulica 5, 2000 Maribor; www.zelena-japka.si. This women-led, Maribor-based zero-waste store champions local produce, such as the Styrian apples from which it takes its name.

Dragon Bridge, Ljubljana

# BALKAN BREEZE
## A road trip from Zagreb to Sarajevo

Starting in the capital of Zagreb, explore the forests of mainland Croatia, with soaring peaks, lush valleys and rare wildlife. As you traverse the spectacular hairpin bends towards Zadar, you'll find yourself on the Jadranska Magistrala, one of Europe's most stunning roads. The 'Adriatic Highway' zigzags along an extraordinary coastline, and pine-forested islands come and go like apparitions. Stop off in Zadar, Split and Dubrovnik for a taste of contemporary life on the Med. Then it's on to Montenegro for a stay in cobblestoned Kotor before swerving inland to Bosnia and Herzegovina to discover the ancient Ottoman town of Mostar, then Sarajevo, a capital with a complex history.

Spanning Croatia, Montenegro, and Bosnia and Herzegovina, this cross-border route traverses over a thousand kilometres of the Balkans. From forest to mountains and sea, every striking landscape feels like a world apart from the next. Though this journey is easier by car, coach services are reliable and comfortable – and the journey is just as scenic.

## SLAVIC METROPOLIS

Although capital of an independent Croatia only since 1991, Zagreb has served as the cultural and political focus of the nation since the Middle Ages. The city grew out of two hilltop medieval communities, Kaptol and Gradec, divided by a (now dried-up) river. Zagreb grew rapidly in the nineteenth century, and many of the city's buildings are well-preserved, peach-coloured monuments to the self-esteem of

Zadar, the ancient capital of Dalmatia

the Austro-Hungarian Empire. Nowadays, with a population reaching almost one million, the city is the boisterous capital of a changing nation. Always home to a thriving scene of alternative music, edgy fashions and eccentric nightlife, Zagreb is currently having a bit of a moment, with a flourishing dining scene and an arts renaissance. Brilliantly located for transport connections to the Balkans and the Adriatic, Zagreb is a quietly understated experience. This isn't a place to rush around ticking off big-hitting sights. It's an authentic city pursuing its own, idiosyncratic path. Third-wave cafés, grungy bars and inventive museums define the cultural offerings of Croatia's capital. Gradec plays host to the checkerboard-roofed St

**PRACTICAL INFORMATION**

**Distance covered:** 400km

**Recommended journey time:** 7 days

**Transport details:**

- There are two main London–Zagreb rail itineraries: the first is via Paris, Lausanne, Milan, Venice and Ljubljana; the second via Brussels, Cologne, Salzburg and Ljubljana. The total journey is around 30hr; buy an Interrail or Eurail pass for the best rates. Sarajevo has direct trains to Zagreb and Ploče; the routes to Belgrade and Budapest are currently suspended (travel via Zagreb).

- There are few places in Croatia that you can't reach by bus (www.buscroatia.com). For bus timetables in the Balkans, visit www.balkanviator.com. To buy tickets: www.busticket4.me for Montenegro; www.busbosnia.com for Bosnia.

- Car rental in Croatia costs around 600Kn/€80 per day to 1500Kn/€200 a week. The major rental chains have offices in the cities and at Zagreb airport.

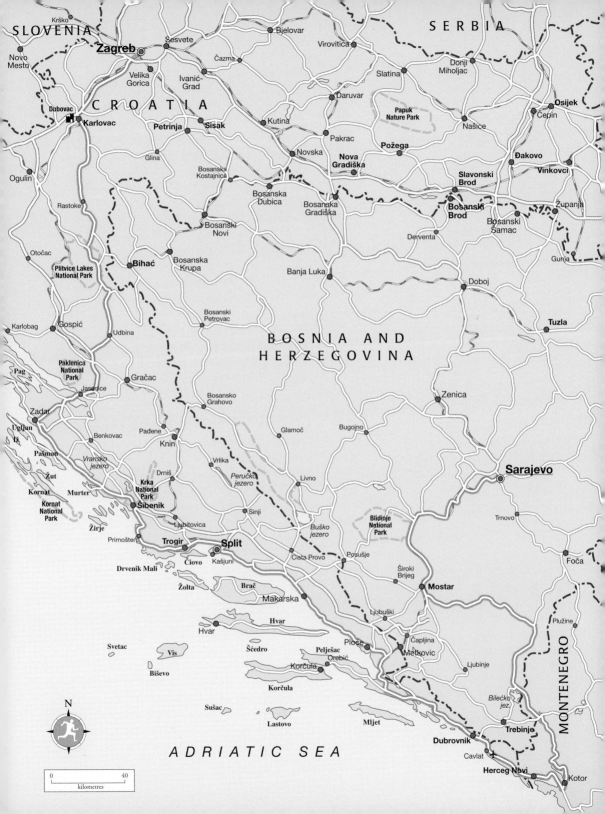

## Balkan breeze

- ◉ **Zagreb**
- ● **Karlovac**
- ● Rastoke
- ● **Zadar**
- ● Šibenik
- ● **Split**
- ● Kašjuni
- ● **Dubrovnik**

CROATIA
MONTENEGRO

MONTENEGRO

- ● **Kotor**

BOSNIA AND
HERZEGOVINA

- ● **Mostar**
- ◉ **Sarajevo**

villages and the occasional hilltop medieval castle. After around an hour, stop for lunch at Dubovac, a perfectly preserved Renaissance-era castle with views of the historic fortress town of Karlovac, the last frontier of the Homeland War of 1991–95. Continue on to Rastoke, a fairy-tale village sitting at the confluence of the Korana and Slunjčica rivers, beneath Slunj's towering fifteenth-century castle. A huddle of wooden-roofed houses clings to the travertine riverbanks, connected by walkways that cross foam-tipped waters.

From here, a 25-minute drive takes you to Croatia's main calling card: Plitvice Lakes National Park, an 8km series of sixteen turquoise lakes strung between densely forested hills. Stay overnight in Rastoke and visit the park early the following morning before the hordes of tourists arrive by coach. Take in the ever-shifting landscape of waterfalls and lakes from the wooden pathways above, marvelling at the chameleon emerald and cerulean waters. Nearby are rafts of unexplored forest and crystalline waters where you can swim, kayak and fish.

## DUBROVNIK'S QUIETER SIBLING

From here, it's just over an hour to Zadar. Turn off the A1, and you'll arrive on the Jadranska Magistrala, or Adriatic Highway, one of Europe's finest drives. Karst-grey peaks of the Dinaric Alps float majestically in the distance, against the sparkling sea.

The ancient capital of Dalmatia, Zadar is an animated jumble of Roman, Venetian and modern architecture, with a bustling café life, a vibrant bar scene and ahead-of-the-curve architectural projects (such as the *Sea Organ* and the *Greeting to the Sun*), plus fabled sunsets. Popular, but not as over-touristed as Dubrovnik, it's a lived-in city whose busy central alleys are crammed with medieval churches. If you have time to take things slowly, it's very easy to spend a night or two here. Nearby, the ninety or so islands of the Kornati archipelago – a national park since 1980 – are scattered like pebbles around the 35km-long island of Kornat. Continuing along the Jadranska Magistrala, you'll pass the laidback island of Murter, joined to the mainland by a small bridge, and Šibenik,

Mark's Church, and unpretentious restaurants tucked into medieval courtyards. Strossmayerovo šetalište, a leafy promenade offering fine views of the city, twists down towards Trg bana Jelačića (Governor Jelačić Square), site of the Dolac daily food market. Tkalčićeva springs to life after dark when pavement bars serve *rakia* (brandy) to a youthful crowd. Cult speakeasies and nightclubs are dotted around the centre and further afield in the easygoing suburbs of Trešnjevka and Maksimir. Don't miss the Museum of Broken Relationships, a collection of objects connected with all aspects of break-ups, donated by former lovers with a synopsis of why their love didn't last. It's surprisingly moving, and the adjoining coffee shop is a good place to pick yourself up afterwards.

## THE BUCOLIC HEART OF CROATIA

From the capital, the road trip heads south, skirting the socialist-era outliers of Novi Zagreb before plunging into Croatia's bucolic interior, passing farmyards,

whose surprising blend of Mediterranean architecture, island beaches and festival culture makes it one of Dalmatia's most underrated cities. The maze-like medieval centre is as evocative as any on the Adriatic, and the cathedral is one of the finest monuments in southeastern Europe.

## SIZZLING SPLIT

An hour further along the coast, Split is where ancient history meets urban sprawl. Croatia's second city has a unique heritage, having grown out of the palace built here by the Roman Emperor Diocletian in 295 AD. It remains the city's central ingredient, having been gradually transformed into a warren of houses, tenements, churches and chapels by the various peoples who came to live here in later years. Swish restaurants and boutiques have carved out a presence within these ancient walls. Beyond the Roman and medieval tangle are stately rows of socialist-era housing blocks that look like something out of a modernist architectural stylebook.

The seafront Riva, dotted with palm-shaded cafés, is where locals gather over a leisurely coffee, channelling the spirit of *fjaka* – the Dalmatian philosophy of aspiring to nothing. The main urban beach Bačvice is a bar-flanked sandy swathe popular with families by day, partygoers by night. For a quieter idyll, head to Kašjuni, a ten-minute drive west of town, on the south side of the pine-cloaked Marjan peninsula. Reached by an unmarked side road around 1km beyond the Ivan Meštrović Museum, the fine shingle strip faces out towards the green island of Čiovo.

## THE PEARL OF THE ADRIATIC

As you continue along the dramatic twists and turns of the Adriatic Highway, coastal mountains press in from above, stark and ominous. At the foot of the bone-grey karst Cetina gorge is Omiš, a tiny town and former pirate stronghold cradled among Jurassic peaks. Pause for lunch at the family-run bistro *Arsana*; try the squid and polenta stew. The surrounding landscape is made for high-octane adventuring, from mountain climbing and ziplining to rafting down the River Cetina.

Back on the road, cross the Pelješac Bridge (opened in 2022) over the Pelješac Peninsula and rejoin the D8 near Zaton Doli. It's then an hour on to Dubrovnik, one of Europe's most perfectly preserved walled towns. Trace the battlements for an ideal vantage point of the city's medieval and Baroque splendours. Catch the sun setting over the Adriatic from *Buza*, a hole-in-the-wall bar carved into the rockface. Before you move on, visit the Red History Museum for a fascinating glimpse of the consumer-communism that flourished under Tito's Yugoslavia, evoked through displays of vinyl records, colour magazines, comic books and film posters.

## ON TO KOTOR

As you navigate the last stretch of the Croatian coast, impeccable views of the Bay of Kotor unfurl before you.

Thirty-five kilometres south of Dubrovnik, the road arrives at the border with Montenegro. It's then an hour's drive to Kotor, a handsome city with a palatial parade of Romanesque churches, cobblestoned piazzas and ancient fortifications. The Venetian city walls snake alongside the 1350 steps up to St John's Fortress, from where beautiful views of the fjord-like bay unfold below. Back in town, sample spicy Montegrin fish soup *(riblja čorba)*, washed down with a glass of crisp Malvasia wine.

## SARAJEVO

The drive from Montenegro to Bosnia and Herzegovina takes you from the glacial folds enveloping Podgorica to the rocky canyons beyond Plužine. As you travel north through the barren plains of Bosnia and Herzegovina, cloaked in mountain scrub, the landscape is unremarkable yet strangely mesmerising. Break up the five-hour journey with a stop in Mostar, a pretty town centred around a medieval bridge that hunches over the Neretva. From here, the final push to Sarajavo is two hours by car, three via bus.

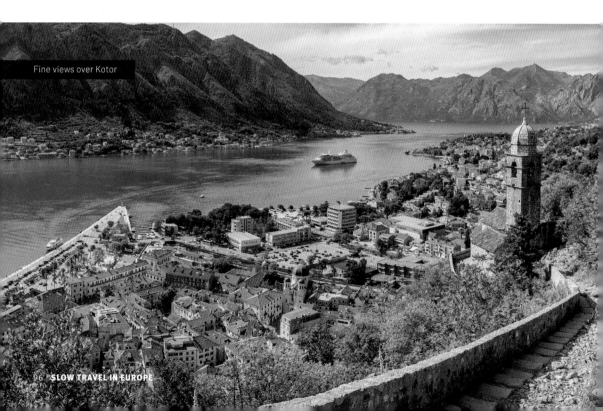

Fine views over Kotor

Fairy-tale village of Rastoke

Bosnia and Herzegovina's river-threaded capital is a jumble of socialist-era futurist architecture and Ottoman mosques. Wedged between three mountains, and often shrouded in early-morning mist, the wooden-riveted Baščaršija Mosque is its headline act. The surrounding streets are a feast for the senses, with aromatic notes of coffee and sizzling *ćevapi* lingering in the air. The sprawling Baščaršija bazaar stretches up to the hillside, a labyrinth of wardrobe-width shops and bakeries selling *burek* and steaming cups of *salep,* made from hot milk, cinnamon and ground orchid root. The Alifakovac Graveyard is a sobering reminder of recent history. For context, visit the affecting War Childhood Museum, in which the Bosnian War is regaled through the children who lived through it. A fitting end to a trip through the Balkans, whose dignified and resilient facade belies the scars of its storied past.

## LIKE A LOCAL

### STAY

**Esplanade** Mihanovićeva ul. 1, 10000, Zagreb; www. esplanade.hr. Once a stopover for Orient Express passengers, the *Esplanade* oozes luxury. Sip coffee in the Art Deco tearoom for a taste of Habsburg elegance.
**Falkensteiner Resort Punta Skala** 23231 Petrčane; www.falkensteiner.com. With infinity pools that blur into the turquoise sea, the *Falkensteiner* is one of the most luxurious hotels in northern Dalmatia. Located at the tip of Punta Skala, it's a 20min drive from Zadar.
**Hotel Mirjana & Rastoke** Donji Nikšić 101, 47240 Slunj; www.mirjana-rastoke.com. A year-round activity hub and 30-room guesthouse, offering white-water rafting, kayaking, off-road vehicles and horseriding.

Green Market in Split

## EAT

**Beštija** Masarykova ul. 11/1, 10000 Zagreb; www.bistro-bestija.com. Combining fresh ingredients from the Med with modern European culinary styles, *Beštija* remains one of the best bistros in Zagreb.

**Bokamorra** Trumbićeva obala 16, 21000 Split; +385 99 417 7191. Featuring 48hr-aged dough with lashings of San Marzano tomatoes and fresh local toppings, *Bokamorra* is the best pizzeria in Split.

**Bota Šare** Ul. od Pustijerne, 20000, Dubrovnik; www.bota-sare.hr. With oysters caught from the nearby bay of Mali Ston, this destination restaurant offers sublimely fresh sushi, and an enviable location in Dubrovnik's Old Town.

**Dvor** Put Firula 14, 21000 Split; +385 21 571 513. A long-standing Split institution. Enjoy views of the Šolta and Brač islands while you dine on caught-that-day fish and seafood, cooked over an open grill outdoors.

**The Four Rooms of Mrs Safije** Čekaluša 61, Sarajevo 71000; www.sarajevoin.ba. Run by a TV chef with an infectious passion for vegetarian cooking (in a very meat-leaning country), this tiny six-table restaurant provides an intimate dining experience. The *borscht* (beet soup) is impeccable, as are the celeriac 'steaks'.

**Galion** Šuranj bb, Kotor 85330; www.galion.me. Fine dining with second-to-none views of the Bay of Kotor. Offering exquisitely cooked fish adorned with red caviar and various foams and jus, *Galion* is worth the splurge.

**Kornat** Liburnska obala 6, 23000 Zadar; www.restaurant-kornat.hr. Set on the marina, *Kornat* pairs top-tier northern Dalmatian cuisine with white tablecloth service. It's on the pricier side, but for the location and ambience, warrants the outlay.

**Nostress Bistro** Narodni trg, 21000, Split; www.bistro-nostress.com. Despite its location among a sea of tourist traps on one of Split's busiest streets, *Nostress* is one of the most inventive eateries in town, with a seasonal menu championing fresh Dalmatian ingredients.

**Pizzeria Tri Bunara** Ul. Jurja Bijankinija 8c, 23000 Zadar; +385 23 250 390. This Zadar pizzeria has been around for decades –and thanks to its top-quality ingredients and laidback atmosphere – shows no signs of letting up. The starters are worth a look-in too, with quality *paški sir* (Pag cheese) and *pršut* at affordable prices.

**Pod rastočkim krovom** Rastoke 25b, 47240 Slunj; www.rastoke-croatia.com/accomodation. The centrepiece of Rastoke is this family-owned restaurant, with an open-air terrace set above the cascading water. Order the grilled trout, and a glass of peachy Graševina wine.

## DRINK

**Academia Club Ghetto** Dosud ulica 10, 21000 Split; www.facebook.com/AcademiaClubGhetto. Set in a candlelit courtyard with ivy-clad walls, this atmospheric hangout is a great setting for live music. It's also one of Split's only queer-friendly bars.

**Buza** Crijevićeva ul. 9, 20000 Dubrovnik. One of two hole-in-the-wall bars on the cliff, *Buza* is the most atmospheric location to watch the sunset.

**D'vino Wine Bar** Palmotićeva ul. 4a, 20000 Dubrovnik; www.dvino.net. A stellar choice to round off an evening in Dubrovnik, with an excellent selection of regional and national Croatian wines.

**The Garden Brewery** Slavonska Avenija 26/1, 10000 Zagreb; www.thegarden.hr. The Garden Brewery has set the gold standard for Croatian craft beer, and its Zagreb-based taproom is stunning, set in a giant glass atrium with indoor trees.

**Mon Ami Old Winery** 483 Zanatska, Kotor. Offering a best-of-the-region wine list and charcuterie boards, *Mon Ami* occupies an easygoing central spot away from the crowds.

**The Nitrox Pub** 263, stari grad kotor, Kotor 85330; www.thenitroxpub.com. Trendy brewpub in Kotor with atmospheric low lighting and rock'n'roll memorabilia. The cocktails are excellent, and the prices affordable.

**The Swanky Bar** Ilica 50, 10000 Zagreb; www.stayswanky.com. A hostel-restaurant-club hybrid, Stay Swanky is an enterprising Zagreb outfit. *The Swanky Bar* offers the best cocktails in town, best enjoyed in the wood-decked courtyard with adjoining pool.

**Zlatna ribica** Kaptol 5, Sarajevo 71000; +387 33 836 348. Translated as *The Goldfish Bar*, this is one of the most atmospheric watering holes in Sarajevo, if not the Balkans. Intricately and whimsically decorated in a fin-de-siècle theme, the attention to detail is stunning. Make sure to visit the bathroom, where you'll be transported to a full-scale 1920s vanity room, with a black-and-white TV screening nature documentaries.

## SHOP

**Green Market** Ul. Stari pazar 8, 21000, Split. If you're looking to pack a picnic for the beach, stop off at Green Market on the eastern side of Diocletian's Palace. Gleaming fresh fruit and seasonal vegetables are harvested from Dalmatia and Montenegro, and you'll also find olive oil, white cheese and plump figs to add to the spread.

**Natura Zara** Ul. Brne Karnarutića 5–7, 23000 Zadar; +385 98 888 585. Cute family-run boutique store with an excellent selection of Dalmatian wines, olive oil, lavender and honey.

**Š'mek** Rastoke 22, 47240 Slunj; +385 91 502 0092. A traditional deli set in an old farmhouse, this is the place to grab cottage cheese, *ajvar* (bright-red aubergine and pepper relish) and freshly laid eggs.

Eriskay ponies

# SCOTLAND'S WILD HEART
## Exploring the remote Outer Hebrides

Beyond Skye, across the unpredictable waters of the Minch, lie the Outer Hebrides, officially known as the Western Isles. A 210km-long archipelago stretching from Lewis and Harris in the north to the Uists and Barra in the south, the islands appear as an unbroken chain when viewed from across the strait, hence their nickname, the Long Isle. Car ferries make it easy to hop between the handful of islands that are inhabited. This is a land on the edge, where the turbulent Atlantic smashes against a coastline of tiny bays and sandy beaches. The islands' interiors are equally dramatic, bare mountaintops soaring above flat, treeless peat moor and pewter lochans.

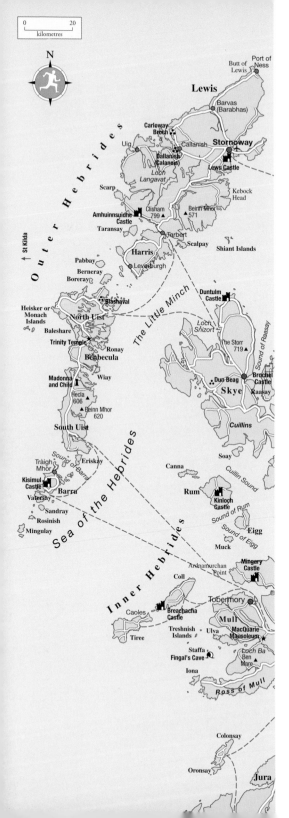

0     20
kilometres

# THE JOURNEY

Shaped like the top of an ice-cream cone, Lewis is the largest of the Western Isles. Nearly half of the island's inhabitants live in the crofting and fishing villages strung along the northwest coast, between Callanish (Calanais) and Port of Ness (Port Nis), in one of the country's most densely populated rural areas. On this coast you'll also find the best-preserved prehistoric remains – Dun Carloway (Dùn Charlabhaigh) and the Callanish standing stones. The landscape is mostly peat bog – hence the island's Gaelic name, from *leogach* (marshy) – but the shoreline is more dramatic, especially around the Butt of Lewis, the northernmost tip. The rest of the island's population live in Stornoway, on the east coast, the only real town in the Western Isles. In July, the streets come to life for the Hebridean Celtic Festival, a celebration of Celtic music held in Lews Castle grounds and at the An Lanntair arts centre. To the south, where Lewis is physically joined with Harris, the land rises to over 550m, providing an exhilarating backdrop for the excellent beaches that lace the isolated western shores around Uig.

## THE LONELY ROAD TO NESS

The A857 crosses the vast, barren peat bog that characterises the interior of Lewis, an empty, undulating wilderness riddled with stretch marks formed by peat cuttings and pockmarked with freshwater lochans. The whole area was once cloaked in forest, but these disappeared long ago, leaving a deposit of peat that continues to serve as a valuable energy resource, with each crofter being assigned a slice of the bog.

Twenty kilometres across the peat bog, the road wends towards the west coast of Lewis and splits, swerving southwest towards Callanish or wiggling northeast through Barvas (Barabhas). A few kilometres beyond Barvas, you skirt past the 6m-tall monolith of Clach an Truiseil, the first of a scattering of prehistoric sights between the crofting and weaving settlements of Ballantrushal (Baile an Truiseil) and Shader (Siadar).

Heading southwest from the crossroads near Barvas brings you to the Westside. The main road lies a couple of kilometres inland from the coast, but a string of villages meanders down towards the sea. At Arnol and Garenin (Gearrannan) there are beautifully preserved blackhouses to explore, and, at Callanish (Calanais), the islands' most dramatic prehistoric ruins. Overlooking the sheltered, islet-studded waters of Loch Roag (Loch Ròg), the Callanish standing stones are some fifty slabs of gnarled and finely grained gneiss (the oldest rock in Britain) reaching heights of up to five metres. The behemoths were transported here between 3000 BC and 1500 BC, but their exact function remains a mystery.

## BRITAIN'S WESTERNMOST ISLAND CHAIN

The St Kilda archipelago, 65km from North Uist, is dominated by Britain's highest cliffs and sea stacks. Hirta, the main island, was occupied until 1930 when the last 36 Gaelic-speaking inhabitants were evacuated at their own request. The island was then bought by the Marquess of Bute, to protect its huge population of nesting seabirds. In 1957, having agreed to allow the army to build a missile-tracking radar station here linked to South Uist, the marquess bequeathed Hirta to the National Trust for Scotland (NTS).

St Kilda is one of only two-dozen UNESCO World Heritage Sites with a dual status reflecting its natural and cultural significance. Despite its inaccessibility, several thousand visitors make it out here each year. Between mid-May and mid-August, the NTS organises volunteer work parties, which either restore and maintain the old buildings or take part in archaeological digs. Several companies offer boat day-trips, though the sea journey (8hr return) is not for the faint-hearted and there's no guarantee that you'll be able to land.

## UIG'S GLORIOUS SANDS

It's a long drive along the B8011 to the remote district of Uig, which suffered badly from the Clearances. The landscape here is hillier and more dramatic than

A *cleit* (storage hut) on St Kilda

## PRACTICAL INFORMATION

**Distance covered:** 280km
**Recommended journey time:** 7 days
**Transport details:**

- To reach Scotland from elsewhere in Britain, from Ireland or even northwest Europe, you can travel easily enough by train, bus or ferry.
- CalMac car ferries run two services daily from Ullapool to Stornoway; one or two daily from Uig, on Skye, to Tarbert and Lochmaddy; and operate daily from Oban to Barra and Mallaig to South Uist (www.calmac.co.uk).
- A series of causeways makes it possible to drive from one end of the Western Isles to the other with just two interruptions – the ferry from Harris to Berneray, and from Eriskay to Barra. If you're going to take the ferry, it's advisable to book in advance (www.calmac.co.uk). Note that petrol stations can be a long distance apart (and might be closed on Sundays). If you'd rather not drive, the islands have a decent bus network (www.cne-siar.gov.uk), though note that there are no services on Sunday.
- The dual-aspect long-distance Hebridean Way launched in 2017, opening up the archipelago further to hikers and cyclists. The 250km walking trail and the 300km biking trail (National Cycling Route 780) cover different ground but each stretches from Vatersay in the south to Lewis in the north (the hike ends in Stornoway; the cycle route at the Butt of Lewis). You'll need to know the ferry schedules and although it's remote, there are places to rest and pick up supplies. For a stress-free trip, allow four to six days for cycling and ten to twelve days for walking (see www.visitouterhebrides.co.uk for details).
- The wind makes cycling something of a challenge – head from south to north to catch the prevailing wind. It's free to take bikes on all ferry services, or if you prefer to hire wheels, there are rental outlets in Barra and Stornoway.

elsewhere: wild cliff scenery giving way to patches of pristine golden sand. Offshore, myriad islets stand sentinel among the thrashing waters, fragments of the mainland half-lured to sea by the wiles of the horizon. The main road slices through the narrow canyon of Glen Valtos (Glèann Bhaltois) to Timsgarry (Timsgearraidh), overlooking Uig Sands (Tràigh Uuige), the largest and most prized of all Lewis's golden strands, where the sea goes out for miles at low tide; the best access point is from the cemetery car park in Ardroil (Eadar Dha Fhadhail), a few kilometres south of Timsgarry.

## HARRIS: A TOUCH OF NATURAL DRAMA

Harris, whose name derives from the Old Norse for "high land", is much hillier, more striking and much more immediately appealing than Lewis, its boulder-strewn slopes tumbling to aquamarine bays braided by white sand. The shift from Lewis to Harris is almost imperceptible, as the two are, in fact, one island, the "division" between them embedded in a historical split in the MacLeod clan, lost in the mists of time. Harris itself is more clearly divided by a minuscule isthmus, into the wild, inhospitable mountains of North Harris and the gentler landscape and sandy shores of South Harris.

North Harris was run like some minor feudal fiefdom until 2003, when the locals managed to buy the land for a cool £2 million. If you're travelling from Stornoway on the A859, it's a spectacular introduction to Harris, its bulbous pyramids of ancient gneiss looming over the fjord-like Loch Seaforth (Loch Shìphoirt). The peaks of South Harris are less dramatic, though the scenery is no less attractive. There's a choice of routes from Tarbert to the ferry port of Leverburgh, which connects with North Uist: the east coast, known as The Bays (Na Baigh), is rugged and seemingly inhospitable, while its western counterpart is endowed with some of the finest stretches of golden sand in the whole of the archipelago, buffeted by the Atlantic winds.

Don't miss the award-winning Isle of Harris Distillery whose gin is infused with hand-harvested local sugar kelp (you'll see the distinct rippled bottles everywhere you go in the Outer Hebrides). It is also a whisky distillery, and guests can enjoy tastings of its single malt during tours.

## THE UISTS

Compared to Harris, North Uist – 27km long and 20km wide – is much flatter. Over half the surface area is covered by water, creating a distinctive peaty-brown lochan-studded 'drowned landscape'. Visitors come for the smattering of prehistoric sites, the birds, the otters, the sheer peace of the island and the solitude of its vast sandy beaches, which stretch – almost without interruption – enticingly along the north and west coasts.

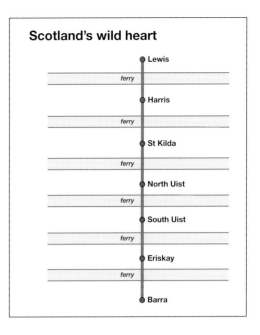

### Scotland's wild heart

Lewis
*ferry*
Harris
*ferry*
St Kilda
*ferry*
North Uist
*ferry*
South Uist
*ferry*
Eriskay
*ferry*
Barra

Baleloch beach, North Uist

Berneray, in the Sound of Harris

Blink and you could miss the pancake-flat island of Benbecula (put the stress on the second syllable), sandwiched between Protestant North Uist and Catholic South Uist. The latter is the largest and most varied of the southern chain of islands. The west coast boasts some of the region's finest machair and beaches – a necklace of gold and grey sand strung 32km from one end to the other – while the east coast in sculpted by a ridge of high mountains rising to 741m at Beinn Mhòr. There are few places to stop for food and drink, until you reach the south of the island.

The Reformation never took a hold in South Uist (or Barra), and the island remains Roman Catholic, as is evident from the various roadside shrines. The only blot on the landscape is the Royal Artillery missile range, which dominates the northwest corner of the island. Whatever you do, however, don't make the mistake of simply driving down the main A865 road, which runs down the centre of the island, otherwise you'll miss out on the natural highlights of its wild coastal contours.

## WILD PONIES AND WILDER BEACHES

Famous for its patterned jerseys and a peculiar breed of pony, originally used for carrying peat and seaweed, the barren, hilly island of Eriskay has been connected by a causeway to South Uist since 2001. The pretty speck, which measures just over three kilometres by one, shelters a small fishing community of about 150.

For a small island, Eriskay has had more than its fair share of historical headlines. The main beach, Coilleag a Phrionnsa (Prince's Cockle Strand), was where Bonnie Prince Charlie landed on Scottish soil on 23 July 1745 – the sea bindweed that grows here to this day is said to have sprung from the seeds Charles brought with him from France. The prince, as yet unaccustomed to hardship, spent his first night in a local blackhouse and ate a couple of flounders, though he apparently couldn't take the peat smoke and chose to sleep sitting up rather than endure the damp bed.

Eriskay's greatest claim to fame, however, came in 1941 when the SS *Politician*, or "Polly" as she's fondly known, sank on her way from Liverpool to Jamaica, along with her cargo of bicycle parts, £3 million in Jamaican currency, and 264,000 bottles of whisky.

## SANDY RUNWAYS AND GAELIC CULTURE

Six kilometres wide and 13km long, Barra is the Western Isles in miniature: sandy beaches backed by machair, mountains of Lewisian gneiss, prehistoric ruins, Gaelic culture and a laidback, welcoming population of around 1200. A kind of feudal island state, it was ruled over for centuries, with relative benevolence, by the MacNeils. Unfortunately, the family sold the island in 1838 to Colonel Gordon of Cluny, who had also bought Benbecula, South Uist and Eriskay. The colonel deemed the starving crofters 'redundant' and offered to turn Barra into a state penal colony. The government declined, so the colonel called in the police and proceeded with some of the cruellest forced Clearances

in the Hebrides. In 1937, the 45th chief of the MacNeil clan bought back most of the island, and in 2003 the estate was gifted to the Scottish government.

Two huge yellow smiles of sand wrap around the north end of the island: the dune-backed west side takes the full force of the Atlantic breakers and is a wonderful hidden spot for a stroll, while the east side boasts the crunchy shell sands of Tràigh Mhòr, better known as Cockle Strand. The beach is also used as the island's airport, with planes landing and taking off according to the tides, since at high tide the beach (and therefore the runway) is covered in water. As its name suggests, the strand is also famous for its cockles and cockleshells.

From Barra, it's possible to travel to the Scottish mainland by catching a ferry to Oban, or perhaps extend your journey with a visit to Mull and its nearby pilgrimage centre of Iona.

Parking up on the Isle of Lewis

# LIKE A LOCAL

## STAY

**Ardroil campsite** Ardroil, Uig, Lewis (Eadar Dha Fhadhail); 01851 672248. The location, on Lewis by one of the most remote and incredible sandy beaches in the Western Isles, is unbeatable. There's a small utilities block with showers and sinks for washing dishes plus a very handy electric socket. The nearest shop is a 10min walk away.

**Beul-na-Mara** Seilebost, Harris; www.beulnamara. co.uk. This is a perfectly decent B&B run by an excellent host, but what makes it particularly special is the stunning location, overlooking the golden sands of Luskentyre Bay (Tràigh Losgaintir) on Harris.

**Hamersay House** Lochmaddy, North Uist; www. hamersayhouse.co.uk. One of Outer Hebrides' more upmarket hotels, this North Uist bolthole is stylish inside and out. The brasserie has lots of pricey seafood options like langoustines while the vegetarian option is usually more economically palatable.

A carpet of wildflowers on North Uist

**Kneep campsite** Kneep (Cnìp), Lewis; www.kneep campsite.co.uk. Small campsite by the wonderful sandy Reef Beach (Tràigh na Beirghe) and an ideal place to take a kayak to explore the tiny islands around Lewis. The community-run site's only facility is a small unisex toilet block with coin-operated showers.

**Polochar Inn** Polochar (Poll a' Charra), South Uist; www.polocharinn.com. One of the best places on South Uist to hole up in, right on the south coast overlooking the Sound of Barra, and with its own sandy beach close by; the rooms all have sea views, and there's a good pub and attached restaurant.

**Scurrival campsite** 3 Eoligarry (Eòlaigearraidh), Barra; 01871 890292. This is a lovely, simple campsite on Barra with showers and toilet facilities, overlooking the sea and close to the wide sandy beach of Scurrival (Tràigh Sgurabhal) in the north of the island.

## EAT & DRINK

**Am Politician** Rubha Ban, Eriskay. The island's purpose-built pub named after the SS *Politician* is unlikely to win any design awards. However, it offers great views out to sea from its pub garden, where you can dine on scallops with black pudding as well as the usual pub grub options. Decent range of single malts. Ask to see one of original bottles from the shipwreck.

**An Lanntair** Kenneth St, Stornoway, Lewis; www. lanntair.com. Stornoway-based arts venue with a stylish, modern café-bar-restaurant that serves simple food all day.

**Barra Airport Café** Tràigh Mhòr, Barra. Wonderful café with views of the planes landing and taking off from the beach airport. Coffee, cake and specials. Open for fish suppers on Friday and Saturday nights in summer.

**The Good Food Boutique** 59 Cromwell St, Stornoway, Lewis; www.thegoodfoodboutique.co.uk. Deli counter and storeroom in Stornoway with quality international and local produce. Takeaway sandwiches and salad boxes are available (think porcetta with apple and chilli chutney), or there's everything you need for a picnic (cheese, olives, meat, marinades, bread, wine).

**Isle of Harris Distillery** Tarbert, Harris; www.harris distillery.com. Isle of Harris Gin, produced here, is making waves across the UK: the concoction uses nine botanicals, including sugar kelp, which is foraged from the local lochs. The whisky is also on its way, already ageing in the barrels. Tours are run on a regular basis and best booked in advance.

**North Uist Distillery** Baile nan Cailleach, Steadings Benbecula; www.northuistdistillery.com. Over on Benbecula, the North Uist Distillery is shaking things up in its new lodgings, where whisky is now brewing alongside its award-winning Downpour gins.

**Temple Harris** 22 Northton (Taobh Tuath), Harris; www.templeharris.com. Artisan coffee roastery, café and deli in a hobbity stone and timber building right on the water's edge. Stop by for an excellent brew and a baked treat, which might be chocolate cake, machair buns or heather biscotti depending on what's fresh from the oven that day. Later in the day, nab one of the outdoor tables and linger over a Harris gin and tonic overlooking the sea. Be sure to pick up some tasty goodies on the way out, perhaps some wildflower granola or wild whisky marmalade.

**Uig Sands** Timsgarry, Uig; www.uiglodge.co.uk. With large windows framing views of Uig Bay, this restaurant-with-rooms is one of the finest places to eat on Lewis. The menu is determined by what the fisherfolk bring in that day. Expect dishes like crab claws served with garlicy butter, Hebridean seafood chowder and half lobster salad.

## SHOP

**Hebridean Smokehouse** Clachan, North Uist; www.hebrideansmokehouse.com. Two of North Uist's most abundant natural resources are put to good use by the Hebridean Smokehouse: peat and fish. The salmon and sea trout are caught around the Hebrides, while the lobster and scallops are fished around North Uist.

**The Blue Pig Studio** 10 Upper Carloway; www.bluepig studio.co.uk. Out of decay and decline comes the birth of artist Jane Harlington's creative works. Using mixed media including painting, printing and collage, she channels traditional values encountered in crofting and fishing, both of which are in steady decline on the island, into her art. Call in advance (01851 643225) before visiting as opening hours can be erratic.

Prenzlauer Berg, an artsy enclave in Berlin

# CULTURAL CAPITALS
## Berlin to Stockholm by sleeper train

If one city could be said to be the gritty and creative heart of Europe, it's Berlin. But the core of sleek, minimalist chic? Stockholm, without a doubt. One at the maximalist end of the fashion scale; the other at the demurer pole. And now they're linked by sleeper train, taking overnight passengers from the glamour and industry of Germany's capital to the cobbled streets and waterways of Sweden's in little more than sixteen hours. From frenetic Berlin to fashion-forward Stockholm, this route trundles 1446km across three countries. It is even possible – with a high pulse rate and no delays – to get from London to Stockholm in just over a day.

# THE JOURNEY

As one of the most fun-loving, happening cities in the Europe, the lure of Germany's capital is obvious. Berlin's pace is brisk: nightlife is frenetic, trends whimsical; graffiti is everywhere and the air crackles with creativity; even brilliant exhibitions and installations are quickly replaced. After a tempestuous twentieth century, with the forces of renewal and regeneration calming, Berlin has entered a new phase where, among the cranes and the concrete, an exciting mix of modern buildings, thoughtful monuments and world-class museums have appeared. Thankfully, many fascinating reminders of the city's past remain, too. Yet it's not all heavyweight history and high culture; Berlin is also endlessly vibrant: there's always something new, challenging and quirky going on and every year it is a little more cosmopolitan, international and mesmerising.

At the other end of the spectrum, Stockholm is one of Europe's more sedate cities (and one of its most beautiful). Built on no fewer than fourteen islands, where the fresh water of Lake Mälaren meets the brackish Baltic Sea, clean air and open space are in plentiful supply here. Broad boulevards lined with elegant buildings are reflected in the deep blue water, and rows of painted wooden houseboats bob gently alongside the cobbled waterfront. Yet Stockholm is also a high-tech metropolis, with futuristic skyscrapers, a bustling commercial heart and one of the world's hottest start-up scenes. It's undeniably stylish and, like its German counterpart, has creativity at its core. What better duo could be paired on a cool cultural trail, with an overnight sleeper train connecting the two in just over sixteen hours.

Oberbaum Bridge connects Kreuzberg and Friedrichshain

## Cultural Capital

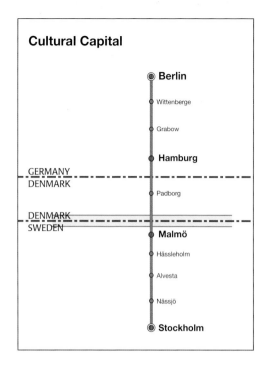

- ◉ **Berlin**
- ○ Wittenberge
- ○ Grabow
- ◉ **Hamburg**

GERMANY
DENMARK

- ○ Padborg

DENMARK
SWEDEN

- ◉ **Malmö**
- ○ Hässleholm
- ○ Alvesta
- ○ Nässjö
- ◉ **Stockholm**

### THE OTHER CITY THAT NEVER SLEEPS

Assuming you're travelling from south to north, your journey will begin at Berlin. You could spend the next 72 hours straight partying before emerging squinting into the sunlight to catch the sleeper train out of the capital, or you could have a rather more laidback trip. It's certainly worth taking the time to explore the rich sociopolitical history of this once-divided city. And a day spent burrowing through heaps of vintage clothing, wandering the streets from one pavement café to the next is time well spent.

In the immediate vicinity of Berlin's train station is Mitte, the central district where ornate and historic buildings stand wall to wall with modern utilitarian architecture. Turn south to find some of the best-known sights such as the Brandenburg Gate, the Holocaust Memorial and the Reichstag, all near the vast, green Tiergarten. Heading northeast lands you in Prenzlauer Berg, a laidback, cobblestoned enclave of cosy cafés and vintage shops. Or let your feet lead you southeast to Kreuzberg and Friedrichshain, the city's euphoric, creative heart where, deep inside a former power station, you'll find *Berghain*, one of the world's most infamous clubs.

### SETTING OFF

Note that two Swedish operators run night trains to Stockholm: Snälltåget leaves from Berlin Hauptbahnhof (Hbf) and SJ EuroNight from Berlin Gesundbrunnen, so arrive at the right station in plenty of time and with plenty of snacks. While there is an on-board kiosk it doesn't come close to rivalling the stacked sandwiches and fluffy pastries you can pick up in the city. On board, there are four different classes: seats, six-berth couchettes, and first- and second-class sleeping compartments.

Shortly after 6.30pm, the train rumbles out of the station, through the western suburbs and into acres

Denmark's Great Belt Bridge connects Zealand and Funen

In midsummer, suspended in the perpetual twilight of the northern latitudes, it might not even be dark at this point. Open the window for a faceful of fresh sea air.

The next scheduled stop is Copenhagen Airport shortly after 3.30am but delays, while the driver stops to let higher-speed services pass, are not unusual. In these cases, a train operator will check whether anyone wants to disembark and, if not, you'll fly on through. Now comes one of the most exciting parts of the journey, where the train shoots off the edge of Zealand into a tunnel, emerging on the narrow artificial island of Peberholm. Here, it joins the 7.8km-long Øresund Bridge to Sweden. This is a combined railway and motorway bridge, with the road running across the top and the train passing between girders beneath. Nevertheless, it's worth negating the whole point of sleeper trains and awaking to watch the sun, a hot pink ball, rise over the luminous Øresund strait. Halfway across the bridge, you enter Sweden.

## SWEDISH SCENES

It would be very understandable to put your head back down at this point but if you're too excited to sleep, peer outside to glimpse the flashing scenes beyond the window. Check for the 191m-high neofuturist twisted skyscraper, Turning Torso, marking your arrival in Malmö. After making its stop, the train glides through the tower blocks and construction sites of the outer district, passes Lund and enters the Swedish countryside. Look out for characteristic wooden houses with the double-angled gambrel roof and distant turreted churches gleaming white in the sun. North of Hässleholm the scenery becomes more wooded and wet, passing stands of pine and silver birch and gleaming blue lakes dotted with forested islands. Low humped hills rise to the east and west.

Somewhere between Alvesta and Nässjö, hunger pangs are likely to hit. Those in a sleeping compartment receive a complimentary breakfast – a bread roll and little packets of jam, butter and cheese tucked inside a box with a carton of juice and a hot drink. It's a spartan meal so it's worth bringing your own. The first sight you'll see of Stockholm is an industrial

of countryside. You'll pass redbrick Wittenberge, push through Grabow, and, in summer, approach Hamburg Hauptbahnhof just as the last colour of the sky fades to a dark dusky blue. People often board here, so if it's been quiet expect some neighbours. The train departs Hamburg just after 10pm, the glimmering city lights reflected in the waters of Binnenalster.

## CROSSING DENMARK

The first border crossing, into Padborg, Denmark, comes at around 1am, when you might be woken for a not-especially-welcome passport check. If you're wise, you'll have your head down and eye mask on when the train leaves the mainland to cross over onto Funen. But if the gentle rock of the carriage stimulates rather than soothes and you happen to be awake around 2.30am, peep out the window. You'll see the lights of the Great Belt Bridge twinkling over the Danish straits.

sprawl, before the train crosses to Södermalm, where you'll experience a fleeting glimpse of Gamla Stan, a medieval jumble of cobbled streets and narrow alleyways huddled together on a triangular-shaped island. And shortly after, at around 10am, the train draws into Stockholm Centralstationen.

## STYLISH STOCKHOLM

If you've had a good night's kip, head straight to one of the city's cool coffee shops, and if you haven't, the same. Bypass the usual chains in favour of *Fabrique*, known for its freshly baked cinnamon buns, or *Chokladkoppen*, a fabulous café overlooking Gamla Stan's main square (order the blueberry pie).

There are plenty of places to stay in Central Stockholm, and Gamla Stan is only a two-minute train journey south. The medieval quarter gets a lot of attention and it's no wonder – the alleyways and colourful buildings are mesmerising. Just as worthy of your footfall, though, is the subway. Decorated with murals, funky sculptures and ornate mosaics, it's been dubbed the world's longest art exhibit.

To the south of the Old Town, the island of Södermalm was traditionally the working-class area of Stockholm but is now a hipster haven. Its grids of streets, lined with lofty stone buildings, create a more homely ambience than the grand, formal buildings of the city centre. It's here, in a fashionable enclave known as SoFo (south of Folkungagatan) that you'll discover some of the city's best bars and restaurants. Crossing the narrow neighbouring island of Långholmen, known for its beaches, you'll reach Kungsholmen, fast becoming a rival to its southern neighbour for its trendy food and drink scene.

Whether on foot, by ferry or electric scooter, exploring really is the best, and often cheapest, way to spend your time in Stockholm. It's for more than one reason that you'll leave with heavy feet.

Playful *Hobo* in Stockholm

# LIKE A LOCAL

## STAY

**Castanea Hostel** Kindstugatan 1, 111 31 Stockholm; www.castaneahostel.com. Tucked away down a narrow cobbled alley in Stockholm's Old Town, this cosy hostel is housed in a pair of eighteenth-century buildings. Rooms are simple and airy and range from private singles to sixteen-bed dorms.

**EastSeven Berlin Hostel** Schwedter Strasse 7, 10119 Berlin; www.eastseven.de. Situated in Berlin's bougie bohemian Prenzlauer Berg, *EastSeven* is consistently highly rated thanks to its friendly staff, airy rooms and leafy courtyard. An excellent budget stay.

**Ett Hem** Sköldungagatan 2, 114 27 Stockholm; www.etthem.se. A tiny boutique bolthole in an elegant Stockholm townhouse with a courtyard garden. At the pricey end, but service and the decor are sublime.

**Hobo** Brunkebergstorg 4, 111 51 Stockholm; www.hobo.se. Fun and function collide in this bright Stockholm

For currywurst, head to Berlin institution *Konnopke's Imbiß*

boutique hotel with gadgets like Chromecast in your room, luggage-storage lockers and a delicious breakfast spread.

**Michelberger Hotel** Warschauer Straße 39–40, 10243 Berlin; www.michelbergerhotel.com. Stylish comfort within hobbling distance of some of Berlin's biggest clubs, *Michelberger Hotel* is the aesthete's option. Also has a restaurant serving local, organic food from its own farm.

**Orania.Berlin** Oranienstrasse 40, 10999 Berlin-Kreuzberg; www.orania.berlin. This boutique hotel in Berlin's creative Kreuzberg has luxurious rooms, local musicians playing on the ground floor, and a breakfast club serving seasonal dishes into the afternoon.

## EAT

**Aleppo Supper Club** Wühlischstraße 21, 10245 Berlin; www.aleppo.supper.club. Find fresh Aleppine cuisine from Syrian refugee Samer Hafez in Berlin's buzzy Friedrichshain district. Feast on plates of pomegranate salad, creamy houmous and stuffed aubergine in a relaxed dining space.

**Konnopke's Imbiß** Schönhauser Allee 44B, 10435 Berlin; www.konnopke-imbiss.de. Located in a kiosk beneath Magistrate's Viaduct, this Berlin institution has been serving currywurst to a well-guarded family recipe for eighty years.

**Nystekt strömming** Kornhamnstorg, 111 27 Stockholm; www.facebook.com/Nystektstromming. A food truck doling out fresh fried Baltic herring with creamy mashed potatoes, pickles and onion. This is simple, inexpensive and very Swedish fare.

**Rosendals Trädgård** Rosendalsvägen 38, 115 21 Stockholm; www.rosendalstradgard.se. Pick a table on the outdoor terrace or in the greenhouse draped with vinery at *Rosendals Trädgård* in Stockholm's Djurgården enclave. Season-led lunches made with fresh, organic ingredients plucked from its own biodynamic allotments.

## DRINK

**Café Pascal** Norrtullsgatan 4, 113 29 Stockholm; www.cafepascal.se. One of the best places to indulge in the Swedish tradition of *fika*: a chat and a snack over coffee. As well as its fresh brews, this laidback hangout is renowned for its freshly baked cinnamon buns and pastries.

**Velvet** Ganghoferstraße 1 12043 Berlin; www.velvet-bar-berlin.de. Seasonal cocktails infused with locally foraged plants – think pinecone extract, walnut bitters and hogweed seeds. Concoctions are fleeting, unique and delicious.

## SHOP

**Hornsgatan Street** Slussen Station, Södermalmstorg, 116 46 Stockholm. For a morning browsing independent art shops showcasing the work of local talent, followed by a leisurely afternoon sifting through thrift stores, head directly to Hornsgatan Street and Mariatorget on Södermalm island.

**Iris Hantverk** Västerlånggatan 24, 111 29 Stockholm; www.irishantverk.se. Residing alongside a slew of touristy shops is this artisan gem which, alongside its own paintbrushes made by visually impaired craftspeople, sells an array of textiles, crafts and other locally made goods.

**Mankii Vintahe** Gormannstraße 16, 10119 Berlin; www.instagram.com/mankiivintage. Berlin is blessed with thrift shops such as the multilevel chain HUMANA but for a more refined selection, rifle through Mankii's vintage and designer secondhand pieces.

**Marabouparken Art Gallery** Löfströmsvägen 8, 172 66 Sundbyberg; www.marabouparken.se. Catch the train 10min northwest of Stockholm city centre to roam this sculpture park and contemporary art gallery nestled in a beautiful small park.

**Mauerpark Markt** Bernauer Straße, 13355 Berlin; www.mauerpark.info. Every Sunday, half of Mauerpark in Prenzlauer Berg turns into a giant flea market-cum-festival with scores of vendors, live music, food stalls and a legendary karaoke spot.

**She Said** Kottbusser Damm 79, 10967 Berlin; www.shesaid.de. This queer feminist bookstore might be small but its handpicked selection is mighty, and there's a café where you can settle in with your new read and a coffee.

# 8-14 DAYS

# EMERALD ISLE
## Driving Ireland's Wild Atlantic Way

The name Wild Atlantic Way perfectly describes the 2500km route from Ireland's northwest to southeast. Clinging to the rugged western coast, it passes through some of the most beautiful scenery on earth. Isolated beaches, misty mountains, and tumbling rivers fill the view. Ferocious waves, unchecked in their progress across the vast Atlantic, crash against some of Europe's highest cliffs. Along the way, lovely towns and villages show off the richness of Ireland's history, food and hospitality. By bringing visitors to this remote west coast, the trail is a driving force behind sustainable tourism, helping to preserve its cultural and natural heritage.

# THE JOURNEY

The official starting point of the Wild Atlantic Way (WAW) is Kinsale, a pretty seaside town full of art galleries and equally artistic restaurants. In summer, it's packed with visitors — a victim of its own success — so the Atlantic wildness really starts in West Cork. Here, the village of Schull is a long-time refuge for those escaping to the remote west. A sailing-mad community, full of artists, spreads out across the Mizen Peninsula. (From this point on, assume that any part of this western coast is rugged, and has picturesque beaches hidden away in tiny coves.)

Visit Mizen Head Signal Station to learn more than you need to know about maritime navigation and communication. This is the furthest southwest you can go in Ireland. The next headland is Sheep's Head, at the end of a peninsula known for its walking trails, including the Sheep's Head Way. This 93km-long route takes you as far as the historic West Cork market town

Cable car to Dursey Island

## PRACTICAL INFORMATION

**Distance covered:** 2500km
**Recommended journey time:** 14 days+
**Transport details:**

- For those not used to driving on the left, the recommended direction for the WAW is clockwise, as this gives the driver a better coastal view. It also helps you acclimatise to narrow, twisting roads before you hit the vertiginous cliffs of Kerry, Clare and Donegal.
- The WAW can be done by bus or bike but a car or campervan is more usual; the whole WAW would take about ten days of non-stop driving to see, so most people linger over one or two sections. Car-hire companies, including Hertz (www.hertz.com) or Avis (www.avis.com), are at all of Ireland's airports. Campervan hire (€90–€200 per day) is available from Lazy Days (www.lazydays.ie), Vanderlust (www.vanderlust.com), and Ireland West Motorhomes (www.iwmotorhomes.ie); most will arrange pick-up/drop-off at airports.
- Major ferry operators serve Ireland: Stena Line connects Holyhead and Dublin, Fishguard and Rosslare, and Liverpool and Belfast (www.stenaline.com); Irish Ferries serves Holyhead and Dublin, Pembroke and Rosslare, and Cherbourg and Rosslare (www.irishferries.com); P&O Ferries links Cairnryan, Scotland, and Larne, Ireland; and Brittany Ferries connects Roscoff/Cherbourg with Cork/Rosslare.
- The west of Ireland is served by airports at Cork, Kerry, Shannon, Knock, Donegal and Derry. There are connections to Dublin, London or Glasgow from Ryanair (www.ryanair.com), Aer Lingus (www.aerlngus.com) and Loganair (www.loganair.co.uk).
- Trains connect Donegal and Belfast (4hr; 4–6 daily; from £25; www.translink.co.uk) and Ulsterbus (via Derry or Enniskillen).

# Wild Atlantic Way

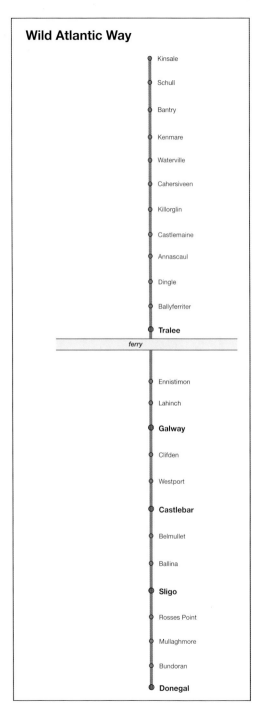

- Kinsale
- Schull
- Bantry
- Kenmare
- Waterville
- Cahersiveen
- Killorglin
- Castlemaine
- Annascaul
- Dingle
- Ballyferriter
- **Tralee**

*ferry*

- Ennistimon
- Lahinch
- **Galway**
- Clifden
- Westport
- **Castlebar**
- Belmullet
- Ballina
- **Sligo**
- Rosses Point
- Mullaghmore
- Bundoran
- **Donegal**

of Bantry. From here, the road signs point to Kenmare, in County Kerry. However, the WAW first takes in the Beara Peninsula, a worthy rival to the better-known Ring of Kerry. The Beara Way is one of Ireland's longest hiking routes at almost two hundred kilometres.

Eyeries is known for its colourful houses, and is close to the many walks in the Slieve Miskish Mountains. Hop on the cable car to Dursey Island, a firm favourite with birdwatchers and hikers for its quietness and coastal views.

## COASTAL SCENES

You enter County Kerry through Kenmare, a town it's easy to fall in love with for its candy-coloured street fronts, many sheltering cosy pubs and cute shops. From here, the WAW follows the Ring of Kerry road past some of Ireland's best coastal views. Ireland is scattered with unexpected statues, and Kerry particularly so. Along the Ring of Kerry, you'll find a bronze Charlie Chaplin standing on the seafront in Waterville where he used to holiday, while Sneem has delights such as Steve "Crusher" Casey, once a world champion wrestler. This region, part of the Iveragh Peninsula, is — like most parts of Ireland — a treasure trove of both natural and man-made delights.

A good base is the town of Cahersiveen, opposite Valentia Island, to which it is linked by ferry and road bridge. The town has seen better days but is now facing an awakening thanks to Ireland's most beautiful cycle way. The South Kerry Greenway [opening in 2025] runs to the tiny village of Glenbeigh along a disused railway line. Take a snorkelling tour of Ballinskelligs Bay or join a seashore safari of Inny Strand or Mannix Point with the energetic team at Sea Synergy (www.seasynergy.org).

After Killorglin, the Ring of Kerry presses on to Killarney before closing the circle by skirting Ireland's highest mountains in the MacGillycuddy's Reeks. This whole area is an outdoor playground, rebadged in recent years as the Reeks District. From Killorglin, famous for its annual Puck Fair, the road to Dingle beckons. You can reach Dingle from the village of Castlemaine, supposed birthplace of Jack Duggan from the Irish-Australian folk ballad *Wild Colonial Boy* — whose pistol-packing statue

stands by the town's supermarket. An alternative is to continue to Tralee, home of Mary O'Connor, the "Rose of Tralee", immortalised in a ballad by William Pembroke Mulchinock about his forbidden love for Mary; a statue of the mooning pair stands in the town's park.

## RUGGED VISTAS

The Dingle Peninsula in County Kerry is one of the most picturesque parts of Ireland's rugged west. Known for its Gaelic-speaking community, this mighty crooked finger of land and its villages, cliffs, mountains and hospitality is a microcosm of the whole WAW. In recognition of its natural beauty, large swathes of the peninsula gained protection under Ireland's newest national park, Páirc Náisiúnta na Mara, in 2024. The peninsula is circled by a road that has the Atlantic on its north side, and the calmer Dingle Bay on its south. The town of Dingle sits to the south, with a large fishing port taking advantage of this sheltered position in its own bay. The town is known for its brightly

painted houses, some of which face the harbour to create a colourful frontage of musical pubs, seafood restaurants and souvenir shops. It's an obvious base for the area, with good hotels and B&Bs.

Entering the peninsula from Castlemaine, along the southern shore, the first major sight is Inch Beach, a yawning sandy swathe disappearing into Dingle Bay, with an excellent surf school. At nearby Annascaul, the *South Pole Inn* is where Irish polar explorer Tom Crean quietly lived out his last days. Still run by his family, the inn is a museum of Antarctic exploration, not to mention serving good food and drink.

Beyond Dingle Town, the WAW wraps around Slea Head. Follow the recommended clockwise one-way route for some of the best views in Ireland. Look out for the Blasket Islands, now deserted but once a bastion of the Irish language. Learn more at the fascinating Great Blasket Centre and then walk along the coast to see the crumbling school built for 1970 film *Ryan's Daughter*. Another must-visit is Dunquin Pier, a popular spot with photographers. Beyond Ballyferriter is the well-preserved Gallarus Oratory, an ancient stone church dated to the seventh century. Its beehive shape reflects those dotted across famous island monastery Skellig Michael. At Conor Pass, you cross the highest mountain pass in Ireland. The views from the summit are remarkable, if the weather allows.

Brandon Bay is laced by five beaches, three of which braid together to form 18km of unbroken sand. There are plenty of seabirds here, and a visit to Tralee Bay Wetlands offers ornithological context. While Dingle is a great base, Tralee lets you see a "real" Irish town – warts and all. Connected by train to Dublin, it also runs bus services (www.buseireann.ie) throughout Kerry.

## OTHERWORLDLY LANDSCAPES

A short ferry ride from Tarbert crosses the wide estuary of the River Shannon, and into County Clare. Pointing west is the Loop Head Peninsula, tipped by a lighthouse of 1854. A drive here offers big Atlantic vistas. The road onwards leads to the Cliffs of Moher, a rocky spine spanning 14km in length, and up to 214m in height. With a million visitors a year, these much-photographed sea cliffs suck the air out of Clare's other attractions. These include the Burren, an unworldly expanse of limestone rock carved into large slabs by the elements. The Burren National Park protects its unique flora, fauna and historical landmarks.

You will find similar landscapes, including plunging sea cliffs, on the Aran Islands. Take the ferry from Doolin, where you can enjoy Irish traditional music "sessions" in pubs such as *McDermott's* and *McGann's*. The three tiny specks of the Aran archipelago – Inishmore, Inishmaan, Inisheer – are home to around 1500 people whose main language is Irish. Take a guided bike or walking tour of the largest, Inishmore, to learn more.

Back in County Clare, Ennistimon is a picturesque market town, known for the remarkable Cascades, a rocky staircase of frothy rapids on the Inagh River. It is also another stronghold of traditional Irish music.

Conor Pass, Ireland's highest mountain pass

Nearby, Lahinch, a seaside village with a pretty beach, is an escape for local surfers. Take a surf lesson with the team under Irish champion surfer John McCarthy at Lahinch Surf School.

## GLORIOUS GALWAY

The county city of Galway, with its traditional pubs and pastel-toned shops, is very much part of the WAW experience. Wander along the Salthill Promenade for fine views across Galway Bay. From Galway, the WAW leads on to Roundstone, self-dubbed "Ireland's most picturesque village". It's certainly a contender thanks to its dinky harbour, thatched cottages and sublime beaches. It's also a gateway to Connemara, a wild region known for its green marble fashioned into jewellery, and other beautiful objects. Explore the 2000-hectare Connemara National Park and hike up Diamond Hill for panoramic views over toothy mountain range Twelve Bens, and Kylemore Abbey, a Victorian-era lakeside castle with walled gardens.

Discover a different landscape of blanket peat bog and unique plants at Derrigimlagh Bog. It was here that pioneer aviators Alcock and Brown found a soft landing after the first transatlantic flight in 1919.

Clifden, the "capital of Connemara", is strung along the banks of the Owenglin River, with its salmon and trout fishing. The annual Clifden Arts Festival highlights the cultural credentials of a town well-known for its art galleries and craft shops. From here you can explore Mannin Bay Beach and the Coral Strand. It's a starting point for the circular Sky Road, plaited with isolated beaches, and views over the tiny offshore islands of Turbot and Inishbofin. Go coasteering on Connemara's shoreline with Real Adventures (www.realadventures.ie), which also offers kayaking and surfing.

Inishbofin, the first Irish island to be granted the ecotourism award by the Global Sustainable Tourism Council, is best explored on a self-guided walking tour.

## PILGRIM SITES AND DESERTED VILLAGES

The tree-lined streets of Westport make a fine entrance to County Mayo. The town is a gateway to Clew Bay, peppered with hundreds of small islands. Overlooking the area is Croagh Patrick, named for Ireland's patron

Roundstone, self-dubbed "Ireland's most picturesque village"

saint. For centuries, pilgrims have climbed the 764m-high mountain but the views from the top are enough reward for the more secular.

Mayo's county town, Castlebar is built around the thirteenth-century castle of its name. It's worth the diversion to see the National Museum of Ireland – Country Life, which showcases Ireland's rural past.

Back at Westport, the Great Western Greenway runs for 42km along the shores of Clew Bay to Achill, Ireland's largest island. Visit Keem Bay, where basking sharks are regularly seen, and the deserted village at the foot of Slievemore, with its one hundred abandoned stone cottages.

The loneliest place in Ireland, though, has to be the Nephin Beg mountain range in Wild Nephin National Park. Walk or tour this vast 15,000 hectares of uninhabited wilderness, and the Owenduff, one of Western Europe's last untouched blanket bogs.

From Belmullet to Ballina is perhaps the loveliest stretch of the Wild Atlantic Way. Headlands include the Mullet Peninsula, entered through Belmullet, an outdoor haven for active types. At Downpatrick Head, you'll find teetering sea stacks and the Dún Briste blowhole. Nearby, just outside Ballycastle, is the Céide Fields Visitor Centre. Its history of Irish farming is up to date with a study of climate change. The tidy heritage town of Westport is a good base for the surrounding Mayo countryside and beaches. Discover the story of Grace O'Malley (1530–1603), the "Pirate Queen" who faced down England's powerful Queen Elizabeth I in the seventeenth century, at the Granuaile Centre.

## YEATS HERITAGE AND SEAWEED BATHS

Sligo is Yeats country, the inspiration for the first Irish Nobel laureate in literature, poet W.B. (William Butler) Yeats. A pilgrimage to his graveside at Drumcliff Cemetery, in the shadow of flat-topped Benbulben mountain, is practically mandatory.

However, on this journey, Sligo town comes first. It's a good centre for exploring sites such as the 1253-built Sligo Abbey, or driving around scenic Lough Gill. The freshwater lake is a beautiful place for boating or fishing. Sligo town's Benbulben is Knocknarea, a

Slieve League, among Europe's highest sea cliffs

slab-crowned limestone monolith from whose summit you have views of Sligo, Leitrim and Donegal. Only 327m high, it still looms over the surrounding flat countryside; it is an easy walk of around six kilometres.

Strandhill Beach, home to Ireland's 2023-opened National Surf Centre, welcomes novice and seasoned surfers alike. The sandy stretch also hosts the Voya Seaweed Baths, a traditional bathhouse where a long, hot soak will warm the coldest of bones.

North along the rolling Sligo coastline are the villages of Rosses Point and Mullaghmore. The former was a favourite holiday spot for W.B. Yeats and his brother, the artist Jack Butler Yeats. It also has several Blue Flag beaches. Overlooked by picturesque Classiebawn Castle, Mullaghmore has a glorious 3km-long beach. Strike out on the Mullaghmore Head Walk, a 5km loop with amazing views of massive Atlantic waves rolling in.

## SLOW ADVENTURES IN COUNTY LEITRIM

Blink-and-you-miss-it Leitrim has just under five kilometres of coastline. Its main attraction is Glencar Waterfall, pretty in itself, and the start of a path that climbs the sheltered south face of Benbulbin. Leitrim's lakes and mountains lend themselves to outdoor pursuits, and the county is fast becoming Ireland's capital of slow adventure. Lough Allen is perfect for boating, fishing and scenic drives. The Sliabh an Iarainn mountain range is threaded with walks, starting at the informative visitor centre. Kayaking on the River Shannon, or foraging for a wild menu are among other activities on offer here.

## THE DIZZYING HEIGHTS OF DONEGAL

The end of your WAW adventure may be near, but there are still some amazing sights to see. The biggest of these, literally, is Donegal's Slieve League: just over 600m in height, these are some of the highest sea cliffs in Europe. The summit offers breathtaking views of the Atlantic. Keep an eye out for fulmars, razorbills, dolphins and seals. Catch your breath first in the interesting seaside resort of Bundoran, or handsome Donegal town on the River Eske. Stroll around Donegal's charming Diamond square, and listen to traditional music in one of its pubs. From here, the coast-hugging road wends through a string of tiny – and often quaint – villages, and so many miniscule beaches you are overwhelmed with choice. This wild stretch of coast relies on its lighthouses, and the most scenic can be found at Fanad Head. Ballymastocker Bay's wide smile of a yellow beach (Portsalon) is frequently voted one of the most beautiful in the world.

A two-hour drive around Lough Swilly, through Letterkenny, leads to Malin Head. The WAW officially ends here, at the point where Banba's Crown marks Ireland's most northern point. The winding, clifftop drive is not for the faint-hearted but, by now, you are ready for anything Ireland's roads can throw at you.

Home of the famed Irish playwright Brian Friel (1929–2015), Greencastle is a lively port town poised on placid Lough Foyle. Near Burt, the Grianán of Aileach is a restored hilltop stone ringfort with fantastic views over Londonderry, Donegal and Tyrone.

# LIKE A LOCAL

### STAY

**The Ashe Hotel** Maine St, Tralee; www.theashehotel. ie. A Tralee four-star that shows how charmingly Ireland can do grand hotels.

**Ballyboes B&B** Eleven Ballyboes, Greencastle; +353 74 932 5839. A luxurious Greencastle home demonstrating Ireland's high reputation for hospitality.

**Clifden Eco Campsite** Claddaghduff Road, Clifden; www.clifdenecocamping.ie. With its zero-carbon footprint, this Clifden-based campsite is a pioneer in eco-holidays. Be sure to try a seaweed hot tub.

**Eyeries Glamping Pods** Pallas Strand, Eyeries; +353 87 775 4535. Sleep in two-person pods tucked away on a working farm, with some neighbourly animals, very close to Eyeries village.

**Ocean Breeze B&B** Station Rd, Lahinch; +353 65 708 1616. A warm welcome awaits at this small Irish B&B in central Lahinch. Serves an excellent breakfast.

**Pier Head Hotel** The Harbour, Mullaghmore; www. pierheadhotel.ie. This landmark hotel and spa has been a Mullaghmore fixture since the early 1800s.

**Sive Townhouse** 15 Newmarket St, Cahersiveen; www. sivebudgetaccommodation.com. Private guest rooms and shared dorms at a simple, budget-friendly hostel in central Cahersiveen.

### EAT

**Dursey Deli** +353 86 366 2865. This food truck sells some of the best fish in Cork, if not further afield.

**Eithna's by the Sea** The Harbour, Mullaghmore; www.eithnasrestaurant.com. Local fish, shellfish and seaweed is transformed into remarkable Irish dishes in this cosy Mullaghmore favourite.

**Hugo's** Ennistimon Rd, Lahinch; +353 85 161 4389. Excellent sandwiches, coffee and custard tarts in this blue-fronted Lahinch deli.

**Kealy's Seafood Bar** Eleven Ballyboes, Greencastle; www.kealysseafoodbar.ie. An award-winning family-run pub in Greencastle with great seafood chowder.

**Mitchell's Restaurant** Market St, Clifden; www. mitchellsrestaurantclifden.com. Award-winning kitchen specialising in sustainably sourced seafood.

**The Oratory Pizza & Wine Bar** Main St, Cahersiveen; www.theoratorywinebar.com. A former church turned airy restaurant in Cahersiveen dishing up great pizzas.

**Seven Wanders** Bridge St, Louisburgh. Owners Louis and Trina Freiter have transformed a traditional pub into a breezy breakfast, brunch and lunch spot known for its imaginative dishes.

**Wild Café** The Mall, Tralee; +353 66 712 7503. Outstanding service in a teal-painted corner café serving up everything from pancakes to pulled pork.

## SHOP

**Burren Smokehouse** Lisdoonvarna; www.burren smokehouse.com. Look out for Burren Smokehouse's products, such as organic Irish salmon, in shops around County Clare.

**The Clifden Bookshop** Main St, Clifden; www. clifdenbookshop.com. A literary treasure trove for Connemara, including maps and local history.

**Irish Atlantic Sea Salt** Lickbarrahan, Cahermore; www.irishatlanticsalt.ie. Keep an eye out for this handcrafted salt made on the Beara Peninsula.

**Green Castle Kelp** Ballymacarthur, Greencastle; www. greencastlekelp.com. Organic seaweed products for eating as well as beauty and wellness.

**Skellig Soaps** Main St, Cahersiveen; www.skellig soaps.com. Co-owner Alice Dennehy's outstanding photography decorates this sweet-scented Cahersiveen shop selling natural soaps, handmade from ingredients such as seaweed.

**St. Vincent De Paul** Friary Ln, Tralee; vincents. fltralee@svp.ie. "SVP" is a charity shop where you'll find everything from secondhand books to preloved tweed coats.

**Terrybaun Pottery** Bofeenaun, Ballina; www.terrybaun pottery.com. Ireland's oldest pottery is still producing hand-spun designs inspired by the country's landscape and wildlife.

*Kealy's Seafood Bar* spotlights the bounty of the ocean

# PORTUGAL'S EDEN
## Island-hopping in the mid-Atlantic

On the edge of Europe, formed by volcanic eruptions 1400km off Portugal's coast, the Azores is a wild paradise. Dizzying hydrangea-fringed trails tumble to *fajãs*, ocean-touching flats formed by lava flows. Craggy coastlines harbour natural pools sculpted and soundtracked by the Atlantic. Of the nine main islands, three specks – Faial, Pico, São Jorge, or the 'triangle' – are connected year-round by ferry. As you traverse this cinematic trio, Mother Nature remains a constant humbling presence. You'll quickly discover, though, that the Azores' true protagonist is her people, who have harnessed this inhospitable land into a welcoming home.

## PRACTICAL INFORMATION

**Distance covered:** 260km

**Recommended journey time:** 12 days

**Transport details:**

- Reaching the Azores flight-free is near-impossible, other than by joining a sailing (www.santamariamanuela.pt) or, with much difficulty to arrange, a cargo route (www.gslines.pt). To minimise internal flights, fly directly from Lisbon to Pico or Faial (2 weekly; www.azoresairlines.pt). Azores Airlines offers direct seasonal flights from London, Barcelona, Milan and Paris to Ponta Delgada (São Miguel), thus requiring an onward interisland connection. To avoid connecting flights from North America, utilise Azores Airlines' non-stop, weekly summer routes from Boston, Oakland, New York and Toronto to Terceira, and then the onward seasonal Linha Branca ferry to Faial (9hr; June–Sept 2 weekly; €29.50).

- Atlântico Line's Linha Verde ferry (atlanticoline.pt) links the three islands year-round (daily, with additional summer services). Book tickets in advance for Faial to São Jorge (2–3hr via Pico; €15.50) and São Jorge to Pico (1hr 15min; €10.20). Limited weekday commuter bus services (2 daily; www.transportes.azores.gov.pt) operate mainly as island loops from the main towns, including Faial's Horta, São Jorge's Velas and Calheta, and Pico's Madalena and São Roque. Bus journeys are rarely longer than 30min and cost just a few euros, payable on board by cash. Alternatively, taxis and transfers (www.visitazores.com/en/explore) are helpful for linear trails.

Horta, Faial's capital

This remote volcanic archipelago in the mid-Atlantic is an outdoor adventure playground. Canyoning, coasteering and abseiling afford adrenaline-pumping access to extremities, and sperm whales dance in the deep blue beyond. Sadly, flight-free travel is complicated; ferries no longer connect all nine islands. Thankfully, three lesser-visited specks – Faial, Pico, São Jorge, known as the 'triangle' – retain ferry links year-round, and can be explored by e-bike, bus and on foot.

## A SLOWER PACE ON FAIAL

Arriving on Faial, 1700km west of Lisbon, you'll be greeted by the island's capital, Horta, a laidback terracotta-roofed, whitewashed town that wouldn't look amiss on the Portuguese mainland. Yet those iridescent emerald slopes beyond are distinctively Azorean. These vivid colours define the mid-Atlantic archipelago: cobalt oceans and green hills punctuated by overgrown calderas. Faial, dubbed the *Ilha Azul* (Blue Island) by Portuguese poet Raul Brandão, is garnished with an abundance of hydrangeas from spring until early autumn.

The other most immediate difference from Portugal's capital is the slower pace on Faial. Fittingly, the island's outline faintly resembles a turtle. But fight off the urge to sink into the sun-warmed volcanic sands of Praia do Porto Pim and refrain from sipping a few in the legendary, marina-facing *Peter's Café Sport*. Those indulgences are best saved for a lazy leg-rest day. Instead, pick up your e-bike from Ecomoov (pre-book via www.ecomoov.pt) and delve straight into the island's heart, cycling the turtle's sloping back.

It's an uphill schlep to Caldeira, a gaping dormant stratovolcano whose highest point, Cabeço Gordo, reaches 1043m above sea level. Assist mode will aid the ascent, the urban world fading away after the stone chapel of Ermida de São João. The final zigzagging stretch climbs steep slopes, scented with the sweet perfume of blue hydrangeas between May and September. From the *miradouro* (viewpoint) at the top, peek inside the caldera and relish far-reaching ocean panoramas. Descending into the crater's sunken belly requires an authorised guide, but a two-hour trail circles the rim. On the return journey to Horta, cycle through the dense ancient laurel forest of Reserva Florestal do Cabouco Velho.

Exploring Faial's perimeter is the next morning's challenge, a cycle ride best spread over two days. Reaching the west, the Vulcão dos Capelinhos's otherworldly dusty, taupe-coloured headland is a stark contrast. Here, walk across Portugal's youngest landmass, created by a thirteen-month eruption in 1957. Continuing clockwise along the ocean road, the journey is one of verdant pastures and huge Atlantic breakers. Diminutive villages stud the coastline. Pull over at pebbly Praia da Fajã beach for a refreshing dip in the sea.

## EXPLORING SÃO JORGE'S VINEYARDS AND COFFEE FARMS ON FOOT

If Faial is a turtle, São Jorge takes the shape of an elongated dolphin: a slender, verdant landmass rising sharply from the Atlantic, its fins the ridged

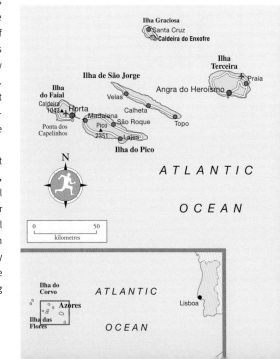

## Portugal's Eden

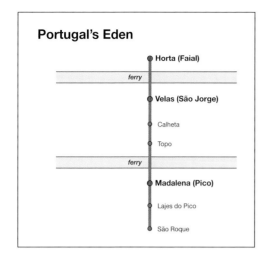

Horta (Faial)

*ferry*

Velas (São Jorge)

Calheta

Topo

*ferry*

Madalena (Pico)

Lajes do Pico

São Roque

Gruta das Torres, Pico

*fajãs* created by lava flows and landslides. Speaking of cetaceans, keep an eye on the waters swirling around these shores, home to playful dolphins that often follow in the wake of ferries connecting the archipelago. On approach by boat, first glimpses of São Jorge inspire awe; its topography is daunting – cycling these sheer flanks demands stamina. Many choose instead to hike the glorious trails that clamber up ridges and descend through gnarled tracks. The impressive 38km Great Route runs from east to west, but breaking the journey into bite-size chunks can be more appealing.

Docking in sleepy Velas, the largest of São Jorge's communities, reclaim your land legs with a stroll towards the Jardim da República before taking a coastal bus to even sleepier Calheta. From here, you're well-placed to explore some of the island's best hikes via short taxi transfers. First, venture to one of Europe's only commercial coffee farms at Fajã dos Vimes. It's a 10km linear route stringing two individual trails together. The first stretch tracks the road to the Miradouro da Baía – not that there's a lack of panoramas en route, including a fine frame of Mount Pico across the waters. From the viewpoint, loop up to Portal to join the PR09 SJO trail. A steep, weathered staircase descends to Fajã da Fragueira, where vineyards and ruins await, followed by a dirt track to Fajã dos Vimes. Duck inside *Cafè Nunes* for an espresso and a tour of the coffee plantation, before doubling back to Calheta.

The following day, tackle São Jorge's most dazzling day trek, the 9km-long PR01 SJO. Taxi to the trailhead at Topo, the start of the sloping trail at around 690m above sea level. It's a breathtaking descent wrapped in greenery, the Atlantic an omnipresence. On the coastal plains, the track braids three of the most remarkable *fajãs* together: Caldeira do Santo Cristo with its scenic lake, Fajã do Belo and, finally, Fajã dos Cubres. From here, head up the road for photogenic vistas back across Cubres and an afternoon bus return. The next day is for rest: board a bus to Norte Pequeno, followed by a downward stroll to Poça Simão Dias, a sensational natural swimming pool framed by basalt columns.

Otherworldly São Jorge

## AN ELEMENTAL LANDSCAPE

Cruising towards Pico Island, Portugal's highest peak looms ahead. At 2351m, the stratovolcano of the same name is a challenging climb worth reserving a day to tackle, either guided or alone. Pico is the destination where the elements are at their most powerful, and from the cloud-raking summit of Mount Pico, you'll experience pure Azorean air.

Disembarking in the quaint town of Madalena, veer south to the Paisagem da Cultura da Vinha, following the pretty trail through Pico's mind-boggling and backbreakingly built UNESCO-listed vineyards. To protect the fragile vines from the harsh Atlantic winds, ingenious vintners chiselled into the volcanic rock to plant their grapes and built a web of stone walls to shelter the precious bounty. Post-walk, sample these mineral-rich wines at the long-standing 1949-founded Pico Island Wine Cooperative.

Circumnavigating Pico is a treat, and after picking up an e-bike from Pico447 (www.pico447.com), set off in search of the two remaining elements. First up, fire – the scars of scorching lava. Plunge underground at Gruta das Torres – Portugal's longest lava tube – to witness the Azores' volcanic nature up close by headlamp. Then, track the coastal road to Lajes do Pico, where the island's former whaling industry is recorded at the Museu dos Baleeiros. Better still, take to the water on a boat tour with responsible and reliable operator Futurismo (www.futurismo.pt) to see whales how they're meant to be seen: free in their wild habitat.

On reaching Pico's other side – either by tracing its coastal contours or crossing the volcano-flanked interior road – bathe in the rugged natural pools of São Roque before returning to the vine-combed landscapes around Lajido. Casa dos Vulcões, a small museum with an earthquake-replicating vibrating platform, is the penultimate stop before heading next door to the vineyard's interpretation centre – it's time to raise a final glass to your Atlantic adventure.

The Azores is one of Europe's best whale-watching destinations

## LIKE A LOCAL

### STAY

**Azul Singular** Rua da Granja 61, Faial; www.azul singular.pt. This cluster of glamping yurts and fully equipped wooden cabins hides among palm trees just 5km outside of Faial's Horta.

**Cantinho do Piano** Rua de São José 23, São Jorge; www.facebook.com/cantinhodopianosjz. Expect a warm welcome at this central São Jorge guesthouse, with helpful owners, kitchen and stellar views across the waters to Mount Pico.

**Engenho** Rua Manuel Paulino de Azevedo e Castro 5, Lajes do Pico, Pico; www.hostelengenho.com. This whitewashed eighteenth-century building has been restored as a modern boutique hotel in Lajes do Pico. The airy rooms have mountain or sea views.

**Fajã do Belo Kuanza** São Jorge; www.fajadobelokuanza. pt. This smattering of secluded traditional stone houses – reachable on foot or by quad bike – promises a rural escape on São Jorge. It's a good stop between hikes if you don't mind a two-night minimum stay.

**Hotel Solmar** Rua Domingos de Oliveira 4, São Jorge; www.housity.net/hotel/residencial-solmar. Close to Calheta harbour, this B&B has simple, spacious rooms. It's a decent base for short transfers to hiking routes.

**Paraíso do Triângulo** Rua do Lagido, Lajido, Pico; www.paraisodotriangulo.pt. Sleep among Pico's UNESCO-listed vines in one of these small, self-contained stone abodes with kitchens. Throw in the Atlantic views from the terraces, and you have a sensational self-catering bolthole.

**PÁTIO Ecolodge** Rua da Igreja, Cedros; www.patio. pt. This eco-hideout in Faial's north offers rooms, apartments and pitches. Trails are on the doorstep, rock pools beyond, and horseriding is available on site.

*Fajã do Belo Kuanza, São Jorge*

**Porto Pim Guest House** Rua do Monsenhor António Silveira de Medeiros 6, Faial; www.naturalist.pt. Seconds from Praia do Porto Pim, this cosy, central stay has spacious rooms and well-equipped common areas, including a terrace and kitchen.

**Vila Barca** Caminho da Barca, Madalena, Pico; www.vilabarca.com. This contemporary three-star hotel is a short walk from Madalena. Rooms and apartments are modern, but the ocean views shine brightest.

## EAT

**Café Calhetense** Calheta, São Jorge; +351 295 416 507. Cheerful service and a local atmosphere define this open-sided, ocean-facing restaurant serving up affordable and plentiful plates of freshly grilled fish.

**Cantina da Praça** Rua Serpa Pinto 38, Faial; +351 967 753 565. Adjoining Horta's market, this clean-lined restaurant pairs classic Azores flavours with a culinary twist. The seared tuna is excellent.

**Restaurante Fornos de Lava** Travessa de São Tiago 46, São Jorge; www.fornosdelava.pt. Set on a São Jorge farm, which provides ingredients for the kitchen, this restaurant's fire-cooked dishes and views of Mount Pico are worth the elevated prices.

**Restaurante Rumar** EN1-1A Praia do Norte, Faial; www.rumarsnackbar.com. This no-frills restaurant is ideal for a well-priced feast of local flavours after visiting Praia da Fajã or before cycling back from Capelinhos.

**Taberna do Canal** Av. Padre Nunes da Rosa, Madalena, Pico; +351 918 409 397. Stone walls, framed photos, aged trinkets and heaving terracotta plates – this is a proper Azorean experience for a post-vineyard lunch.

## DRINK

**Café Nunes** Fajã dos Vimes 138, São Jorge; +351 295 416 717. Tour one of Europe's only commercial coffee plantations before enjoying an espresso or buying a bag of rare beans to take home with you.

**Cella Bar** Rua da Barca, Madalena, Pico; www.cellabar.pt. This curious wine bar is reminiscent of a piece of driftwood from the outside and a wooden boat inside. Bag a table on the rooftop for ocean views.

**Cooperativa Vitivinícola da Ilha do Pico** Av. Padre Nunes da Rosa 29, Madalena; www.picowines.com. Tour the Azores' oldest wine cooperative and meet the makers while tasting volcanic wines and hearing behind-the-scenes stories of backbreaking work.

**Peter's Café Sport** Rua José Azevedo 9, Faial; www.petercafesport.com. No visit to Faial is complete without a beer in Horta's legendary century-old marina meeting place. Try the team's own locally produced gin or visit the museum to browse a small collection of scrimshaw pieces from the old whaling days.

## SHOP

**Artes em Basalto** Rua da Igreja 9, Santo Antońio, Pico; +351 924 349 526. In this studio, owner Nídia shapes small sculptures and crafts jewellery pieces from the island's signature volcanic basalt.

**Bambu** ER1 312, São Roque do Pico, Pico. Stop by this unassuming roadside shop for handmade souvenirs crafted from bamboo driftwood – there's a forest on São Miguel.

**Cooperativa de Artesanato Senhora da Encarnação** Ribeira do Nabo 9800, São Jorge. Traditional weaving equipment sets the scene in this women-led cooperative where talented hands have been embroidering for over thirty years.

**Lava Studio** Rua das Angústias 66, Faial; www.facebook.com/lavastudioazores. Ornate handmade ceramics, paintings and trinkets – all from the Azores or mainland – in a well-curated boutique.

**Uniao de Cooperativas Agricolas de Lacticinios** Canadinha Nova, Beira, São Jorge; www.uniqueijo.pt. Take a tour of the cheese factory and then sample and buy São Jorge *queijo* straight from the source.

*Azul Singular*'s luxury yurts, Faial

Biertan's UNESCO-listed fortified church

# HIKING VIA TRANSILVANICA

## A trek beyond the vampire lore

Transylvania: it looms in the imagination as a shadowy realm of creepy castles and bloodthirsty vampires, where jagged mountain peaks and fog-draped forests set the stage for Gothic tales. There's more to the region than vampire lore, and an ambitious army of volunteers has set out to prove it with Via Transilvanica, a new walking trail that delves into the heart of the real Transylvania, through wild forests, time-forgotten villages and twelve UNESCO sites. The 1400km route crosses Romania diagonally from Putna to Drobeta-Turnu Severin and is marked by individually carved andesite stones; it's an epic art installation and a nod to the creativity of the Romanian people.

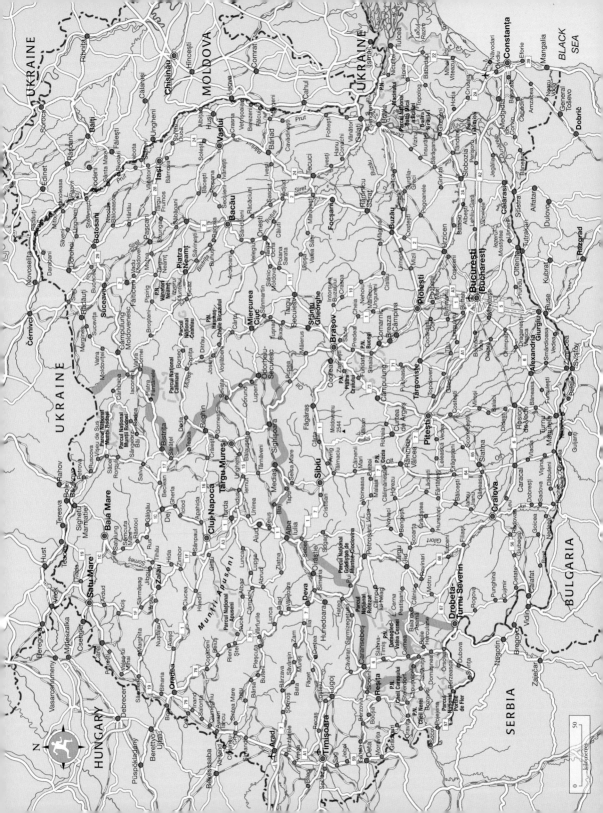

# THE JOURNEY

Transylvania's new walking trail starts in Bucovina on the slopes of the Eastern Carpathians, a region that spills over Romania's northern border into Ukraine. It's famed for its painted monasteries, whose beautiful fifteen- and sixteenth-century frescoes depicting scenes from the bible and the Siege of Constantinople are some of the best-preserved masterpieces of Byzantine art in the world. From Bucovina, the route rolls southwesterly for 1400km, finishing eventually on the banks of the Danube; next stop: Serbia. All in, Via Transilvanica makes the Camino de Santiago look like a walk in the park, but thankfully, you don't have to complete the whole thing to gain a taste of authentic Transylvania.

## FOLLOWING IN THE FOOTSTEPS OF THE SAXONS

This hike begins in Via Transilvanica's middle section, in a village called Micăsasa, the gateway into so-called Saxon Land. Transylvania's Saxons settled in the twelfth century when the Hungarian king offered them incentives to secure their help in defending the land's eastern borders from raiding nomadic tribes. The Germanic people brought with them their language, culture and medieval customs, all of which endured in Transylvania for over eight hundred years. But after the fall of Ceauşescu's communist regime in 1989, Romania's borders were flung open, and most of Transylvania's Saxons accepted Germany's offer of

Symbol marking Via Transilvanica trail

## PRACTICAL INFORMATION

**Distance covered:** 118km

**Recommended journey time:** 8 days

**Transport details:**

- Trains arrive at Micăsasa from the Transylvanian city of Sibiu (1hr 20min–2hr 10min; 3 daily; from €2.10; www.bilete.cfrcalatori.ro) with a change at Copsa Mica.

- For a no-fly journey, consider travelling by rail through Eastern Europe and taking the overnight train from Budapest. Multiple operators run services from London St Pancras to Budapest with journey times from 16hr 15 min (from €140). The sleeper train from Budapest leaves daily at 7.10pm and arrives in Sibiu at 6am (from £40 for a second-class seat/£90 for a bed in a shared sleeper compartment; www.

bilete.cfrcalatori.ro/en-GB/Itineraries).

- Sighişoara's train station is well-connected to other Transylvanian cities like Braşov (3hr 15min) and Cluj Napoca (3hr 30min) as well as Bucharest (5hr 30min).

- The Via Transilvanica website offers planning advice and a comprehensive day-by-day guide to the trail (www.viatransilvanica.com).

- The Via Transilvanica trail is all about taking things slow, but if you're interested in shifting up a few gears, local guide Peter Lorand offers e-bike and mountain-bike tours from his home village of Bazna (www.trailguide.ro). You can choose the self-guided option, but it's better to cycle with Peter for a fascinating insight into local culture.

Painted frescoes of Voroneţ Monastery in Bucovina

citizenship and headed back to the fatherland. The Saxons' legacy in Transilvania lives on in the fairy-tale villages they left behind.

Wander next into Şeica Mică, where a heavily fortified church towers over the village's matchbox houses. Hundreds of Gothic churches like this one stud the Via Transilvanica, all bearing the Saxons' architectural hallmarks of ochre-tiled roofs, whitewashed walls and hefty turrets. But although the Saxons have moved on, these are no ghost towns: in the years following their exodus, communities of Romanians, Hungarians and Roma have taken up residence here. Today, local town squares host hawkers flogging their wares, and horse-drawn carts clatter along dirt roads in a cloud of dust.

The walking trail leads out of Şeica Mică, along an unpaved path that slices through rough pastureland. It's another 11km until the next village, and thankfully the way is clearly marked by signposts bearing Via Transilvanica's logo – a tangerine "T" in a white circle. The same symbol can be seen on the andesite columns that mark every kilometre along the route; each milestone is a unique artwork, sculpted especially for this project. It's a reassuring sign you're on the right track.

Across sweeping meadows bursting with wildflowers, the Via Transilvanica wends through fields of golden corn, and forests bathed in the dappled glow of the sun. In the wild stretches between villages, it's rare to see another human soul. Bumblebees and butterflies busy themselves among the orchids. A symphony of songbirds soundtracks the walk, led by the unmistakable call of cuckoos.

Via Transilvanica has generated a lot of buzz – and not just from the pollen-gatherers hovering above the flower meadows. In 2023, the walking route won the Public Choice Award at the European Heritage Awards in Venice. It's important recognition for the trail, which was dreamt up by local non-profit Tăşuleasa Social. More than just a sustainable tourism initiative off Transylvania's beaten track, it's first and foremost a social project, designed to highlight and preserve the country's cultural heritage by connecting the different ethnic communities that make up the population of modern Romania.

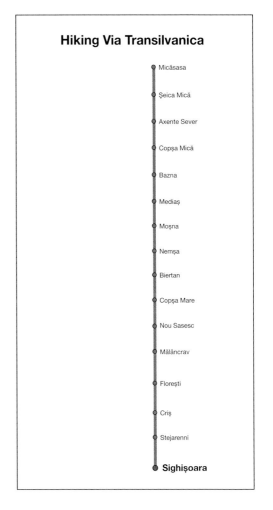

## Hiking Via Transilvanica

- Micăsasa
- Şeica Mică
- Axente Sever
- Copşa Mică
- Bazna
- Mediaş
- Moşna
- Nemşa
- Biertan
- Copşa Mare
- Nou Sasesc
- Mălâncrav
- Floreşti
- Criş
- Stejarenni
- **Sighişoara**

## UNESCO CREDENTIALS

In Transylvania, a red-capped church is as ubiquitous in a Saxon village as a McDonald's might be on a UK high street. The fifteenth-century church in Biertan, however, with its six towering turrets, three concentric walls and gilded altarpiece, is particularly impressive. UNESCO World Heritage Site levels of impressive, in fact – Biertan's is one of seven fortified churches that have earned a place on its list. Day-trippers flock from the bigger nearby towns to admire the village's picture-perfect pastel-coloured buildings and, of course, its magnificent religious centre. Horse and carts clop past on roughly cobbled roads. The heavy cameras that tourists yield here is an anachronism; a technology at odds with a place that belongs to a different time.

## ENGINES OF CHANGE

Back on the trail, and back in the countryside, where the rhythms of Transylvanian pastoral life drum to the same beat as they have for centuries. Farmers cut grass with long-handled scythes that are little changed since the Middle Ages. Headscarf-adorned women cradling wicker baskets pluck pears from low-hanging boughs in wild orchards. Shepherds wearing shaggy fleeces and felt *clop de paie* hats graze their flocks on hilly pastures. It seems more like Hobbiton than a Hardy novel, but these bucolic scenes bely the struggles of life in the Romanian countryside.

The engines of change are inevitable, even in Transylvania. Development projects have already dragged swathes of this region into the twenty-first century, bulldozing picturesque villages to make way for modern housing. Smallholder farmers have been muscled out of business by the onset of industrial-scale agriculture. It's no surprise that the youth are leaving the countryside in droves for Romania's cities or the bright lights of Western Europe. In Saxon Land, the Romanians and the Roma feel little connection to the archaic traditions of the Germanic people who built their towns.

But the old ways die hard, as seen in Mălâncrav. This sleepy village shelters over a hundred of Transylvania's few remaining Saxons, who live alongside Romanians, Hungarians and Roma in houses painted in washed-out shades of blues, pinks and greens. It's a multiethnic community of just over one thousand, and, thanks to a project funded by the Mihai Eminescu Trust, it's also a living museum where residents breathe new life into authentic traditional practices.

Sitting on piles of logs, swift-handed Roma twist hazel into wicker baskets. In workshops flanking a gravel road, seamstresses sit at wooden looms, weaving brightly coloured threads of wool into patterned folk skirts. Shopkeepers sell jams and juices made from fresh fruit picked in the village eco-

orchard. Meanwhile, up in the hills, shepherds delight in trading stories and sharing their ways with travellers over a warm bowl of soup or a glass of *palincă* (fruit spirit), and there's always a spare bed – or space in the hay barn, at least – for a weary walker.

It helps that these local heroes championing sustainable tourism have a powerful ally. Britain's King Charles III was so enchanted by Transylvania's rustic charm and wild landscapes on his first visit here in 1998 that he endeavoured to return every year after, and to help protect its precious ways of life. As a patron of the Mihai Eminescu Trust, and through various other foundations, including his own, King Charles has helped to safeguard hundreds of historical buildings across Transylvania through the training of young architects and craftspeople in time-honoured traditions.

Many have been lovingly restored as guesthouses, including a smattering in Mălâncrav, and some are personally owned by the king himself: you can spend the night at his private nature retreat in nearby Zalánpatak, with proceeds supporting the local community. All this, together with his support for farmers and artisans, has helped to revive Transylvania's villages.

## A BLOODTHIRSTY LEGACY

The last day on this section of the Via Transilvanica is a long one: a final push of almost thirty kilometres, from Mălâncrav to the historic town of Sighișoara, the believed birthplace of the real-life inspiration behind Stoker's Dracula: Vlad Țepeș, the Wallachian prince with a penchant for impaling. On a forest trail between the two towns, deep lacerations on the trunk of old beech trees are a startling reminder that brown bears roam these woods. If that doesn't inspire your tired legs to pick up the pace, nothing will.

A steep descent through the forest, and medieval Sighișoara draws into sight, the dark needle spire of its Gothic clocktower piercing the skyline. It's one of the grandest and most-visited medieval fortress towns in all of Saxon Land, and there are some interesting curiosities to discover here. The Spoonman is part

shop, part-gallery, dealing in authentic Romanian folk art; behind every linden-carved spoon is a story that its owner revels in sharing. Visitors can learn about the importance of the Saxon guilds, from tailors to tinsmiths, at the interesting history museum housed in the clocktower. The panoramas from the top are mightily impressive.

Down on the cobbled streets of its UNESCO-protected Old Town, throngs of tourists revel in the legend of big, bag Vlad the Impaler. Souvenir shops peddle fridge magnets and tacky t-shirts emblazoned with his face, complete with blood-dripping fangs. The house where Vlad III was supposedly born is now a kitschy restaurant, serving up dishes with names like "Dracula stew" and "Dracula chicken roll". Room for dessert? Order the "Dracula pancakes", of course. Mercifully, plans to build a Dracula-themed amusement park here in the early 2000s were quashed.

You can't blame the town for playing up its connections to the infamous Count. Vampire tourism has helped to put Transylvania on the map, bringing all-important dollars to a country with one of the highest poverty rates in the European Union (EU). But those who only follow the Dracula trail risk missing out on Transylvania's more authentic charms. Better to take the road less travelled, through rolling woods and time-warped villages. There might not be any vampires, but there's plenty more at stake.

# LIKE A LOCAL

## STAY

**Casa Dornröschen** Coşbuc 25, Biertan; 07366 37121. The most restful place to stay in Biertan is actually within the church grounds (down the path from the archway at the church entrance) – the rooms are simple, aimed at returning Saxons rather than more demanding tourists.

**Mălâncrav 276A** Mălâncrav 276, 557117; www.experiencetransylvania.ro/guesthouse/malancrav-276. In Mălâncrav, the painstakingly renovated *conac* or manor house of the Apafi family is now a guesthouse, with five en-suite bedrooms, a library and a stately drawing room. It is owned and managed by the Mihai Eminescu Trust, which has half a dozen other accommodations in the village, as well as an organic orchard with ancient varieties of apple, pear, plum and walnut, producing wonderful juices. Home-cooked meals come courtesy of a housekeeper. Proceeds help to support the trust's cultural heritage projects.

**Medieval Apartments Frauendorf** Principala 316, Axente Sever, 557025; https://booking.turistin transilvania.com. Hunker down in one of the former supply rooms at Axente Server's fourteenth-century fortified church for a unique Saxon-style stay.

**Pensiunea La Teo** Şcolii 14, Sighişoara; www.delateo.ro. Set around a flower-filled inner courtyard in Sighişoara are three elegant neo-Baroque-furnished rooms with marble-finish bathrooms.

## EAT & DRINK

**Casa Ardeleana** Greweln no. 1, Mediaş, 557050; www.casaardeleanamedias.ro/despre. The golden wines of

Traditional Transylvanian cuisine

Mediaş receive a name check in Stoker's iconic novel, *Dracula*. Try it for yourself at *Casa Ardeleana*, a cosy little restaurant that serves up traditional Transylvanian fare.

**Stana de pe coline** Principală, Floreşti, 557116; +40 741 633 814. On the road to Sighişoara, stop off at shepherd Florin's homestead near Floreşti for a hot meal cooked with produce fresh from the farm. If you want to break up the journey, consider overnighting here, and mucking in with the farm work the next morning for an authentic shepherd's experience.

**Unglerus** 1 Decembrie 1918 1, Biertan; www.unglerus. com. Just below Biertan's church, the medieval-themed *Unglerus* restaurant is good for a hearty meal, though rather group-oriented; all the usual meaty suspects, from roast chicken and smoked sausages to veal stew with polenta.

## SHOP

**Obiecte Traditionale** Casa Venetiana, Piața Muzeului 6, Sighişoara 545400; www.obiectetraditionale. ro. Mark 'The Spoonman' Tudose runs a gallery in Sighişoara where you can admire traditional Romanian folk art fashioned by local craftspeople. It's also a souvenir shop that's actually worth visiting.

Södermalm, Stockholm's trendy quarter

# OFFBEAT SCANDINAVIA
## *Friluftsliv* between two capitals

Direct trains connect Stockholm and
Oslo in under six hours, but breaking
up the journey allows you to discover
charming small towns and to embrace
the Nordic concept of *friluftsliv*
('outdoor living') in the forests, flower
meadows and pristine lakes in between
the two capitals. Industrialisation came
late to Scandinavia, meaning that many
city-dwellers still cherish their ties
to the countryside. Around half of all
Swedes and Norwegians have access to
a log cabin (*fritidshus* or *sommarstuga*),
and during the summer, cities empty
out as the locals retreat to reconnect
with nature. Follow their lead and take a
detour into the heart of Sweden.

# THE JOURNEY

Bookended by offbeat tours revealing a different side to two well-trodden capital cities, this journey also takes in charming small towns, seemingly endless forested countryside, and a lake shaped by a meteorite. Time your trip for summer to make the most of the long days, or visit in early autumn to glimpse the vast woodland ablaze in fiery hues. Whenever you visit, embrace the Nordic concept of *friluftsliv* ('outdoor living') and spend as much time as you can exploring walking trails and plunging into (or on) the water. This breezy alfresco vibe is made easy by *allemansrätten*, 'everyman's right' to roam and even camp in nature.

## AN INSIDER TOUR OF STOCKHOLM

Start your visit in Gamla Stan, the city's Old Town, where pastel-coloured buildings line the streets. Beyond the big-hitting Royal Palace, you should also spend time ducking down the side alleys to stumble across local haunts; Mårten Trotzigs gränd is the narrowest in Sweden.

Södermalm is the city's hipster quarter, brimming with vintage shops and a wide range of bars and cafés, the latter filling the streets with the scent of cinnamon and strong coffee, particularly in the trendy Nytorget neighbourhood. For a glimpse of the island's working-class past, head to Nytorget, Svartensgatan and Master Mikaels gata to see traditional architecture dating back to the 1700s, including some of the few remaining wooden workers' houses.

The viewpoints at Monteliusvägen or Skinnarviksberget frame classic postcard vistas of the city, and there are lovely walks along either the north or south shore of the island. Another scenic amble is along Norr Mälarstrand, wrapping around the southern shore of Kungsholmen. This island is largely residential and you'll likely be joined by locals jogging or pushing prams on the route from the City Hall – an imposing building inspired by Venice's Doge's Palace – to Rålambshovsparken. Here, you can take a dip in the lake, or rent a kayak or stand-up paddleboard to see Stockholm from the water.

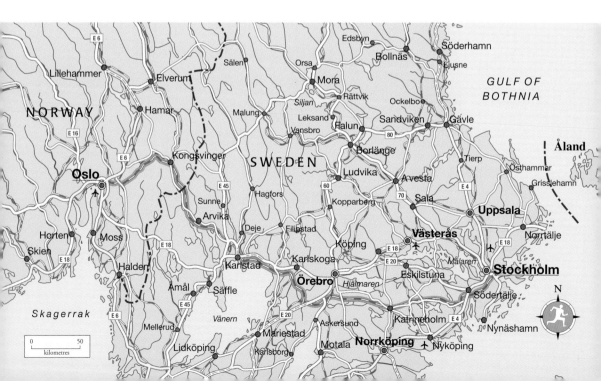

One activity you should fit into your stay is a boat trip; skip the tourist excursions and catch one of several commuter ferries. The most popular route links Slussen on Gamla Stan with Djurgården, a lush green island peppered with museums as well as being a good place for strolls in nature.

## DALARNA

Dalarna is Swedish for 'the valleys' and this is the place you probably have in mind when you picture Sweden: red houses and log cabins punctuating a landscape of lakes and forests. Your journey here follows a historic migration route in reverse; generations have traversed the Dalkarlsvägen (Dalarna Way) to reach the capital city for work opportunities. On the final stretch of the three-hour train journey from Stockholm to Rättvik, don't miss the views of deep blue Lake Siljan, created millions of years ago when a meteorite crashed into the earth.

The charming lakeside town of Rättvik makes an excellent base, with varied accommodation options as well as the chance for boat rides or swims in the lake. Långbryggan, a 628m-long pier – the longest in Scandinavia – jutting over Lake Siljan, makes for a lovely evening stroll to watch the late sunset. Longer walks include the 10km lakeside path to Vikarbyn (hop on the bus back) or, for a more challenging route with excellent views, follow the 7.5km Tre Toppar trail to take in the peaks of Hedsåsberget, Lerdalsberget and Hökolsberget (you can turn back after just one or two if you prefer). Another beautiful town just a short train ride away is Tällberg, a cluster of flower-draped wooden cottages on a promontory in the lake.

You can't visit Dalarna without descending into the depths of the huge copper mine in Falun, an hour's bus ride from Rättvik. At its peak, this site produced two-thirds of Europe's copper, and you can thank the mineral ore for the distinctive red colour of the houses in rural

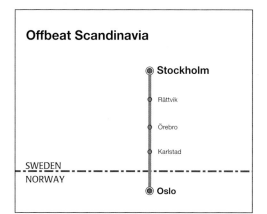

## Offbeat Scandinavia

◉ **Stockholm**

◦ Rättvik

◦ Örebro

◦ Karlstad

SWEDEN
NORWAY

◉ **Oslo**

Sweden (called 'Falu red'). For local culture, the Museum of Dalarna in central Falun offers an introduction to the region's folk art, the Dala horse, dresses and music, as well as a reconstruction of the wood-panelled study where Swedish author and the first woman to receive the Nobel Prize in literature Selma Lagerlöf worked when she moved to Falun in 1897.

### ARTY ÖREBRO

A two-and-a-half-hour train journey from Falun will take you to the university town of Örebro and, depending on the season, it's a good short stop-off. If you happen to be visiting between mid-June and early September in

## PRACTICAL INFORMATION

**Distance covered:** 830km

**Recommended journey time:** 8 days+

**Transport details:**

- It is possible to reach the Swedish capital without flying by taking trains: for instance, by taking the Eurostar from London to Brussels, followed by a train to Hamburg and a sleeper service to Stockholm Central Station. Getting to Sweden by train is more expensive than flying, however, with no through tickets from the UK so it's worth buying a rail pass instead; a global Interrail or Eurail pass are the best options. From London, trains to Sweden travel via Brussels, Cologne, Hamburg and Copenhagen. A typical journey will involve changing trains four or five times and take around 24hr, so might be most suitable for those planning a multi-city trip. For a dependable summary of the options of getting to Sweden by train, check out www.seat61.com.
- Oslo has direct trains to Hamburg, as well as ferry links to Kiel in northern Germany, with the latter taking you along the stunning Oslofjord.
- Vy (www.vy.se) and Swebus Express offer train and bus services through Sweden and Norway (FlixBus also covers some routes),

while national train operator SJ (www.sj.se) operates an extensive train network across Sweden. Routes include Stockholm to Rättvik (3hr 20min; 2 daily; second-class tickets from £18); Falun to Örebro (2hr 30min; hourly, every 2hr Sat & Sun; second-class tickets from £18); and Karlstad to Oslo (2hr 30min; 3–5 daily; second-class tickets from £11). Bus services link Rättvik and Falun (1hr; hourly, every 2hr Sat & Sun; from £5).

- Long-distance bus operator Vy Bus4You connects Örebro and Karlstad via multiple direct services each day (#850; 1hr 40min; from £11). To travel by train, take the Vy Nattåg Regional if it suits your timing (1hr 20min; 1 daily on Sat & Sun eve only; from £11), or change at Hallsberg (1hr 40min–2hr 40min; 8–12 daily; from £11).
- This route is possible by car, which gives you more flexibility, especially in rural central Sweden. If you choose to drive, perhaps venture further north into Dalarna, and make up the time by driving straight from Falun to Karlstad. Car-rental companies include all the usual suspects: Avis (www.avis.com); Europcar (www.europcar.com); Hertz (www.hertz.com) and SIXT (www.sixt.com).

an even-numbered year, you can experience OpenArt, an outdoor festival that transforms the whole town into an open-air contemporary art gallery. At other times, the Örebro konsthall – the museum behind the biennial – hosts a range of exhibitions. Otherwise, Örebro's fortified thirteenth-century castle steals the show, forming a magnificent backdrop to the water-lily-studded Svartån River.

The open-air museum Wadköping is also worth a visit. An entire village of centuries-old wooden cottages and shops was brought to the site in the 1950s, when urban planning was threatening the historic dwellings with demolition. A local man, Bertil Waldén, campaigned to save the better ones, and relocated them here at Wadköping on the banks of the river. The extremely pretty little 'high street' is flanked with low eighteenth-century buildings on one side, and on the other with taller houses dating from after the town fire of 1854. Some of the cottages are now lived in again, while others are used for small exhibitions, and for artisans to demonstrate traditional trades such as blacksmithing and silversmithing.

## RIVER-THREADED KARLSTAD

Around two hours by bus or train from Örebro, Karlstad is strung along the northern shore of Lake Vänern, which covers a whopping 5600 square kilometres (four times the size of Greater London), stretching 140km in length from Trollhättan, northeast of Gothenburg, up to Karlstad. The quaint summer-only water buses are the perfect way to explore the 'sunshine city': the Mariebergsskogen nature park is ideal for families, while an island-hopping adventure to Jäverön or Västra Långholmen is great for walks and swimming in the archipelago. Back in the city centre, wander along the river, or head out on foot or bike along a stretch of the Klarälvsbanan trail.

*Mälardrottningen Yacht Hotel,* Stockholm

The Värmlands Museum offers a comprehensive account of the province's life and times; it's small but its temporary exhibitions in particular are excellent, or discover the work of one of Scandinavia's leading watercolourists, Värmland-born Lars Lerin, who has returned to his homeland and lives in Hammarö, just south of Karlstad.

## OSLO, NORWAY'S LEADING LIGHT

Once you've had your fill of Karlstad, it's time for the final leg of the trip: a two-and-a-half-hour train ride to Oslo, a modern metropolis with plenty of gems to discover. Highlights in the city centre are the 2022-opened National Museum; MUNCH, a museum dedicated to Norway's most famous artist; and a dizzying walk on the roof of the Operahuset (Opera House) for fine views of the city and the fjord. If you happen to be in town on a Sunday, it's worth pre-booking tickets for the Emanuel Vigeland Museum, one of the most offbeat spots you'll find in the Norwegian capital. The artist – whose elder brother sculptor Gusta is behind the better-known Oslo sight of the sculpture-dotted Vigelandsparken – actually designed the room to be his own tomb, covering the walls in eerie frescos.

Just east of the centre, Grünerløkka is one of the best spots for ambling, either along the river or in and out of the independent boutiques and chilled-out cafés that are giving the district a reputation as the cool side of the city. Formerly a rundown working-class district, Grünerløkka has been reinvigorated in a boho sort of way, popular among artists and students. The main drag, Thorvald Meyers gate, is dotted with retro shops, bars and restaurants – plus a couple of pocket-sized urban parks – and people come here from all over the city to eat and drink.

Lesser visited is the Rodeløkka neighbourhood, a formerly industrial enclave whose wooden houses have been well preserved. Their bright facades exude a fairy-tale vibe, intensified by the often-present aroma of chocolate drifting over the red rooftops from the Freia factory, one of Norway's leading confectionary brands.

The glittering Oslofjord

If you're looking to pack more natural landscapes into your trip, it's a short uphill walk to Ekebergparken, a small city park framing the view that inspired Edvard Munch to paint *The Scream*. Alternatively, you can catch the metro to Frognerseteren, a wild pocket of wooded hills and lakes offering panoramic views over the city and hiking trails suitable for a range of abilities. And of course, there's the Oslofjord, necklaced by an archipelago of low-lying, lightly forested islands, to the south of the city centre. The sheltered waters are best explored by boat, kayak or stand-up paddleboard, dipping into the nooks and crannies of the islet-studded channel.

Also close by are Hovedøya, a pretty island with its mosaic of pastures and woodland, Cistercian monastery ruins, and shingle beaches; Lindøya and its scattering of candy-coloured wooden cottages; and Gressølmen, which attracts a young crowd in summer. Hop between the three to round off your Nordic adventure.

MUNCH, an Oslo museum dedicated to the iconic Norwegian artist

# LIKE A LOCAL

## STAY

**Bruntegården** Vålsvedsvägen 51, Rättvik; www.xn--bruntegrden-38a.se. Dating back to 1868, this typically Swedish guesthouse run by a local chef offers lake views, a restaurant with top-quality locally sourced food, and proximity to Rättvik's summer toboggan run.

**Livin Station Hotel** Östra Bangatan 3, 703 61, Örebro; www.livinstation.se. You can't get closer to Örebro's train station than this railway-themed boutique hotel.

**Mälardrottningen Yacht Hotel** Riddarholmskajen 4, 111 28 Stockholm; www.malardrottningen.se. Stockholm is a city best seen from the water, so why not book a night on one of its floating hotels? This refined choice has a bar and restaurant on board.

**Oslofjorden Friluftsråd** Hovedøya; www.oslofjorden.org. From a non-profit that works to protect the Oslofjord's environment, this cabin-rental scheme offers self-catering accommodation in former shops, post offices and railway buildings. It's a choice for intrepid travellers only; most cabins require guests to supply their own bedding, though a rowing boat is often included in the rental. Two are on Hovedøya close to the centre.

## EAT & DRINK

**Kafé Rosteriet** Tolagsgatan 1, 652 24 Karlstad; www.lofbergs.se/kaffebar. Traditional Swedish coffee fresh from the Löfbergs roastery next door – you can also book coffee tastings or guided tours. Löfbergs is a Swedish institution and has a focus on sustainability.

**Lisas Grabb Café & Hembageri** Blekingegatan 36, 118 56 Stockholm. Serving up some of the best cinnamon buns in Stockholm, this café is a gem. There are other spots nearby for barista-made coffee; here you'll get filter coffee or tea, with a choice of home-made classic bakes, all self-serve with an ambience that feels like someone's living room. Owner Niklas (Lisa's 'boy' or *grabb*) is continuing the family tradition.

**Pub Stallyktan** Södra Strandgatan 3B, 702 10 Örebro; www.stallyktan.se. Cosy spot to try the traditional dish of *pyttipanna*, a meat, potato and onion hash.

**Renbiten Deli** Holmgatan 32, 791 71, Falun; www.renbiten.se. Family-run Falun shop and café selling crafts and food typical of Sweden's Sámi population.

**Rest** Kirkegata 1-3, 0153 Oslo; www.restaurantrest.com. A (pricey) zero-waste fine-dining experience in Oslo.

**Sopköket** Söderhallarna, Medborgarplatsen 3, 118 26 Stockholm; www.sopkoket.se. In an unassuming food hall in the south of Stockholm, *Sopköket* creates tasty lunches from ingredients that would otherwise be binned, and leftovers feed the city's unhoused people.

**Vippa** Akershusstranda 25, 0150 Oslo; www.vippa.no. A food hall with nine stalls offering diverse cuisines. It's also a social enterprise, using ethically sourced food from local farms and pairing up experienced chefs with restaurant entrepreneurs to support them.

## SHOP

**A World of Craft** Hornsgatan 58, 118 21 Stockholm; www.aworldofcraft.se. Three Stockholm branches selling artisanal goods by makers in developing countries across Africa, Asia and Latin America.

**Brudd** Markveien 42A, 0554 Oslo; www.brudd.info. In Oslo's Grünerløkka district, scratch your shopping itch at Brudd, where crafts are made by its twenty-strong artists' collective, or at the Sunday market at cultural venue BLÅ (Brenneriveien 9C; www.blaaoslo.no).

**Handslaget i Rättvik** Torget, 795 30 Rättvik; www.handslaget.nu. The place for souvenirs, from jams and cheeses to ceramics and woodwork, almost all produced by Dalarna makers. Look out for typical Swedish flavours like lingonberry jam.

**Lisa Larsson Second Hand** Bondegatan 48, 116 33 Stockholm; www.lisalarssonsecondhand.com. Sweden has plenty of vintage stores (Myrorna, Emmaus, Stadsmissionen) and this one in the capital is a gem, focusing on designer items.

**Papercut** Krukmakargatan 24, 118 51 Stockholm; www.papercutshop.se. A haven of books, art and design.

**Värmlands Hemslöjd** Västra Torggatan 18, 652 24 Karlstad; www.varmlandshemslojd.se. Homeware and Swedish souvenirs, many produced in Värmland.

St Mary's, Kraków

# POLISH PILGRIMAGE
## A slow train from Gdańsk to Kraków

This grand rail tour visits some of Poland's most captivating – and often underappreciated – cities. Bypass faster trains in favour of slower ones to take in the scenery as you travel from Gdańsk, a historically pivotal northern metropolis, to Kraków, the former royal capital whose Old Town was honoured by UNESCO as one of the twelve original World Heritage Sites in 1978. In between, call at youthful Poznań to soak up its lively café culture; the lesser-visited city of Wrocław and its unexpected architectural riches; under-the-radar Łódź for its surprising arts and cultural scene; and the shape-shifting capital city of Warsaw, a symbol of destruction and regeneration.

# THE JOURNEY

It is fair to say that Gdańsk, one of Poland's oldest cities, has played a definitive role in European history. It was in Gdańsk where the Thirteen Years' War ended in 1466 with the defeat of the Teutonic Knights. It was in Gdańsk, following the German attack in 1939, that marked the beginning of World War II. It was in Gdańsk, at the Lenin Shipyard in 1980, that the trade union Solidarity was founded, which eventually led to the collapse of communism in Poland. Following a century of sociopolitical upheaval, the city has finally settled into a new role: as the epicentre of tourism in Pomerania, Poland's northern land.

The windswept Baltic city can largely be divided into two parts. Its vibrant Old Town (Stare Miasto), in the north of the city, may look medieval but it was almost entirely flattened during World War II and has since been rebuilt; nearly all of its present buildings are completely reconstructed. Authenticity aside, the brick Gothic churches, Renaissance-era city gates and narrow eighteenth-century merchants' houses still look the part and are charming, nonetheless.

The other half of town is the bustling waterfront area with its retro blend of colourful quayside buildings and shipyard industry focused around the National Maritime Museum. Here you'll find the fifteenth-century port crane, the largest in medieval Europe; an exhibition on primitive boats; the SS *Sołdek*, a retired Polish coal and ore freighter; and, of course, the famous Gdańsk Shipyards, birthplace of the trade union Solidarity.

Wrocław's Rynek (market square)

## Polish pilgrimage

- Gdańsk
- Poznań
- Wrocław
- Łódź
- Warsaw
- Kraków

Manufaktura, textile mill turned arts centre in Łódź

### BOHEMIAN POZNAŃ

Around a three-hour train journey south of Gdańsk, Poznań is the ideal overnight stop. Diverse, lively and bohemian, the small city crams in a lot. At its core is the Old Town centred around its ever-busy market square (Stary Rynek) lined by restaurants, cafés and bars; in spring and summer, tables spill out onto the cobblestones. If you have time, there is a clutch of interesting museums and galleries, such as the Historical Museum of Poznań and the futuristic Porta Posnania Interactive Heritage Centre, as well as a handful of monuments and landmarks including Poland's oldest cathedral, the Basilica of Sts Peter and Paul, on the peaceful holy island of Ostrów Tumski.

Even if your train arrives in Poznán well after the sun has set, you won't be disappointed by the city's dynamic bar and club scene.

### WROCŁAW: A LESSER-VISITED GEM

Traded back and forth for a millennium by various duchies, known as Breslau for centuries while occupied by Germans, decimated during World War II, and then rebuilt and restored as thousands of Poles returned after the preceding nightmare – the history of Wrocław (pronounced '*Vrots-waff*') is certainly a catalogue of trials and tribulations.

Despite its turbulent past, the city is delightful. Aside from its picturesque location on the River Odra, its twelve islands, 130 bridges and riverside parks, Wrocław has a captivating Old Town. Its cobblestone streets maintain a gentle mix of Gothic and Baroque architecture, while a significant student population affords the town its youthful energy and ensures there are plenty of restaurants, cafés and bars. What's more, the city doesn't suffer from the tourist crowds of Warsaw and Kraków.

In the heart of the Old Town is the fairy-tale Rynek market square with its collection of fascinating architecture, including the turreted thirteenth-century town hall and its ornate facades; St Elizabeth's Church with its iconic 90m-high tower; and the quaint Baroque houses known as Hänsel and Gretel (Jaś i Małgosia). Further afield, there is the Jewish quarter,

## PRACTICAL INFORMATION

**Distance covered:** 1150km

**Recommended journey time:** 12–14 days

**Transport details:**

- By train the fastest option from London is to take the Eurostar to Brussels, and then continue across Belgium and Germany to Berlin, from where express services run to Warsaw, Poznan, Wrocław and Kraków (return trip will cost from £180; www.bahn.com). None of these options takes longer than 24hr, but you might like to break up the journey with stops in Brussels and Berlin. Alternatively, all the usual suspects offer flights to Gdańsk and Warsaw from the UK.

- In Poland, PKP InterCity (www.intercity.pl) is the big-hitter, overseeing a range of express intercity services plus EuroCity (EC) and TLK trains. PolRegio (www.polregio.pl) runs local and crosscountry trains at slower speeds than their PKP equivalents and stop at more stations en route; rates are noticeably cheaper, however.

- Onward tickets can be bought at city train stations or in advance at www.polrail.com; consider buying an Interrail or Eurail (www.eurail.com) for multi-destination trips.

- Dedicate at least two days to each city, more if time allows.

Stalinist-era architecture in Warsaw's Constitution Square

the university district and its huddle of handsome Baroque and Neoclassical structures, and the pretty river islands of Wyspa Piasek and Ostrów Tumski. Throw in a spirited cultural scene of theatres, popular festivals, museums, galleries, clamorous nightlife, and you have a thriving metropolis with the air of a city on the move. Wrocław is moreish, so make the most of your time here.

## YOUTHFUL ŁÓDŹ

Heading east now into the green heart of Poland, it's on to Łódź: a city that remains a mystery to most travellers despite its substantial size. Nineteenth-century industry behemoth turned arts and culture hub, Łódz is one of the country's most changed faces. It is a relatively young city, having grown rapidly over the last two hundred years from an obscure village to Poland's third-largest metropolis.

During its rise, the city collected some nicknames, from the 'Polish Manchester' for its textile boom, to 'Holly-Łódź' (pronounced 'Holly-woodge') as a nod to its famous film school that churned out talent like Roman Polański, Krzysztof Kieślowski and Andrzej Wajda. Its huge red-brick factories, many now reimagined as restaurants, shopping centres, bars and heritage centres, are immortalised in Wajda's Oscar-nominated film, *The Promised Land*, an adaptation of the mill-town tale written by Nobel laureate Władysław Reymont.

There is an embarrassment of Art Nouveau architecture and a host of contemporary art museums (Leopold Kindermann Villa, Łódz Art Museum, Łódz Art Center, Manhattan Transfer) to keep you regaled for an afternoon, making it an ideal spot to break up the journey from Wrocław to Warsaw.

## WARSAW: A STORY OF DESTRUCTION AND REGENERATION

Warsaw: a city that has endured so much, yet still manages to flourish. At first glance, it may be easy to forget that 85 percent of the city was destroyed during World War II. Warsaw today is modern, fashionable, important and thriving – everything you would desire

from a contemporary European city. But glance around a corner, catch an inscription on a building, spot a museum from a tram, and you'll see that this city wears its history on its sleeve.

Warsaw was the seat of the Polish monarchy for centuries; the home of classical composer Chopin; a brave resister to the Nazis in 1944 during the gallant but tragic Warsaw Uprising; and a testament to Poland's efforts to reconstruct itself from almost nothing after being razed to the ground during World War II.

In reality, at least a couple of days are needed to scratch beneath the surface of this multilayered city. There is the UNESCO-listed Old Town, painstakingly reconstructed brick by brick after World War II, but still charming nonetheless; the enormous red-brick Royal Castle; the haunting Jewish Cemetery, filled with the graves of over 250,000 people; the splendid landscaped parks; the unique University Library Roof Garden; and the Stalinist-era architecture such as Palace of Culture and Science – a 'gift of friendship' from the Soviet Union. And then there are the museums. Too many to list here, but if you visit only one make it the POLIN Museum of the History of the Polish Jews, located amid the former ghetto.

Despite or perhaps because of its past, Warsaw is a city of reinvention. Even today, it refuses to stand still, giving rise to cutting-edge architecture and museums, a gourmand dining scene and new nightlife districts.

## KRAKÓW

The former royal capital was Poland's only major city to escape World War II virtually undamaged. Since then, its gorgeous Old Town was honoured by UNESCO as one of the twelve original World Heritage Sites, first listed in 1978. The Old Town effortlessly fuses European architectural styles – including Romanesque, Gothic, Renaissance, Baroque and Art Nouveau – with a jumble of narrow cobbled streets, elaborate churches and palaces, and grand medieval sights. Add in delicious food, heavenly gelato and endless cocktails in Europe's largest medieval town square and the result is simply exquisite.

The city is easily explored on foot beginning at the buzzing Rynek Główny, Europe's largest medieval town square, overlooked by the striking St Mary's or Mariacki Church (Kosciół Mariacki) and the soaring fifteenth-century Town Hall Tower. Other highlights include the eye-catching Wawel Cathedral and castle complex – the former seat of the Polish monarchy – and Rynek Underground, a vast subterranean museum beneath the market square, whose tunnels, medieval stalls, alcoves and long-forgotten compartments were discovered during excavations that took place when the Rynek was being repaved in 2005–08.

For a sobering insight into Poland's darkest days, Auschwitz-Birkenau is a harrowing day-trip from Kraków. Historians estimate that over 1.1 million people were murdered between 1940 and 1945 in the concentration camp. Guided tours take in the notorious gas chambers, the death wall where thousands of prisoners were killed by firing squad, and roll-call square where the daily headcount could last for hours. But don't let this be the final vignette of your journey. Allow at least another day in Kraków to process the experience and sow some more uplifting – but no less indelible – memories into your tour of Poland.

## LIKE A LOCAL

### STAY
**Art Hotel** Kiełbaśnicza 20, 50-110 Wrocław; www.arthotel.pl. Just steps from the epicentre of Wrocław's Old Town, the *Art Hotel* is an uncomplicated yet stylish hotel where guests instantly feel at home.

**Ester** Ul. Szeroka 20, Kraków; www.hotel-ester.krakow.pl. In the heart of Kazimierz, opposite the Old Synagogue, and within walking distance of Wawel Castle, the *Ester* is an intimate bolthole (only fifty guests fit in when full) with friendly staff, mural-

Porta Posnania Interactive Heritage Centre in Poznań

Café Bristol, Warsaw

adorned rooms and a smart restaurant serving up Polish and Jewish cuisine.

**H15 Luxury Palace** Św. Jana 15, 31-017 Kraków; www.hotelh15palace.pl. Right in the heart of Kraków's Old Town, just 200m from Rynek Główny, this chic hotel was built into the sixteenth-century Lubomirski Palace.

**Hotel Bristol** Krakowskie Przedmieście 42/44, 00-325 Warsaw; www.marriott.com. Greats such as concert pianist turned prime minister Ignacy Jan Paderewski and Picasso have stayed here – for good reason. A Warsaw landmark and the city's most elegant hotel.

## EAT & DRINK

**Bar Mleczny Stągiewna** Stągiewna 15, 80-750 Gdańsk; www.barstagiewna.pl. A *bar mleczny* (milk bar) serves traditional Polish food – and plenty of it. A Gdańsk institution and one of Poland's finest milk bars.

**Brasserie L'Olympique** Pijarska 13, 31-015 Kraków; www.hotelfrancuski.pl/en/bon-appetit. Wrap up your trip with an exquisite repast at 1912-born L`Olympique. Cute patisserie by day, classic French brasserie by night.

**Café Bristol** Krakowskie Przedmieście 42/44, 00-325 Warsaw; www.cafebristol.pl. If you can't stretch to a room, then drop by for a morning croissant instead.

## SHOP

**Manufaktura** Drewnowska 58, 91-002 Łódź; www.manufaktura.com. Textile mill turned arts and retail hub.

**Sukiennice (Cloth Hall)** Rynek Główny 1/3, 31-042 Kraków. Former seat of Kraków's medieval clothing trade, turned bustling arts and crafts market.

**Ziemiosfera Zero Waste Shop** Romana Dmowskiego 10, 80-264 Gdańsk; www.ziemiosfera.pl. Patrycja and Franswa are behind this eco-friendly shop and café.

# DUTCH BIKE TOUR

## Cycling the Netherlands' wild coast

You don't need to be a member of the Lycra brigade for this two-wheeled jaunt up the Dutch coast, which could plausibly be done on your grandma's old three-speed. Bookended by the overnight ferry between England and Hoek van Holland, the 160km cycle skirts past colourful tulip fields, rugged national parks and beaches that look like they should be in southern Europe, not facing off against the indomitable North Sea. Overcrowded Amsterdam is conspicuous by its absence. But you won't miss it: Haarlem, The Hague and Alkmaar are just as cosy, with canals and culture of their own. The final stop: Texel, a glorious dune-swept island, before returning by rail via Delft.

# THE JOURNEY

You've got to hand it to the Dutch. While the rest of the world went gung-ho for cars in the post-war years, they crisscrossed their country with cycle lanes, and now, half a century later, the rest of the world is playing catch up. You could forgive them for feeling a little smug. Is that what it is: smugness? Or simply a look of contentment on their faces as they cycle by on rickety old bikes, groceries stuffed in baskets, kids riding pillion. There's ample time to admire the enviable Dutch lifestyle on this two-wheeled trip up the Netherlands' coastline, which begins with an annoying wake-up jingle. Stena Line plays it to rouse passengers as day breaks in Hoek van Holland, the Dutch port where the overnight ferry from Harwich, Essex, docks around dawn, disgorging red-eyed passengers. After riding through passport control – a fun novelty in itself – it's tempting to crack on immediately and start ticking off the miles. But Hoek van Holland is worth lingering in, if just for a day, especially in summer, when Rotterdammers flock to the beach bars along the North Sea shore. Who needs the Med?

The concrete bunkers hidden in the nearby dunes recall more sobering times. The museum at Bunker Bremen en Hamburg offers some historical context to these German war defences. Striking a lighter note is Museum RockArt, a music museum with an exhibition devoted to Dutch pop.

PRACTICAL INFORMATION

**Distance covered:** 160km
**Recommended journey time:** 10 days
**Transport details:**

- Stena Line ferries connect Harwich and Hoek van Holland, including an overnight service (7–8hr; 2 daily; from £49 one-way for day ticket/£106 for overnight service; www.stenaline.co.uk).
- Teso runs ferries between Den Helder and Texel (€7.50 for cyclists and their bikes; 23 daily in summer; www.teso.nel; reservations are not necessary).
- Dutch national rail operator NS runs trains from Den Helder to Delft, with one change in Amsterdam (2hr 30min; 4 hourly; from €24; www.ns.nl; book in advance and reserve a space for your bike).

### A BREEZY START

The urge to press on soon kicks in. The first leg is easy. From Hoek van Holland, it's a gentle 20km ride along coastal cycle paths to The Hague. That includes a small detour to Scheveningen, the kiss-me-quick beach resort that evokes Brighton. There's a pier, an esplanade and pretty nineteenth-century seafront properties that will have you scrolling Rightmove. It's fun in the sun, forlorn in the rain; tacky in places, but charming. It also has one curious claim to fame: during World War II, resistance groups tested suspected Nazi infiltrators by making them say "Scheveningen" – an impossible feat for Germans, apparently, and not much easier for English-speakers either (try a throaty *s-khay-ve-ning-uh*). The town is home to an outstanding sculpture museum, Beelden aan Zee, and hosts a lively programme of special events, most memorably an international sand sculpture competition in May.

The Hague's pretty downtown – a fifteen-minute ride away – is arguably a better base, especially if you're sniffing out culture. Escher in Het Paleis, a gallery dedicated to the work of Dutch graphic artist Maurits Cornelis Escher (1898–1972), showcases his psychedelic take on the landscapes that await later in the trip. At Mauritshuis, it's all about the Dutch Masters, notably Vermeer, Rembrandt and Steen.

### REWILD THE RIDE

The first big test of the calf muscles is the 50km ride from The Hague to Haarlem. Lined with sand dunes, limpid lakes and colourful tulip fields, the route skirts past Nationaal Park Zuid-Kennemerland, where bison have been reintroduced as part of a rewilding project. Also roaming the land are Highland cattle, Shetland ponies and deer.

Haarlem, an old port city, has housed weary travellers for centuries and provides a welcome pit stop on this journey. Its brown cafés, so named because of their nicotine-stained walls, serve strong beers in cosy surrounds, and are a reminder that the Dutch do pubs better than most.

Haarlem has long lived in the shadow of Amsterdam, but you can spend a few days pottering around its cobbled streets before the nearby capital starts to call. The city has a handsome historic centre, great restaurants and big-hitting attractions, not least the Frans Hals Museum, named after the Dutch Golden Age painter, and showcasing an impressive collection of sixteenth- and seventeenth-century art. Among the most notable works are Hals's famous twin portraits, *Regents* and *Regentesses of the Oudemannenhuis*, which depict the people who ran the almshouse when Hals was living there; Cornelius Cornelisz van Haarlem's (1562–1638) giant *Wedding of Peleus and Thetis*, an appealing rendition of what was then a popular subject; and *Adam and Eve* by Maerten van Heemskerck (1498–1574).

## CHEESE COUNTRY

It's not all tulip fields and sand dunes along this coastal cycle ride. The 32km peddle from Haarlem to Alkmaar cuts through IJmuiden, a smut-belching port city with dirt under its fingernails. A free ferry shuttles cyclists across the River IJssel, which flows through Amsterdam further upstream, and empties out into the nearby North Sea.

Industry soon gives way to farmland and herds of cud-chewing cows on the final push to Alkmaar, a canal-threaded city that flies mysteriously under the radar of tourists, despite having echoes of Amsterdam.

Alkmaar is known across the Netherlands for its *kaasmarkt*, or cheese market, which has taken place on Waagplein since the 1300s. Crowds gather on the square to watch porters (*kaasdragers*) barrow in enormous wheels of the stuff every Friday from

**Dutch bike tour**

Hoek van Holland

Scheveningen

**Den Haag (The Hague)**

**Haarlem**

**Alkmaar**

Den Helder

*ferry*

Texel

**Delft**

March to September. The ceremony starts with the buyers sniffing, crumbling and finally tasting each cheese, followed by intensive bartering. Once a deal has been concluded, the cheeses – golden discs of local Beemster mainly, laid out in rows and piles on the square – are borne away on ornamental carriers for weighing. Curiously, the city also has a Beatles Museum, curated by a local superfan.

A ticket to ride is needed for the next leg of the trip, which involves a ferry ride across the North Sea to Texel. The 45km cycle to the ferry terminal in Den Helder, a naval city, is perhaps the most rugged of the whole route, passing through woods, rolling dunes and weather-beaten villages. A phrase comes to mind along the way: "God created the world, but the Dutch created the Netherlands". It's a hackneyed local saying, but there's some truth in it: over the centuries, the Dutch have painstakingly reclaimed great chunks of land from the sea. Some are still fighting the tide, not least the good folk of Egmond aan Zee, a village built in the shapeshifting sand dunes.

## ISLAND BOUND

A refuge for seabirds, seals and artists, Texel is part of the Wadden Islands; a wildlife-rich archipelago that follows the Dutch coast northeast into German waters

Cheese market in Alkmaar

Spaarne River, Haarlem

and on to Denmark. Catch a ferry from Den Helder for the twenty-minute journey to Texel. The island belies the Netherlands' status as one of Europe's most densely populated countries. Out of season, the weather-beaten native sheep surely outnumber humans. In summer, Dutch and German holidaymakers are among those flocking to the broad sandy beaches that honestly almost look Caribbean – almost. Scattered among the farms and forests inland are arty villages, modern restaurants and the pleasingly offbeat Maritime and Beachcombers Museum, a tribute to strange items that washed ashore nearby.

Back at Den Helder, departing trains chew up in a couple of hours the miles that took days to cycle. Rather than travelling all the way to Hoek van Holland, disembark at Delft. The lively university city has a pretty canal belt and one of the Netherlands' best flea markets, which spills out across the city centre every Saturday. Delft's famous son, the mysterious painter Johannes Vermeer (1632–75), was renowned for capturing life in the Netherlands. A visit to the Vermeercentrum, a museum dedicated to the artist, is then, perhaps, a fitting place to end this trip, before the short cycle south, along the canals, towards the Essex-bound ferry.

## LIKE A LOCAL

### STAY

**AmiCe** Donkere Spaarne, Haarlem; +31 6 30002018. Converted barge moored on the Spaarne in the heart of Haarlem. Berths are cosy; the setting is charming.

**Boutique Hotel de Salon** Noordeinde 140C, The Hague; www.salonvanfagel.nl. Period features abound in the characterful *Boutique Hotel de Salon*, which occupies an endearingly crooked seventeenth-century building along one of The Hague's most prestigious shopping streets.

**De Museumkamer** Burgwal 20, Den Burg; www.museumgalerierat.nl. Housed in the Museum Galerie RAT, this one-room guesthouse offers visitors exclusive viewings of artwork fashioned from flotsam.

## EAT

**Bogor Roemah Makan** Van Swietenstraat 2, The Hague; www.bogorroemahmakan.nl. *Rijsttafel* (Indonesian small plates) is a mainstay at this Hague restaurant.

**Paal 17** Ruijslaan 94–98, De Koog, Texel; www.paal17.com. The beachfront *Paal 17* is open for coffee and cake in the morning but gets fancier as the day progresses with its fine-dining menu. Hosts a dance festival in July.

**Willy's Vis** Wilsonsplein 23, Haarlem. A Haarlem institution serving seafood and sandwiches from a wooden kiosk overlooking the city's Leidsevaart canal.

## SHOP

**Concept Store Nyhavn** Koningstraat 15, Haarlem; www.conceptstore-nyhavn.nl. This sustainable concept store in downtown Haarlem sells secondhand furniture, ethically made fashion, natural cosmetics, and much more. Much of it from Dutch designers.

**Tony's Garage Sale** Westvlietweg 74 A3, The Hague; www.tonysgaragesale.com. Secondhand Scandi and Dutch vintage furniture that's seen better days is given a new lease of life by the upcyclers at this eco-conscious department store.

Toes-in-the-sand *Paal 17* in Texel

# SPANISH FOODIE TRAIL

## A tantalising gourmand experience

Embark on this EV-powered road trip for an introduction to Northern Spain's gastronomy, traditions and show-stealing architecture. Crossing six of Spain's autonomous communities – the Basque Country, Navarre, La Rioja, Castile & León, Asturias and Cantabria – your culinary pilgrimage cruises from coast to city before circling the serrated peaks of Picos de Europa. En route, local ingredients and provincial plates – forget *paella* and *churros* – from authentic kitchens pair perfectly with world-class wines and World Heritage Sites. Beyond the big-hitters, old-world *sidra* houses, cheese caves and elusive gourmand societies allow for a deeper connection with each region's culture.

Bilbao has undergone a cultural renaissance

# THE JOURNEY

Disembarking the ferry in Bilbao – seagulls squawking and engines rumbling – your first impression might be of a gritty, industrial port city. Perhaps true 25 years ago but Bilbao has experienced a beguiling renewal. Forgo the city's metro and dawdle on foot to soak it all in. Amble along the Río Nervión for an architectural feast, passing the Art Deco Mercado de la Ribera, Art Nouveau La Concordia station and the neo-Baroque Teatro Arriaga. Top billing is Frank Gehry's astounding Museo Guggenheim, a landmark of swirling titanium panels crammed with contemporary and modern art. This futuristic space, inaugurated in 1997, is the regeneration's kingpin. If you'd prefer art away from Bilbao's most-visited attraction, visit Museo de Bellas Artes' masterpieces instead.

Hungry? Enter the 700-year-old Casco Viejo (Old Town), where Bilbao's boisterous personality survives. Shirk Plaza Nueva and squeeze into an overspilling side-street bar for provincial plates, such as *bacalao al pil pil* (spiced salted cod), *marmitako* (tuna stew) and *txipirones* (baby squid).

## SIZZLING SAN SEBASTIÁN

San Sebastián is only an hour's drive from Bilbao, but an additional forty minutes will trade half the highway for scenic views. At Elgóibar, exit the AP-8 for the N-634. Windows down, a playlist of gentle waves begins at Playa de Deba. Secondary roads, edged by vineyards slanting to the shimmering Bay of Biscay, wend to the pretty coastal towns of Zumaia and Zarautz before narrow country lanes lead into Spain's culinary capital.

Dining well is built into Donostiarras' DNA; San Sebastián brags the world-renowned Basque Culinary Center, double-digit Michelin-starred restaurants, and first-class finger foods: *pintxos*. To best enjoy the

## PRACTICAL INFORMATION

**Distance covered:** 940km

**Recommended journey time:** 11–14 days

**Transport details:**

- Brittany Ferries offers services from Portsmouth to Bilbao (33hr; March–Nov 2 weekly; from £388 for a car and two passengers without a cabin; www.brittany-ferries.com) or Santander (33hr; 2 weekly; from £362). Sailings also run from Rosslare, Ireland, to Bilbao (29hr; March–Nov 2 weekly; from €175) or Santander (28hr; March–Nov 2 weekly; from €175). Renfe (www.renfe.com) offers direct train connections between Madrid and Bilbao (4hr 45min; from €16pp) and Santander (4hr 10min; from €33pp).
- If you don't bring your own car, you can hire an EV on arrival. OK Mobility offers hybrid rentals from Bilbao and Santander airports (from €20 per day; www.okmobility.com), and Hertz offers EV hire (from €100 per day; www.hertz.com).
- Alternatively, ALSA (www.alsa.es) and La Estellesa (www.laestellesa.com) bus services connect many of the cities and towns: San Sebastián to Logroño (2hr 15min; 2 daily; from €19.45); Logroño to Burgos (2hr; 7 daily; from €9); Burgos to León (1hr 45min; 4 daily; from €6); Oviedo to Picos de Europa (2hr 30min; 4 daily; from €10.30); and Picos de Europa to Santander via Bustio/Unquera (3hr; daily; from €10).
- National trains also link Bilbao and San Sebastián (2hr 40min; 15 daily; from €6.50; www.euskotren.eus), and León and Oviedo (1hr 10min; 5 daily; from €8; www.renfe.com).

latter, bar-hop the Old Town's countertops laden with small plates and skewered bites where bartenders pour *txakoli*, a lightly sparkling wine, from shoulder height. But the most intimate dining experience here is concealed underground. Eating in a *txoko* – long-standing, low-key, member-only communal kitchens – is invite-only, but some Basque chefs and tours can arrange this elusive, unforgettable experience (see page 189). Suitably stuffed, allow San Sebastián's other splendours to unfurl. Sunbathe on the butterscotch sands of La Concha, schlep (or ride the funicular) up Monte Igueldo or less-developed Monte Urgull for sweeping bay views, and learn more about Basque culture and Euskara, the age-old local language, in the Museo San Telmo.

## BOUNTY OF THE VINES IN LAGUARDIA

Next on the menu is the no-introduction-needed wine region of La Rioja. Sidestep the route skirting Pamplona and instead drive via Estella. The first half of

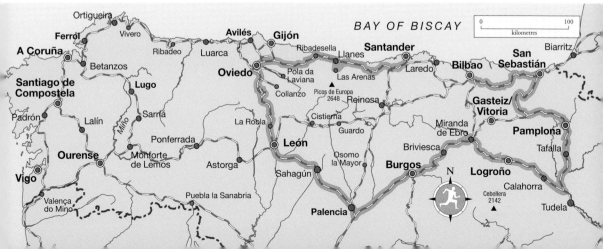

Medieval San Vicente de la Barquera, Cantabria

## Spanish foodie trail

● **Bilbao**

● Donostia-San Sebastián

● Logroño

● Burgos

● **León**

● Oviedo

● Las Arenas

● **Santander**

the journey is uneventful: tunnels and forest-flanked highway. But at Navarre's frontier, the jaw-dropping valley views of the Andía Mountains from Mirador del Puerto de Lizarraga reward the detour. Crossing Urbasa y Andía Natural Park, gushing cascades and karst caves provide pit-stop-worthy pauses.

In Logroño, trade car keys for a bus ticket for the short ride to Laguardia – it's wine-tasting time. This fetching tenth-century, car-free labyrinth camouflages medieval defence tunnels below, many now used for ageing wine. Plunge underground for a tour and tasting with *Bodega El Fabulista* or *Bodegas Carlos San Pedro Pérez de Viñaspre*. Back in Logroño, gain historical context at Museo de la Rioja before another animated evening of *pinchos* (*pintxo* is Basque). Logroño is perhaps the best pub crawl that an epicurean can have, with every bar lining lively Calle Laurell serving its own speciality small plate.

## LEÓN'S ARCHITECTURAL GEMS

The drive from Logroño to León is the longest and (arguably) least impressive, barrelling through patchworks of often-parched farmland. Put the pedal down, playlist on, and beeline to Burgos, a midpoint journey break. Plug in your EV and head for the hulking Gothic Catedral, which took over five hundred years to painstakingly build. Dip down a side street for a typical lunch of provincial *morcilla* (blood sausage) and roasted *cordero lechal* (suckling lamb).

In León, the cluster of architectural feats in the Casco Antiguo (Old Town) could easily fill two days. León Catedral's extensive (1800 square metres) stained-glass windows steal the show – some panels date to the thirteenth century. Ornate eleventh-century frescoes in the Panteón Real are motivation to join a guided tour of the Basílica de San Isidoro. And far from the hordes flocking around Gaudí's whimsical works in Barcelona, his modernist Casa Botines is delightfully devoid of crowds. By dark, Barrio Húmedo (Wet Quarter) buzzes. León is celebrated for its often-complimentary tapas accompanying each drink – the perfect excuse to taste a few Prieto Picudo wines.

## A SLOWER PACE IN OVIEDO

Heading north, travel via the N-630. It's not a road for the faint-hearted – there's enough snow in winter for a ski resort. But the panoramas from the Puerto de Pajares mountain pass – straddling the boundary between provinces at 1378m – are spectacular. Pause for a coffee at the old parador and relish unadulterated Cantabrian Mountain views; Spanish ibex and Iberian wolves hidden in the chasms. Asturias's second city is made for slipping down a few gears. Sure, there are art and archaeological museums and intriguing pre-Romanesque churches to visit. But Oviedo's charisma is best absorbed by strolling its spotless streets to stumble across its many statues. The swooning sound of the *gaita asturiana* (local bagpipe-like instrument) often carries in the air, as does the scent of freshly

Bilbao *pintxo* bar

baked *carbayones* (almond puff pastry) and *moscovitas* (chocolate-coated almond biscuits), the town's signature sweet treats. *Fabada asturiana*, a white bean stew, and *cachopo*, a breaded veal, cheese and ham combo, are meals worth lingering over. Nightfall draws droves to Calle Gascona, the "cider boulevard", where experienced *escanciadors* pour uncarbonated *sidra* from great heights in *chigre* (cider houses).

## ELUSIVE WILDLIFE, PRISTINE NATURE AND MOUNTAIN LIFE IN PICOS DE EUROPA

From Oviedo, the N-634 plunges deep into Picos de Europa National Park. Spread across three autonomous communities, it's a realm of saw-toothed mountains, elusive brown bears, limestone gorges and dense beech forests. Slow down on trails flanked by emerald inclines and recharge in tucked-away, timeless stone villages. The first tempting detour: the glacial lakes of Covadonga. Alternatively, push on to Benia de Onís's visitor centre for an overview of the park's geological features, mountain lifestyle and magnificent bearded vultures.

Wander to *Sidrería El Pareón* for a hearty lunch in a wooden-balconied cider house, or drive to stuck-in-time Asiego for an alternative *sidrería* experience. At Las Arenas, join a pre-booked tour and tasting in the Cueva del Queso de Cabrales. Pinch your nose and enter the cave where wheels of Cabrales, the world's most expensive blue cheese, naturally age. This is an excellent base from which to explore the park; the hamlet of Poncebos is just 6km beyond. From here, the linear and challenging Ruta del Cares is a canal-tracking, ravine adventure. For a more easygoing mountain escape, the Funicular de Bulnes climbs 402m in seven minutes, offering access to isolated mountain village life.

## SANTANDER

Leaving the park, you could speed on to Santander. Better still, spare some time to track the secondary coastal roads instead. Park up at the medieval fishing village of San Vicente de la Barquera. Swim at sensational Playa de Gerra for vistas of verdant pastures and mountain faces. Or detour down diminutive roads leading to serene shore lookouts.

Santillana del Mar, with its rickety overhanging balconies and Caves of Altamira, adorned with palaeolithic cave art, is worth a final detour. Once in Cantabria's capital, head to Playa del Sardinero for a swim or to circle the peninsula's Palacio de la Magdalena, a former royal retreat, before devouring a pre-ferry seafood feast.

## LIKE A LOCAL

### STAY

**Bodegas FyA** C/de Entrena, Logroño; www.bodegas fya.com. A 20min drive from Logroño, this luxury vineyard hideaway offers tastings, tours and a ceramic museum. Bikes and EV chargers are available.

**La Casa de Juansabeli** Barrio Juansabeli, Picos de Europa; www.hoteljuansabeli.com. Roadside yet peaceful, this stone-built hotel has a fine restaurant. There's an EV charger in the adjacent petrol station.

**Gran Hotel España** C/Jovellanos 2, Oviedo; www.gran hotelespana.es. One of Oviedo's oldest and grandest hotels, with well-renovated rooms and EV charging.

**Gran Hotel Sardinero** Pza. de Italia 1, Santander; www.hotelsardinero.es. An elegant period property seconds from Sardinero Beach with sea view rooms and underground EV chargers.

**Hospedaje Magallanes** C/Magallanes 22, Santander; www.hospedajemagallanes.com. A welcoming, basic budget choice close to the city centre and bus station.

**Hotel Gran Bilbao** Avda. Indalecio Prieto 1, Bilbao; www.hotelgranbilbao.com. Modern four-star bolthole with mural-heavy rooms and reliable eco-credentials, including EV chargers, a 15min walk from Bilbao's Casco Viejo.

**Hotel My Palace León** C/San Francisco 13, León; www.mypalaceleon.com. This wood-heavy, design-led hotel is close to most attractions. A spa and underground EV charging are bonuses.

The drum beats to a slower pace in Oviedo

**Hotel Real Colegiata San Isidoro** Pza. de Santo Martino 5, León; hotelrealcolegiata.com. Adjoining the eleventh-century basilica, this heritage hotel is an attraction itself, with cloister-facing rooms, modern amenities and fair prices.

**Hotel Rural El Torrejón** Barrio Del Torrejon, Picos de Europa; www.hotelruraleltorrejon.es. This serene, mansion-style hotel on a working farm is an excellent base for exploring Cabrales' cheese caves.

**Lasala Plaza Hotel** Pza. Lasala 2, San Sebastián; www.lasalaplazahotel.com. Sweeping panoramas of the bay and city from a rooftop swimming pool make this chic four-star abode with EV chargers well worth the splurge.

**El Patio de San Nicolas** C/Marques de San Nicolas 68, La Rioja; www.elpatiodesannicolas.com. This sixteenth-century guesthouse blends modern decor, original beams, and a patio 900m from La Rioja's bus station.

**Pensión Bilbao** C/Amistad 2, Bilbao; www.pension bilbao.es. Affordable, traditionally decorated rooms in a family-run guesthouse, easily reached by *cercanías* from Bilbao's bus station.

**Pensión Donostiarra** C/San Martín 6, San Sebastián; www.pensiondonostiarra.com. A central, second-generation, family-run guest house with modern rooms close to inter-city transport.

**Pensión Fidalgo** C/Jovellanos 5, Oviedo; www.hostal fidalgo.es. This family-run guesthouse offers simple but well-kept rooms at reasonable prices.

## EAT

**Agua Salada** C/San Simón 2, Santander; +34 665 96 00 96. This first-class yet unpretentious, couple-run restaurant offers half-size portions to sample the fusion menu's diversity.

**Basque Gastronomic Societies** San Sebastián; www.sansebastianpintxos.com. Invites to San Sebastián's member-only gastronomic societies are elusive. This long-running local tour operator can pair you with a local chef to get underground.

**Blanco y Negro** C/Laurell, Logroño; www.callelaurel.org. Start your Logroño *pincho* crawl here, in this street's oldest bar, for anchovy-stuffed buns. Then head to *Bar Soriano* for mushrooms and *El Perchas* for pork ears.

**Casa Xurde** Lugar Arenas 217A, Picos de Europa; www.casaxurde.es. A traditional, exposed-brick dining room for hearty mountain recipes and cuts of Asturian beef.

**La Corte de Pelayo** C/San Francisco 21, Oviedo; www.lacortedepelayo.com. This long-term respected restaurant serves typical Asturian dishes, including *fabada asturiana* and *cachopo*.

**La Despensa del Etxanobe** C/Juan Ajuriaguerra 8, Bilbao; www.ladespensadeletxanobe.com. This is the more affordable sibling of Michelin-starred *Etxanobe Atelier*, where Bilbao-born Fernando Canales injects Basque flavours into fair-priced tasting menus.

**Mercado de la Ribera** Erribera Kalea, Bilbao; www.mercadodelaribera.biz. Europe's largest indoor market. Book ESHBI's Escuela de Cocina's cooking class to prepare local dishes such as *bacalao a la vizcaína*.

**Pintxos Crawl** C/31 de Agosto, San Sebastián. Use this street as a *pintxo* crawl starting point. Begin at La Cepa de Bernardo or Karrika Taberna and finish at La Viña for Burnt Basque cheesecake.

**Restaurante del Parador de León** Pza. San Marcos 7, León; www.paradores.es. Housed in a grand heritage building turned hotel (closed to non-guests), an indulgent dinner here allows for a peek inside and the chance to mingle with the exclusive set.

## DRINK

**Barrio Húmedo** C/Ancha, León. León's "Wet Neighbourhood" is brimming with bars serving free tapas with each drink. La Trébede, El Romántico and La Ribera are great starting points.

**Sidrería El Pareón** Lugar Sirviella Onís 8, 33556 Asturias; +34 673 76 98 78. An authentic country house pit-stop between Oviedo and Cabrales for home-made *sidra* and cheese pairings.

**Sidrería Tierra Astur** C/Víctor Chávarri, Oviedo; www.tierra-astur.com. Cider houses are abundant in this corner of Spain, but this over-the-top local chain (especially the El Vasco branch) brings theatre to a cheese and meat feast.

## SHOP

**dendAZ** Pza. Arriquíbar 4, Bilbao; www.azkunazentroa.eus. Inside the Azkuna Zentroa Cultural Centre, this showcase space spotlights up-and-coming Basque designers, artists and creatives.

**El Escribano** C/de Fernando G. Regueral 6, León; www.elescribano.com. Part calligraphy workshop, part medieval museum, chatty artisan Antonio runs this stuck-in-time store.

**Marta Berra Design** C/el Cristo 8, La Rioja; www.martaberra.com. La Rioja has a centuries-long history of pottery. Here, Marta sells her modern ceramics, including jewellery and dinnerware.

**Santander Vintage** C/Cubo 1, Santander; www.santandervintage.com. Two sustainably minded friends established this secondhand clothes store with an ever-changing, high-quality fashion collection.

**Sombreros Gorostiaga** VIktor Kalea 9, Bilbao; www.sombrerosgorostiaga.com. Since 1857, this family-run, time-capsule-like store has been the go-to for handmade *txapelas* (typical Basque berets).

**Vinos Martinez** Narrika Kalea 29, San Sebastián; vinosmartinez.com. Step inside this proper old-school wine shop and let a donostiarra pair you with an expertly selected txakolina to take back home.

Asturian sweets, including *carbayones* and *casadielles*

# IBERIAN ECO-ESCAPADE
## A slow trip from Portugal to Spain

From conservation communities to sustainable surf retreats, flamingo-speckled lagoons to a UNESCO Global Geopark etched with the indentations of ancient jellyfish, this green route shows there's more to Portugal and Spain than sea and sand. Crisscrossing tradition-steeped landscapes alive with fauna, this eco-adventure travels from the fairy-tale forests of Sintra to the culture-rich cities of southernmost Spain. Whether you follow in the footsteps of fisherfolk on one of Europe's most beautiful coastal paths or hire an electric car to whizz down the peninsula's western fringes, explore Iberia the slow way.

The historical Fisherman's Trail

## PRACTICAL INFORMATION

**Distance covered:** 780km

**Recommended journey time:** 14 days+

**Transport details:**

- Lisbon and Malaga are connected to all major European cities by budget airlines, including TAP Portugal (www.flytap.com), Wizz Air (www.wizzair.com), Ryanair (www.ryanair.com) and easyJet (www.easyjet.com). However, the better way to travel by far is by train, with regular high-speed services running to/from Paris and Madrid (3hr; 8–10 daily; from €35) for international train connections.
- Hire an electric or hybrid car from Lisbon airport (from €13 per day for a hybrid); drop-offs in a different town cost more (from €33 per day). Car-rental companies include SIXT (www.sixt.com) and Europcar (www.europcar.com).
- Comboios de Portugal operates train services between Lagos and Faro (1hr 45min; 8–10 daily; from €28; www.cp.pt).
- Buses connect Faro and Seville (3hr; 8–10 daily; from €14; www.alsa.com), and Seville and Tarifa (3hr; 3 daily; from €24.50; www.tgcomes.es).
- For ease of travel, take as little luggage as you can, especially if you plan to walk the Fisherman's Trail.

# THE JOURNEY

In Lisbon, there's no better way to begin your slow travel adventure than by staying the night in a restored nineteenth-century windmill. Just a ten-minute ferry ride across the water from the city centre, *Olá Belém* peeks above the forested slopes on the southern banks of the Rio Tejo. An hour away by train is the UNESCO World Heritage Site of Sintra, a fairy-tale town of turreted castles and thick forests straight out of a pop-up storybook. The traditional summer haunt of Portuguese royalty, the hilltop retreat, surrounded by opulent palaces and country estates, is perched at the edge of the sprawling Parque Natural de Sintra-Cascais. Wander its narrow streets to stumble across hole-in-

the-wall shops filled with local delicacies and antique Portuguese wares. The Palácio da Pena, unmissable in its resplendent yellow, is worth the steep thirty-minute uphill walk (or short shuttle bus ride) to see its ornate medley of domes, statues and towers up close. Built in the late 1840s by the German Baron von Eschwege on the site of a former monastery – whose chapel remains today – the palace was embellished at the request of Queen Maria II's husband, Ferdinand of Saxe-Coburg-Gotha, which explains the medley of architectural styles from Moorish to Manueline.

Don't miss the surrounding park, where you can meet the stocky Ardennais draft horses helping to

## Iberian eco-escapade

- ◉ **Lisbon**
- ⊙ Sintra
- ⊙ Porto Côvo
- ◉ **Lagos**
- ◉ **Faro**
- ⊙ Tavira

PORTUGAL
SPAIN

- ◉ **Seville**
- ◉ **Tarifa**

conserve and regenerate the natural vegetation. A twenty-minute bus ride further into the forest reveals arguably an even more special residence; the fabulous gardens and palace of Monserrate, a remarkable blend of Moorish, Gothic and Indian architecture described as the "first and foremost beautiful place in the Kingdom" by Lord Byron.

## ECO-COMMUNITIES GALORE

Closer to coast but still accessible by bus, Sintra is home to Ecoaldeia de Janas, a permaculture centre teaching visitors how to live more sustainably. The *Eco Surf Resort*, an environmentally conscious retreat run by Sintra Surf School, is a network of stone cottages close to the beach designed to passively store heat in winter and cool occupants down in summer. Classical music enthusiasts around in June and July should keep an eye out for the dates of the annual Festival de Sintra, when local stately homes throw open their doors to welcome internationally renowned performers.

It's a two-hour train journey back through Lisbon to the unassuming Ermidas-Sado train station, from where you can transfer to the *Traditional Dream Factory* in the village of Abela. This co-living space aims to appeal to 'slomads', digital nomads keen to combine remote work and slow travel in a bid to cut

down on flying, stay in sustainable accommodation and contribute to environmental projects. With a focus on ecological conservation, the *Factory* invites guests to help regenerate the land (by planting trees, for instance, or covering deforested areas with nitrogen-fixing crops) or bestow their talents through an artistic residency: with the exception of food and laundry, no money changes hands here. Reserve your spot ahead of time – shared bell tents and campsites are free – at www.traditionaldreamfactory.com.

Alternatively, take a direct bus from Lisbon's Sete Rios station to Porto Côvo (ideally on a weekend, for more departure flexibility) to jump straight into the next stage of the trip.

## IN THE FOOTSTEPS OF FISHERFOLK

Less well-known than some of its pilgrim-heavy European counterparts, the 115km Trilho dos Pescadores (Fisherman's Trail) – part of the longer Rota Vicentina (340km), which runs from Santiago do Cacém in the Alentejo to Cabo de São Vicente in the Algarve – follows coastal tracks long used by the local fisherfolk. As you stride through wildflower meadows and along breathtaking clifftops, flashes of white give away storks building precarious nests, and falcons diving for prey. Despite salt-laden sea winds coating your hair and skin, and your bag growing heavy with home-made *pasteis de nata* picked up from tiny villages studding the route, your heart will grow increasingly light. This route takes you through the little-developed Parque Natural do Sudoeste Alentejano e Costa Vicentina, home to rare species of flora and fauna whose habitats are under strict protection. Here, outside of the summer months, you're unlikely to see another soul, though your encounters with feathered locals will number in their thousands, including nightingales, golden orioles, Egyptian vultures and even the magnificent booted eagle. Look out for the rare Bonelli's eagle.

The Fisherman's Trail officially starts at the tiny, maze-like village of Porto Côvo, wiggling along Portugal's western fringes all the way round to Lagos on the south coast. Requiring around twenty kilometres of walking per day to complete in under two weeks,

it's not for the faint-hearted. If you'd prefer a shorter hike, the original trail – from Porto Côvo to Odeceixe – takes around four days, after which you can catch a bus to Lagos. Timing is key: after staying the night in Vila Nova de Milfontes, start out as early as you can to arrive at Almograve for lunch, then wend your way to Cavaleiro as the sinking sun sets the cliffs aglow.

The trail is extremely well-marked and -maintained: keep an eye out for the green and blue stripes, which show you the way to go. There's no shortage of hostels (*pousada de juventude*), guesthouses (*alojamento* or *hospedaria*) or hotels along the way: it's not usually necessary to reserve these in advance unless you're travelling in summer or around a public holiday. Transfers are available to bring your luggage between stops (visit www.rotavicentina.com for details).

For those unable or unwilling to travel by foot, it's possible to hire an electric or hybrid car in Lisbon and sweep down the Atlantic Coast, but it's by far the more expensive option. Take the high-speed train from Estação do Oriente, which shuttles passengers to Lagos in relative comfort within just four hours. However you make it there, reward yourself with a night in Lagos, one of the Algarve's most attractive and historic towns, its centre enclosed in largely fourteenth-century walls at the mouth of the Ribeira de Bensafrim.

Here, you can enjoy some of the region's best beaches (preferably outside of summer to avoid the hordes of sunseekers) and opportunities for dancing (try the Clube Artístico Lacobrigense). Stay the night before catching the train to Faro.

## ALONG THE BEACH-BEJEWELLED ALGARVE

You can make the journey from Faro to Seville in just under five hours by ALSA bus, but it's more rewarding to travel by electric or hybrid car and take your sweet, slow time. If you've never driven one in Europe before, there's lots of information online to help you avoid loss-of-charge mishaps. One key thing to remember is that braking recharges the car, so long motorway stints can run the battery down fast: download an app like JuicePass or Recarga Pública to view available chargers and pay via phone in Spain (for the Portugal leg, you'll need the likes of Miio or EVIO). Once on the road, you can take your pick of the Algarve's hundreds of golden, windswept beaches and fishing villages to stop at for a night.

If you must choose one, make it Tavira, the most interesting and attractive of the eastern Algarve's towns. Straddling both sides of the broad Rio Gilão, the Old Town is a knot of cobbled lanes and white mansions with hipped roofs and wrought-iron balconies, in the shadow of orange blossoms come spring. For those with more time, wake up to unparalleled views of the Serra do Caldeirão mountain range at *Heaven's Edge* on the outskirts of calm São Brás de Alportel; while you're there, stop at the local Museu do Traje (Algarve Costume Museum) for a weird and wonderful look at bygone eras of Portuguese fashion.

The highlight of this section of the journey is the birdwatching, so double check you've packed your binoculars. Before leaving Faro itself, call by the Parque Natural da Ria Formosa to spy flamingos, chameleons, spoonbills and egrets; as you cross the border into Spain and head away from the coast, moving steadily deeper into forests of oak and cork trees, look for red kites, vultures and even the occasional eagle wheeling above the canopy.

Don't miss the mushroom-hunting paradise of Parque Natural Sierra de Aracena, decked out in wildflowers during the spring. Come autumn, foraging expeditions take place among the golden-hued

Faro Marina

chestnut trees. The *Molino Río Alájar* hotel organises mushroom-picking tours and tasting menus, as well as an Iberian acorn-fed ham cutting class.

## SEDUCTIVE SEVILLE

As you drive east into Sierra Norte de Sevilla, the ground you'll cover is some of the most geologically interesting in the world. Designated a UNESCO Global Geopark, and once an ocean floor – where the indentations of ancient jellyfish can still be found – it's one of the best places for watching the Perseid meteor shower that peaks in mid-August. Goats, deer and wild boar thrive in these mountains, and hiking trails follow the path of streams that feed the land.

For those seeking to deepen their understanding of sustainability in action, it's possible to arrange a training course (usually around a week) at *Ecoaldea Los Portales*, whose solar-powered, self-sufficient community produces its own wine, olive oil, cheese, honey, aromatic herbs and herbal medicines. More casual travellers might head to *Hotel Trasierra*, a family home hidden amid 1215 hectares of orange trees and olive groves. Cooking and flamenco lessons are available by arrangement; alternatively, you can join painting, yoga and riding classes led by members of the resident family, the matriarch of whom lovingly restored the hotel from a crumbling wreck over thirty years ago. Staying the night in Seville, Andalucía's flamboyant capital where Arabic and European cultures collide, is a given. If you do nothing else, find a flamenco bar – try *Lo Nuestro* or *El Rejoneo* – and savour a glass of orange wine as you watch soul-wretching performances of an art form birthed by the city's Roma community as an expression of despair.

## SOUTHERN SPAIN

Leaving the car behind (it's likely you'll have to drop it off at Seville's airport), hop on an ALSA bus to Tarifa: the city at the southernmost end of the Iberian Peninsula, where the mountains of Morocco seem close enough to touch across the Strait of Gibraltar. This wind-lashed outcrop is the windsurfing and kitesurfing capital of Spain, with a plethora of local

Flamingos dot Parque Natural da Ria Formosa

schools offering lessons. And if you look up at the right time of year, you'll see migratory birds getting in on the action, using rising thermal currents for an energy-saving ride across the strait onto the next leg of their annual journey to West Africa.

As you head into the final straight, palm trees throw spiky shadows across the road. Both sides of the asphalt, the landscape unfurls into the last subtropical forest in Europe: Parque Natural de los Alcornocales, a vast expanse of verdant hill country stretching south to the sea and north to El Bosque and covered with *alcornocales* (cork oaks). A haven for large numbers of birds and insects, the park is also threaded with the region's best hikes, in particular the trail tracing the contours of Río Guadalmesí (the 'River of Women', said to have been the former hiding place of local women avoiding kidnap by pirates sailing the strait). The sense of stepping back in time is only enhanced by the mists that wreathe the treetops even in summer, known as barbas del Levante ("the beards of the east wind"). Look out for the rare species of fern and rhododendron that have remained evolutionarily unchanged for millenia.

And, nestled on a sloping hillside populated by goats, chickens and cats, sits an old mill – *Molino de Guadalmesí* – given new life as the home of an ecologically focused experimental community. It's vital to notify the owners ahead of time if you wish to visit, partly to ensure there's space for you to stay and partly to receive directions more reliable than those provided by Google Maps. Once you're given the green light, it's best to use the BlaBlaCar app to navigate the slightly challenging journey to the farm. In exchange for food and work on the extensive gardens and buildings, visitors can learn about sacred geometry, deep ecology and vocal therapy; games, bonfires and communal cooking are plentiful. A fitting end to an eco-adventure across the Iberian Peninsula.

## LIKE A LOCAL

### STAY

**Abacatus Farmhouse** Sítio de São Pedro, 8800-562 Santa Luzia; www.abacatusfarmhouse.com. This out-of-town adults-only farmhouse near Tavira offers yoga classes, massages, bike rental, and a swimming pool set within a lush garden.

**Birds of Paradise Lodge** Urbanização Vale da Telha H177, 8670-156 Aljezur; www.birdsofparadiselodge.com. A co-working and -living space in the winter and a vibrant hostel in the summer, *Birds of Paradise* is a boutique lodge offering surf lessons, yoga sessions and a solar-heated swimming pool. Minimum four-day stay required.

**Casa Vicentina** Monte Novo, 8670-312 Odeceixe; www.casavicentina.com. With easy access to both the Fisherman's Trail and the magnificent Praia de Odeceixe, this guesthouse on a former farm comes with a swimming pool surrounded by pine forest.

**Casinha D'Avó** Praça das Armas 12, 8600-523 Lagos. This converted townhouse offers a tranquil rest in the heart of Lagos; friendly host Mariana bakes an excellent carrot cake.

**Ecoaldeia de Janas** R. do Luzio 15, 2710-267 Sintra; www.numundo.org/center/portugal/ecoaldeia-de-janas. Medieval-style farmhouse and gardens accepting volunteers for anywhere from a day to several weeks, with a live-in population of both humans and animals.

**Eco Surf Resort** R. Nova dos Caniçais Número 23 B, 2705-626 São João das Lampas; www.sintrasurf.com. One of the best places around to learn to surf under the expert guidance of coach Nicholas. You can also stay in one of two traditional stone houses where fresh herbs, fruits and vegetables are yours to pick from the kitchen-garden.

**Hakuna Matata Hostel** R. Dr. Jaurez 1B, 7630-781 Zambujeira do Mar. Low-cost, well-located option near the beach, with comfortable beds for exhausted Fisherman's Trail walkers.

**Heaven's Edge** 8150-128 São Brás de Alportel. Peaceful little homestay with mountain views and easy access to quaint São Brás de Alportel.

**Molino de Guadalmesí** Aldea de Guadalmesí, s/n, 11380, Cádiz; www.molinodeguadalmesi.com. Collaborative living project focusing on biodynamics, nutrition, permaculture and detoxification.

**Molino Río Alájar** Finca Cabezo del Molino s/n, 21340 Alájar, Huelva; www.molinorioalajar.com. A scattering of six stone cottages in the Parque Natural Sierra de Aracena. Pets and children are welcome in this idyllic haven; home-grown produce is served to guests; and hiking trails are abundant.

**Olá Belém** Zinhaga dos Fornozinhos 1 a/b, Caparica; www.olabelem.com. Make yourself at home in this refurbished riverside mill, complete with original millstones used for grinding flour, just 10min from Lisbon by ferry. There's even a treehouse on site to admire sunsets over the city.

**Los Portales** 41230 Castilblanco de los Arroyos, Seville; www.losportales.net. For those serious about studying regenerative agriculture and community-oriented living, *Los Portales* hosts a community of international volunteers to its two hundred hectares of gardens, orchards and greenhouses.

**Quinta da Capelinha** Cx Postal 814-Z, 8800-202 Tavira; www.quintadacapelinha.com. An enchanting *agroturismo* tucked away in an idyllic citrus farm a 20min walk from the centre of Tavira; staff here go the extra mile to make your stay as dreamy as possible.

**Raminhos Guest House** R. Artur Horta 14, 7645-224 Vila Nova de Milfontes; www.raminhosguesthouse. pt. A spotless bolthole beloved of trail walkers; owner Catarina offers unique food and drink recommendations in the local area.

**El Rey Moro** C/Reinoso 8, Casco Antiguo, 41004 Seville; www.elreymoro.com. Plant-filled and light-flooded converted manor house close to Seville's Catedral, with a superb in-house restaurant.

**The Riad Tarifa** Comendador 10, 11380 Tarifa; www. theriadtarifa.com. Seventeenth-century hideaway in Tarifa's Old Town; offers traditional Moroccan massages.

**Traditional Dream Factory** Aviario 7540-011; www. traditionaldreamfactory.com. Describing itself as a "regenerative playground", this community welcomes guests to learn about land regeneration and the future of technology. A 5min walk from the peaceful village of Abela.

**Trasierra** Carretera A-432 km 44,5, 41370 Cazalla de la Sierra, Seville; www.trasierra.com. A home-away-from-home in the heart of Parque Natural Sierra de Hornachuelos, where devices stay in bedrooms and complete disconnection is strongly encouraged.

**Villa Zawaia** R. Conselheiro Joaquim Machado 45, 8600-746 Lagos; www.villazawaia.com. Spacious bohemian property with an indoor pool; just a 5min walk from a cluster of restaurants and bars.

**Yurts Tarifa** Suerte Tierra, Vivienda Turística de Alojamiento Rural, Cañada de Matatoros s/n, Tarifa; www.yurtstarifa.com. Off-grid settlement with Bedouin-style tents. The camp's owners have created

Tarifa's windy shores lure kitesurfers

Nau Palatina in Sintra

an oasis of native plants where migratory birds come to rest and feed.

## EAT

**Ao Largo** Largo 1 de Maio 6, 8670-320 Odeceixe; www.aolargo.pt. Small Lagos café with a big vegetarian selection, succulent desserts and overflowing breakfast bowls.

**Arc da Velha** R. do Ferrador 22, 8600-715 Lagos; www.arcdavelha.wixsite.com/arcdavelha. At this Lagos-based restaurant, only a day's worth of produce is ordered each morning, so join the queue early before ingredients run out.

**Blanca Paloma** C/de San Jacinto 49, 41010 Seville; +34 954 333 640. A lovely local haunt for a creative spin on traditional tapas in a less-touristed corner of Seville; nigh on impossible to put a foot wrong with this menu.

**Casa Piriquita** R. Padarias 1, 2710-603 Sintra; www.piriquita.pt. Sintra-based pastry shop best known for its *travesseiros*, pillow-shaped delicacies filled with almond cream; its *queijadas* (sweet cheese biscuits) are equally delightful and best consumed while strolling the streets.

**Delizia da Ponte** R. 5 de Outubro 9, 8800-327 Tavira; www.facebook.com/GelatariasDelizia. Experimental ice-cream shop in Tavira where freshly made flavour combinations attract long queues: try the delicious fig or the throat-tingling cinnamon.

**Dos de Mayo** Pza. de la Gavidia 6, Seville; www.bodegadosdemayo.com. An alternative Seville option for tapas, where loyal diners return time and time again for the seared tuna and sizable olives.

**Estúdio Vegetariano** R. da Oliveira 30, 8600-315 Lagos; www.facebook.com/estudiovegetariano. Not just for vegetarians and vegans, this popular Lagos Old Town spot offers creative alternatives to typical Portuguese dishes popular with herbivores and meat-eaters alike.

**Nau Palatina** Calçada de São Pedro 18, 2710-501 Sintra; www.naupalatina.pt. Be sure to make a reservation in advance for this small but well-regarded, couple-run Sintra restaurant. Good selection of vegetarian dishes.

**Pastelería La Tarifeña** C/Nuestra Señora de La Luz 21, 11380 Tarifa; +34 956 684 015. Come here for gorgeously layered *milhojas* (cream-filled puff-pastry layers), savoury croissants and juicy *empanadas* (meat-stuffed pasties).

**Picnic** C/Guzmán el Bueno 3, 11380 Tarifa; +34 856 92 80 76. Skilled chefs bring out the best in fresh vegetables, with a special mention for the artichoke flower and tomato salad. Head to *El Lola* next door for flamenco afterwards.

**Porto das Barcas** Estrada do Canal S/N, 7645-000 Vila Nova de Milfontes. A slightly more expensive option to reward a weary Fisherman's Trail walker, the fish options at this restaurant are all superb: as is the dessert plate.

**Restaurante Jorge e Lia** R. do Alto do Cano 19, 8800-406 Tavira; +351 281 325 254. An unassuming front hides a Garden of Eden in the back, where home-made paté, garlicky lamb chops and grilled chicken are served to the sound of birdsong.

**Restaurante O Alberto** R. de Santo Amaro 2, 8600-315 Lagos; www.restauranteoalberto.pt. With over thirty years of service under their belts, the husband-and-wife team here are famous for their friendly welcome and their monkfish *cataplana*.

**Tasca do Careca** R. Primeiro de Maio 4A, Vila do Bispo, near Lagos; www.facebook.com/TascaCarecaVilaBispo. Arrive early at this simple, small-town restaurant where the portions are supersized and the stuffed squid is a highlight of the menu.

**Tascantiga** Escadinhas da Fonte da Pipa 2, 2710-557 Sintra; www.tascantiga.pt. Fresh-as-they-come seafood salads and cheese boards served alfresco on mismatched terracotta kitchenware. Seats fill up fast, so arrive early.

**Veganitessen** C/Pastor y Landero, s/n, Casco Antiguo, 41001 Seville; www.veganitessen.es. Located inside Seville's colonnaded Mercado del Arenal, this vegan haunt doesn't shy away from invention (try the dairy-free take on fried 'eggs') and offers a surprisingly delicious break from meat-heavy menus.

## DRINK

**Bom Bom Bom** R. Angelina Vidal 5, 1170-166 Lisboa; +351 935 327 446. Natural wine bar and record shop in Lisbon hosting monthly Sunday jazz sessions and DJ nights.

**Numero c** Juan Trejo 7, 11380 Tarifa. If a night of sampling local wines has left you in dire need of coffee, head straight to *Numero c*, where beans are roasted in-house and served alongside cheap and delicious breakfast options.

**Sol e Pesca** R. Nova do Carvalho 44, 1200-019 Lisboa; +351 21 346 7203. Open daily from noon until 2am (3am on weekends), this late-night Lisbon bar celebrates tinned fish by serving it in various combinations: the sardine with thyme and apple comes highly recommended.

Seville is famed for its flamenco bars

## SHOP

**Algarve Food Experiences** Algarve; www.algarve
foodexperiences.com/products/beekeeper-for-a-day.
Spend the day learning how to keep bees in São Brás
de Alportel, then taste the local honey paired with
fresh fruit and goats' cheese.

**Arjé Decoración** Pje. Andreu 2, Casco Antiguo, 41004
Seville; www.arjedecoracion.com. Suitcase-friendly,
lovingly made decorative items that serve as perfect
souvenirs of your trip to Seville.

**Atelier Tchonya Badginski** R. Padarias 2, 2710-591
Sintra; +351 21 924 4708. No photos allowed inside
this idiosyncratic Sintra boutique, where designer
souvenirs jostle for space with embroidered bags and
pure wool shawls.

**Atlas Beach Gallery** C/Nuestra Señora de la
Luz 4, 11380 Tarifa; www.atlasbeach.com. Local
photographer Manuel captures Tarifa's waves in all
their foaming glory, selling them in his Tarifa shop as
high-quality prints and phone cases.

**Bodegas Tierra Savia** C/San Benito 20, 41370 Cazalla
de la Sierra, Seville; www.bodegastierrasavia.com. No
better place to stock up on wine, here aged in traditional
clay jars using ancient viticultural techniques.

**El Cachalote Project** C/Sancho IV el Bravo 24, 11380
Tarifa; www.elcachaloteproject.com. Owner Eva
not only sells charming sea-themed recycled gifts
handmade by Spanish artisans, but is also a marine
biology expert more than happy to teach visitors about
the Strait of Gibraltar's aquatic residents.

**Casa das Portas** R. 5 de Outubro 1 3, 8800-327 Tavira;
www.facebook.com/CasaDasPortas. Eclectic gift shop
packed to the rafters with ethical, handmade goods,
all with a story to tell.

Yurts at the *Traditional Dream Factory*

Abacatus Farmhouse, near Tavira

**Caza das Vellas Loreto** R. do Loreto 53, 1200-241 Lisboa; www.cazavellasloreto.com.pt. One of the oldest candle shops in the world. Ornately decorated wooden cubbyholes showcase a wide range of candles carefully crafted by hand in the rear of the shop.

**Casa Orzáez** C/Betis 67, 41010 Seville; www.casa orzaez.com. A haven for fermented foods, where milk from local Florida Sevillana goats is used to make cheese, and animal welfare comes first.

**Cécile \*M** R. Poiais de São Bento 74, 1200-349 Lisboa; www.cecilemestelan.com. The Lisbon home of delightfully colourful ceramics handmade by Cécile Mestelan, who also offers pottery classes.

**conTenedor** San Luis 50, Casco Antiguo, 41003 Seville; www.restaurantecontenedor.com. This restaurant has climbed the ranks of Seville's culinary scene for its committed approach to serving slow food, both in the provenance of its ingredients and the relaxed, unhurried atmosphere created for its diners. Top of the menu is the crispy rice, followed by a slab of the home-made cheesecake.

**LYA Tarifa** C/Batalla del Salado 12, 11380 Tarifa; www. lyatarifa.com. Woman-owned concept store whose racks are filled with clothing designed by the owner, who's more than happy to make personalised style recommendations for shoppers.

**Mercado da Ribeira** R. José Pires Padinha 60, 8800-354 Tavira. Built in 1887, this storied market hall hosts a cluster of cafés and restaurants that are ideal for people-watching.

**Oh! My Cod** Lisbon; www.ohmycodtours.com. Anthropologically focused walking tours run by Lisbon locals that feature slow, seasonal food and sustainable shops selling artisanal products.

**wetheknot** R. de São João da Praça 41, 1000-518 Lisboa; www.wetheknot.com. Independent clothes store in Lisbon featuring sustainable local designers and vegan materials.

OVER
14 DAYS

Tracing the snow-carpeted shores
of Norway's Porsangerfjorden

# ARCTIC ODYSSEY
## Chase the midnight sun to Nordkapp

Embark on this adventure from the vibrant streets of Finnish capital Helsinki to the raw, remote beauty of Nordkapp – all without setting foot on a plane. The Santa Claus Express brings you to Rovaniemi, gateway to Lapland. Go slow and include stops at Scandi sauna capital Tampere and quirky Oulu. North of the Arctic Circle, hop on buses to adventure capital Saariselkä or Inari, the beating heart of Sámi culture. This 1600km journey demands at least a day in each stop, with Helsinki and Urho Kekkonen National Park deserving extra love. In summer, you can continue all the way to the North Cape, travelling under the midnight sun and wild camping along the way.

# THE JOURNEY

Helsinki is all about water and greenery. With 130km of shoreline and forty percent of its total area given over to parks and patches of wilderness, it's no wonder the Finnish capital is considered one of the most liveable cities in Europe. Do as the locals do, hit the urban beaches, brave a (winter) swim, warm up with a coffee from a waterside café or island-hop your way around the archipelago – more than three hundred islands surround the city.

Although less famous than Nordic counterparts Copenhagen or Stockholm, Helsinki is as cool as its climate – world-class architecture, cutting-edge design and exciting culinary experiences all fight for your attention. After it was made Finland's capital in 1812, Helsinki benefited from the astonishing talents of German architect Carl Ludwig Engel, who poured his creativity into Senate Square and its surroundings.

When the city was awarded the World Design Capital in 2012, €16 million was funnelled into architectural projects, including the award-winning Kamppi Chapel of Silence and the Kulttuurisauna public sauna.

Refusing to rest on its laurels, Helsinki has big dreams for the future: its run-down industrial areas and former docklands are in the process of being rejuvenated; the old abattoir quarter is now an epicurean enclave; Suvilahti power plant is a dramatic venue for open-air music festivals; Helsinki Allas is an exciting harbourside development with a spa, saunas and two sea-water swimming pools; and Kalasatama harbour is being transformed into a visionary neighbourhood with eco-designed high rises and floating apartments.

This forward-thinking capital might not be one of the world's biggest cities by any stretch of the

The train to quirky Oulu

imagination, but compared to the remote areas you're headed for, it's a metropolis with a rich cultural scene. Standouts include the Ateneum Art Museum, Kiasma, the National Museum of Finland and the Design Museum. When you've had your fix, head towards the central train station: in all its Jugendstil glory, it's a grand place to start such an epic journey.

## TAMPERE: A CITY REBORN

A train ride through dense pine forests and hay bale-peppered fields brings you to Tampere. Finland's second city straddles a narrow isthmus of land wedged between two lakes, Näsijärvi and Pyhäjärvi. Once dubbed the 'Manchester of the North', the former industrial city has reinvented itself. Redbrick mills and

Northern lights in Oulu

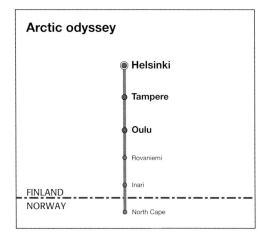

## Arctic odyssey

- ◉ **Helsinki**
- ● **Tampere**
- ● **Oulu**
- ● Rovaniemi
- ● Inari

FINLAND

NORWAY

- ● North Cape

huge factories, formerly the backbone of Tampere's manufacturing prowess, have been transformed into start-up offices, boutique shops, independent cafés, cinemas, tattoo parlours and art galleries.

A good example is Finlayson Factory, once powered by the foaming rapids of the Tammerkoski River. This six-storey building is named after its founder, Glasgow-born Quaker, James Finlayson (1772–1852), who moved to Tampere in 1820 with the backing of the Russian tsar and established his factory making textile machinery, later switching to cotton production. It now houses craft shops, cafés and live music venues, as well as the intriguing Finnish Labor Museum, where you'll find exhibits on the history of industry – including an enormous steam engine – all viewed through a social history lens. Also within the complex is the absorbing Spy Museum, where the sheer range of gadgets, clothing, machines and documents – including a set of now-declassified KGB maps of the Baltic – attest to the rampant espionage on both sides of the Finnish and Russian border during the last century.

The city's industrial heritage also earned Tampere the title the 'Sauna capital of Finland'. Factory owners would use saunas as a way to attract labour – as good a fringe benefit a nineteenth-century blue-collar worker was likely to land. With over fifty public saunas, many by the lake, you're spoilt for choice. *Rajaportti* –

Finland's oldest working public sauna – and *Kuuma*, with its excellent restaurant, are popular options.

For art, don't miss the Sara Hildén Art Museum, built on the shores of Näsijärviand filled with works from 1960s Informalist painters, as well as modern masters such as Klee, Delvaux, Bacon, Lèger – there's even a Picasso. And, of course, you can't visit Tampere without swinging by the world's only Moomin Museum, where some two thousand dolls, models, dioramas, sets and interactive displays recreate scenes from the incredibly popular children's books about the Moomin trolls by Tove Jansson.

### A QUIRKY CULTURAL CAPITAL

In Oulu (pronounced OH-loo), the winter cycling capital of the world, locals commute to work on two wheels even when the streets are carpeted in snow. Which is often. There must be something in the water, how else do you explain such zest among the residents? This is, after all, the same town that organises the annual Air Guitar World Championships (the prize: a real guitar). In quirky Oulu, which has garnered a reputation in recent years as a kind of Finnish Silicon Valley, you're more than likely to bump into a software engineer who works on 6G technology and moonlights as a hot-sauce maker and a drummer in an anarcho-punk band. It's just that kind of city.

The driving force behind Oulu's revitalisation has been its university, whose computing expertise has lured dozens of IT companies to set up in science and technology parks on the outskirts of the city, confirming Oulu's role as national leader in the computing and microchip industries. A handsome series of islands, several highly conspicuous old buildings, and a lively nightlife fuelled by the university's fun-hungry students add colour to an already energetic city.

Oulu has one of Finland's most attractive market squares, dotted with red-ochre wooden shacks and storehouses, which now serve as fine restaurants and local shops, and backed by the sleekly modern library and theatre which rise on stilts from the water. Oulu will be European Capital of Culture in 2026; visit now before the crowds rush in.

## OUTDOOR ADVENTURE PLAYGROUND

After changing from train to bus in Rovaniemi, you'll notice that the landscapes unfurling before the window become ever more barren. Welcome to polar territory. Some 250km north of the Arctic Circle awaits Urho Kekkonen National Park, a huge outdoor playground for intrepid types. The park is one of the country's largest, a 2500 square-kilometre sprawl incorporating the uninhabited wilderness that claws to the Russian border – pine moors and innumerable fells scored by gleaming streams and rivers.

Come winter, busloads of tourists are deposited in Urho Kekkonen for reindeer-sledding, snowshoeing and aurora gazing. However, it is just as worthy of a visit in summer (and not as busy). Rent a fatbike to explore the fells or strike out into the wilderness on foot. With regular bus connections to north and south, the Fell Centre (also known by its Finnish name, Tunturikeskus) is easily the most convenient base. It's at the head of several walking trails, which range from the simplest of excursions to exhausting expeditions using the park's chain of wilderness cabins or designated campsites.

This is one of the wildest corners of Finland, where bears and wolverines roam, and golden eagles soar above the tundra. Here, you can drink straight from crystal-clear rivers – free from the pollution of chemicals and agricultural run-off. Just make sure to bring a hip flask of something stronger to share around the campfire; Finns typically warm up after their first shot.

## SÁMI CULTURE

The short bus journey north to Inari qualifies as one of the most scenic in the country. The road winds around the southern shores of Lake Inarijärvi, the third-largest in Finland, which is transformed into a gigantic ice sheet between November and early June ahead of the late spring thaw – it's a spectacular route at any time of year, though, particularly so if you can coincide your trip with the glorious Lapland *ruska*, a season that takes in late August and early September, when the trees take on brilliant citrus colours that are reflected in the still waters. The scene could be plucked straight from a children's storybook: reindeer graze on lichen by the roadside; tiny islets are scattered across lakes like gems, many adorned with a single majestic pine tree.

Inari, a remote village in the far north, is the centre of Sámi culture in Finland. As the seat of Sámediggi, the Finnish Sámi Parliament, it's a great place to get to grips with the history and traditions of Scandinavia's Indigenous population. The main draw is the captivating Siida Museum, whose considered collection explores the Sámi's intimate bond with the delicate nature of the far north. The principal exhibition includes a timeline tracing the Sámi from pre-history to the present day, detailing all the social, cultural and political changes which have affected them. Admire intricate Sámi handicrafts, carved from reindeer bones with patience and skill, and check out the re-sited nineteenth-century village in the excellent outdoor section. Siida also focuses on the region's famed eight seasons, its wildlife (such as the cute polar foxes that are making a comeback) and the ways climate change affects the landscape. Beyond Siida, there's plenty more to do in the vicinity, from hiking to boat trips and reindeer safaris.

A worthwhile hiking trail of around five kilometres leads through ancient pine forest to the isolated Pielpajärvi wilderness church, dating from 1752, surrounded by whispering birch trees, beautifully sited in a flower meadow on the shores of Iso Pielpajärvi. Fishing trips take place all year on Lake Inarijärvi, and in the winter, guided snowmobile trips set out over the frozen lake.

## NORTH CAPE

Although lonely Inari may feel like it's poised at the end of the road, there's still another 125km to conquer before Finland finally draws her last breath in secluded Utsjoki, a dinky border village strung along the banks of the Tenojoki River.

In the summer months, a daily bus continues from Inari all the way to the bare, treeless and wind-lashed island of Magerøya, home to the steely cliffs of Nordkapp (the North Cape), ostensibly but not actually

Frost-tipped trees in Oulu

Europe's northernmost point: that accolade belongs to Kinnarodden, 80km to the east. Even neighbouring Knivskjellodden, a narrow peninsula also poking out from Magerøya island, pips Nordkapp to the post by 1500m. Nordkapp is more than a destination, though, it's the ultimate bragging right for adventurous travellers. Stand at the end of the world, feel the Arctic wind tousle your hair as you gaze over the Barents Sea in the knowledge that the only thing between you and the North Pole are a few determined seagulls.

## LIKE A LOCAL

### STAY

**Dream Hostel & Hotel** Åkerlundinkatu 2, Tampere; www.dreamhostel.fi. Finland is so proud of its Nordic design that even hostels look like they belong in coffee-table magazines. This one is located near the train station in Tampere.

**Hostel & Apartment Diana Park** Uudenmaankatu 9, Helsinki; www.dianapark.fi. With budget options few and far between in central Helsinki, *Diana Park*'s impeccably clean private and dorm rooms offer good value for budget-conscious travellers. Also a handful of apartments for those with money to spare.

**Hotelli Ville** Hatanpään valtatie 40, Tampere; www. hotelliville.fi. Tucked behind an ivy-clad facade, this self-service hotel offers homely rooms and a green outdoor yard. A 15min walk from Tampere's city centre.

**Jávri Lodge** Tievapolku 9, Urho Kekkonen National Park; www.javri.fi. This adult-only boutique hotel, surrounded by pine trees, has thirteen guest rooms, an indoor swimming pool and multiple saunas. Handily located near Urho Kekkonen National Park's walking trails.

**Klaus K** Bulevardi 2–4, Helsinki; www.klauskhotel. com. Located in an Art Nouveau building in the heart of Helsinki, this design hotel showcases an interior

inspired by the Finnish nineteenth-century epic *Kalevala*. Rooms are individually styled by local artists.
**Rautulampi Reservable Wilderness Hut** 68° 18.802' 27° 38.954', Urho Kekkonen National Park; www.nationalparks.fi/rautulampireservablewildernesshut. Back-to-basics design cottage in Urho Kekkonen National Park, nestled between fells and next to a lake.

### EAT
**Kauppahalli** Hämeenkatu 19, Tampere; https://kauppahalli.tampere.fi. Unless you're a vegetarian, don't miss *mustamakkara*, a blood sausage locals enjoy with red lingonberry jam and a glass of milk. Order at Tampere's *kauppahalli* (market hall); perfect if you're on a budget.
**Kuuma** Laukontori 21, Tampere; www.saunaravintola kuuma.fi. Combine a meal with a sauna and a dip in the lake at this hybrid restaurant in Tampere.
**Luulampi Wilderness Café** 68° 21.2211' 27° 33.2649', Urho Kekkonen National Park; www.nationalparks. fi/luulampidaytriphut. A seasonal wilderness café in Urho Kekkonen National Park, which opens its doors

in spring (for skiers), summer (hikers) and during autumn's *ruska* (nature buffs). Oven-fresh pastries and cakes are brought in daily by quad bike or snowmobile.
**Pirkon Pirtti** Honkapolku 2, Urho Kekkonen National Park; www.pirkonpirtti.fi. If the blazing fireplace doesn't warm you, then the food certainly will. Expect local fish (Arctic bouillabaisse), meat (reindeer), bear pizza and more.
**Shelter** Kanavaranta 7, Helsinki; www.shelter.fi. In an old Katajanokka warehouse, *Shelter* rustles up three-, four- or five-course meals bursting with seasonal flavours. Mixologists create inventive cocktails featuring Finnish berries.

### DRINK
**Café Regatta** Merikannontie 8, Helsinki; www.caferegatta.fi. Grab a cup of coffee and a *pulla* (cardamon bun) and join the locals at this cute red wooden house next to a glittering bay.
**Pyynikin Munkkikahvila** Näkötornintie 20, Tampere; www.munkkikahvila.net. Coffee enthusiasts frequent this café beneath Pyynikki's observation tower in

Tampere. Refill your cup in a forest setting and savour the reputed best *munkki* (doughnut) in the countryside.
**Roasberg** Mikonkatu 13, Helsinki; www.roasberg.fi. Perfectly located – right next to Helsinki's train station – to have one last coffee, lunch (sandwiches and soups) or a glass of wine before boarding the train. A scattering of pavement tables are prime people-watching spots.

## SHOP

**Akateeminen Kirjakauppa** Keskuskatu 1, Helsinki; www.akateeminen.com. Stock up on reading material for the journey in Finland's biggest bookshop, located in an Alvar Aalto-designed minimalist building that's part of Stockmann's (though it has its own entrance on Aleksanterinkatu). Plenty of English titles.
**Hippupuoti Gift Shop** Saariseläntie 5, Urho Kekkonen National Park; www.laplandnorth.fi/en/company/hippupuoti-gift-shop. Tiny boutique offering local handicrafts, leather products, artefacts from reindeer bone, and more. Jovial owner keen to share local tips.

**Iittala** Pohjoisesplanadi 23, Helsinki; www.iittala.com. Finland equals design. Iittala sells iconic tumblers, mugs and cutlery sets, as well as home decor for the chic shopper.
**Partioaitta Saariselkä** Honkapolku 3, Urho Kekkonen National Park; www.partioaitta.fi/myymalat/saariselka. Heading out into the wilderness? This outdoor shop is your last chance to stock up on camping gas or first-aid kits. For hiking maps, check out the nearby K-market.
**Taito Shop** Hatanpään valtatie 4, Tampere; www.taito.fi. Treasure trove of Finnish design, filled with homewares, textiles, jewellery, clothes and local delicacies, affiliated with an artisan association by the same name.
**Tallipihan Suklaapuoti** Kuninkaankatu 4, Tampere; www.suklaapuoti.fi. This beautiful chocolate shop, housed in a charming renovated stables complex, is a dream for those with a sweet tooth. Choose from chocolates and sweets by forty food makers, including artisans from Finland.

Reindeer-sledding in Urho Kekkonen

# BALTIC CITY-HOPPING
## Cultural gains in three cool capitals

An epic rail journey taking in the medieval-meets-modern cities and towns of the Baltics. Experience one of Europe's most underrated capitals, Vilnius; cosmopolitan Rīga, with its excellent art and restaurant scenes; postcard-pretty Cēsis, centred around a huge basilica; and Tallinn and its UNESCO-listed Old Town. United by geography and shared history, yet proudly individual in character, these captivating cities boast picturesque old centres, superb museums, pristine green spaces, hipster neighbourhoods and emerging foodie cultures. Beyond the urban hubs lie unspoiled national parks, eleventh-century castles and ornamental gardens to be discovered.

# THE JOURNEY

The starting point for this Baltic adventure is Klaipėda, a port city in Lithuania. Klaipėda, formerly known as Memel, has a distinctly German air, which is hardly surprising considering it was part of the Prussian Kingdom for hundreds of years. The Klaipėda Revolt finally saw the region gain autonomy in 1923. The compact cobblestoned Old Town is lined with wonky half-timbered buildings built in the traditional German style of *Fachwerkhäuser*. Beyond the city's historic core – which is walkable in a morning – and its moat-protected medieval castle, there isn't much more to keep you in Lithuania's third city for longer.

## THE CURIOUS CITY OF KAUNAS

The sprawling metropolis of Kaunas, Lithuania's second-largest city and a European Capital of Culture in 2022, unfurls along the banks of the Nemunas and Neris rivers as they converge. Between the two world wars, the city was the capital of Lithuania and is still considered by many Lithuanians to be the country's true heart.

The headline act is the delightful Old Town, with a cluster of fifteenth- and sixteenth-century merchant houses crowding its main square. The picturesque Baroque town hall is known as the 'White Swan' for its elegant form, slender 53m-high tower and pristine colour. Wedged between the Old Town and the Neris, the fourteenth-century Kaunas Castle offers a fascinating insight into the country's past.

Kaunas also has a plethora of unique museums and curious exhibitions including the Devil Museum, packed with over two thousand sculptures, masks and artworks depicting the lords of the underworld as well as witches and other mythological figures.

The tiny Republic of Užupis, Vilnius

## Baltic city-hopping

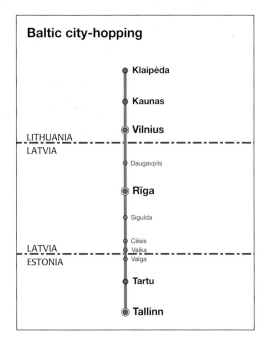

- Klaipėda
- Kaunas
- ◉ Vilnius

LITHUANIA
LATVIA

- Daugavpils
- ◉ Rīga
- Sigulda
- Cēsis

LATVIA
ESTONIA

Valka
Valga

- Tartu
- ◉ Tallinn

'Japan's Schindler' – saved around six thousand Jewish people between 1939 and 1940.

## EDGY VILNIUS

Around an hour and twenty minutes east of Kaunas by train, Vilnius is arguably the Baltics' most underrated capital. Despite slipping under the tourist radar, the city doesn't let this dent its confidence. Beyond the cobbled streets and myriad Orthodox and Catholic church spires of the UNESCO-listed Baroque Old Town (Eastern Europe's largest), Vilnius feels distinctly rebellious in character.

There's the self-declared breakaway Republic of Užupis (an April Fools' Day joke that spiralled into the birth of one of the world's smallest republics, with its own government, constitution and currency); eye-catching murals around every corner; wacky statues like the Frank Zappa monument; and trendy cafés in crumbling period buildings. Then there's the nightlife: a dynamic mishmash of countercultures including punk, goth, dance and rave.

## SURPRISING FINDS IN DAUGAVPILS

Daugavpils' main calling card is that it breaks up the border crossing between Vilnius and Rīga and if there was one destination to get the squeeze on this itinerary, it would be this Latvian city on the banks of the Daugava River. That's not to say it's not worthy of exploration.

Elsewhere, the 1921-founded MK Čiurlionis National Museum of Art hosts a collection of abstract paintings by Mikalojus Konstantinas Čiurlionis (1875–1911), one of Lithuania's finest artists, as well as a curation of sixteenth- to twentieth-century European works. Another must-visit is Sugihara House, where Kaunas-based Japanese diplomat Chiune Sugihara – dubbed

## PRACTICAL INFORMATION

**Distance covered:** 1150km
**Recommended journey time:** 14–16 days
**Transport details:**

- For Lithuania, buy train tickets via LTG Link (www.ltglink.lt); for Latvia, visit Latvian Railway (www.pv.lv); and in Estonia, use Estonian Railways (www.elron.ee). As distances between the cities are small and prices affordable, there's little benefit to buying railcards or round-trip tickets.
- Klaipėda and Tallinn are not as well-connected as other European cities. To avoid flying, take

a bus from Warsaw to Klaipėda (via Vilnius). Warsaw is much better connected to other European cities via train and bus.

- The new Rail Baltica, with a fast service between Vilnius, Rīga and Tallinn (and onwards to Warsaw) is set for completion in 2030.
- Short journey times mean you can make the most of your time without feeling rushed. Avoid lingering too long in Klaipėda or in Daugavpils after entering Latvia. Consider staying longer in the three capitals instead, if time allows.

Head straight to the impressive riverside Daugavpils Fortress, built on the orders of Tsar Alexander I on the eve of the Napoleonic wars.

Here, tucked away in an artillery storage building, is the Mark Rothko Art Centre, an interesting art and culture complex dedicated to Daugavpils' most famous son, none other than the world leader of abstract expressionism (1903–1970). A handful of original works donated by the Rothko family are hung alongside a mushrooming collection of contemporary Latvian art.

Elsewhere is the 1886 red-brick Lead Shot Factory, where ammunition was once manufactured by pouring molten lead from the top of the tall brick tower so that it solidified into spheres by the time it reached the ground; and the city's main synagogue, built in 1850 and restored in 2005.

## ENCHANTING RĪGA

Lively and cosmopolitan Rīga is the largest of the Baltic capitals and the most captivating. The city is a heady mix of old and new: Gothic spires pierce the skyline above a huddle of contemporary art galleries, trendy bars and experimental restaurants.

The heart of Rīga is, of course, its UNESCO-protected Old Town centred around an imposing thirteenth-century red-brick cathedral, home to one of Europe's largest organs. Wrapping around Dome Square is a tangle of cobbled lanes, lined with pastel-hued Art Nouveau buildings and courtyard bars – lively after dark with the hum of patrons.

Just outside the historic core is Rīga Central Market, Europe's largest bazaar, strung across a series of five former Zeppelin hangars. A growing craft-beer scene has given rise to the Beer District (Alus Kvartāls), a

Rīga's cathedral and red rooftops

2.5km trail studded with brewpubs, microbreweries, ale kitchens and even a beer embassy, springing up northeast of the Old Town.

## SIGULDA, GATEWAY TO GAUJA

Northeast of Rīga, the unassuming town of Sigulda is the gateway to Gauja National Park, Latvia's largest protected area. The pristine forested wilderness, threaded by the languid Gauja River, is a natural adventure playground for hiking, cycling, canoeing, rafting, caving, bobsleighing and even bungee jumping. The park is studded with cultural and historical monuments.

Turaida Castle, which means 'God's Garden' in ancient Livonian, is five kilometres north of Sigulda. Despite being Latvia's most-visited museum, it still maintains an air of calm. The eleventh-century red-brick castle is dominated by a tall cylindrical tower and surrounded by a scattering of exhibition spaces, including a wooden church and a folk garden peppered with sculptures of Latvian heroes. There are also landscaped gardens, wildflower meadows and patches of woodland to stroll. Within Sigulda itself, the main draw is the thirteenth-century Sigulda Castle, built between 1207 and 1209 by the Livonian Brothers of the Sword, a Catholic military order established during the Livonian Crusade by Albert von Buxthoeven, the third bishop of Rīga.

## CASTLES OF CĒSIS

Gauja National Park wraps around Cēsis, a pretty town centred around St John's Church, the largest medieval basilica outside Rīga; an immaculate ornamental lake and gardens; and the sprawling Cēsis Castle complex. The site is made up of two fortresses: the dark-stone ramparts and towers of the restored medieval castle, and the elegant white-walled and terracotta-roofed eighteenth-century manor house.

Turaida Castle in Sigulda, Latvia

Founded by Livonian knights in 1214, the original was sacked by Russian tsar Ivan the Terrible in 1577 before being frequently patched up throughout the centuries. Explore the string of halls, dungeons and towers, meandering through dark and eerie passageways illuminated by candlelit lanterns.

The 'new' castle shelters a collection of galleries and exhibits along with a series of reconstructed rooms. Be sure to take an hour or two to mooch around Cēsis' quiet streets and quaint cafés before moving on.

## THE TWIN TOWN WITH A RICH HISTORY

For an example of shared Baltic history, look no further than Valga (meaning 'Walk' in German). Until their separation in 1920, Valga in Estonia and Valka in Latvia were one town. Valga's history stretches back to at least 1286 when the town first appeared

in the Rīga credit register, at which point the regions of southern Estonia and northern Latvia belonged to the Governorate of Livonia. As such, Valga was the geographical centre of Livonia.

When the republics of Estonia and Latvia were formed after World War I, it was impossible to decide which country Valga should fall under. The border issue was eventually resolved in 1920 by Sir Stephen Tallents, a British diplomat, who was sent to the two countries to find a solution. The decision: to chop the town in half on a map.

Once Estonia and Latvia joined the Schengen Agreement in 2007, the towns became somewhat entwined again when all border-crossing points were removed, and roads and fences opened between the two countries in Valga.

The twin town is the perfect border crossing. Wander down to the Latvian-Estonian national boundary for the obligatory photo with one leg in Latvia and the other in Estonia. Other sites of interest include the Valga Museum, occupying a handsome Art Nouveau building, and the Valga Prison Camp Cemetery, where an estimated 29,000 Russians died at the Nazi POW camp Stalag 351.

## YOUTHFUL SPIRIT OF TARTU

Tartu, Estonia's second city, is often referred to as the nation's spiritual capital. You may hear locals refer to a special *vaim* (spirit) created by the traditional wooden houses, eighteenth-century stately buildings, serene public parks and romantic riverfront. Despite its allure, it has somehow managed to avoid the overhyped tourism that swamps Tallinn.

The provincial city (home to fewer than 100,000 residents) is injected with the boisterous exuberance that comes from having a sizeable student population and, after dark, the leafy and historic streets come to life with that characteristic *Tartu vaim*. It is also the gateway to south Estonia, a cultural region rich with local communities, Indigenous languages and long-lasting customs.

Connect with local traditions at festivals like Aigu Om! in Viitina – the brainchild of global music artist Mari Kalkun – and the bonfire-illuminated Night of Ancient Lights.

## TALLINN: A CITY ON THE RISE

Tallinn has fought to win its status as a proud European capital, after centuries of being tossed around by the Danish, Swedish, Polish, Germans and Soviets. Since independence in 1991, it's been a city on the move – and continues to steamroll on relentlessly. In recent years there's been a roll-call of accolades: the Old Town became a UNESCO World Heritage Site in 1997; the wider city hosted the Eurovision Song Contest in 2002; it was named European Capital of Culture in 2011

The pastel facades of Cēsis, Latvia

and won the European Green Capital Award for 2023. Estonia's compact capital is absurdly photogenic.

The Old Town is bursting with fantastic sights, from the glorious Gothic St Nicholas' Church to the onion-domed Russian Orthodox Alexander Nevsky Cathedral – and it's all enveloped within one of Europe's most complete set of city walls. You could easily spend days ambling the medieval streets alone, but that would mean missing out on the city's contemporary face. With its ever-expanding twenty-first-century skyline, emerging foodie scene, shopping centres, cutting-edge art museums, and the futuristic train station set to open in 2030, the city really does tick that travel cliché of old meets new.

It's a fine place to wrap up your breeze through the Baltics before returning home.

## LIKE A LOCAL

### STAY
**Dome Hotel** 4 Miesnieku St, Rīga, Latvia; www.dome hotel.lv. Rīga's premier boutique hotel is tucked away in the heart of Rīga's Old Town. Behind its 400-year-old facade lies a spa complete with Turkish baths, massage rooms and a sauna. Its crowning glory, however, is a rooftop restaurant with gorgeous views of the cathedral.

**Downtown Forest Hostel & Camping** Paupio st 31A, Vilnius LT-11341, Lithuania; www.downtownforest.

Balti Jaama Turg, Tallinn's farmers' market

Canoeing on the Gauja River, Latvia

lt. Playful hostel with a range of sleeping options, offering good vibes and great coffee. It's within walking distance of Vilnius' city centre and close to the Užupis neighbourhood.

**Villa Santa** Gaujas Street 88, Cēsis, Latvia; www.villa santa.lv. This historic hotel overlooking the Gauja River in Cēsis once housed Russian nobility. Recently restored, *Villa Santa* is yet again one of the region's most opulent – but affordable – lodging options.

## EAT & DRINK

**Beer District** (Alus Kvartāls), Centra rajons, Rīga, Latvia; www.beerdistrict.lv. A collection of brewpubs, microbreweries and beer kitchens centred around the Valmiermuiža beer embassy.

**Lee** Uus 31, 10111 Tallinn, Estonia; www.leeresto.ee. *Lee* is an archaic Estonian word meaning to gather around a fire to regale stories and eat. Do it in style at this fine-dining restaurant; a fun twist on a traditional medieval setting.

**Vieta** Šv. Ignoto gatvė 12-1, 01144 Vilnius, Lithuania; www.vieta-restaurant.business.site. Simple and cosy vegan haunt in the heart of the Lithuanian capital plating up delicious, affordable plant-based options.

## SHOP

**Balti Jaama Turg** Kopli 1, 10412 Tallinn, Estonia; www.astri.ee/bjt. The best way to discover what Estonians eat on a day-to-day basis is to visit Tallinn's principal farmers' market, spread across three floors.

**Cukurs** Sigulda J.Poruka iela 14, Latvia; www.cukurs veikals.lv/en. An enchanting gift shop selling locally sourced and made trinkets and wares in Sigulda.

**Užupis** Vilnius, Lithuania; www.uzupiorespublika. com. The Lithuanian capital's trendiest district is home to a string of art galleries and boutique shops.

# HIGH ALBANIA
## Exploring the Accursed Mountains

For any adventurous slow traveller, the Balkans are a dream. Albania offers a rich variety of cultural and natural experiences, and it's easy to cross the border into Kosovo or North Macedonia. This stunning 1100km slow route across the legend-steeped Accursed Mountains allows you to explore historical cities and ancient ruins in three welcoming Balkan countries. Hike through wild mountain landscapes, eat delicious fresh food, and enjoy encounters with the hospitable locals. Avoid the heat and crowds in summer by visiting in spring when the mountain meadows are filled with wildflowers, or in autumn when the farm harvest lands fresh on your plate.

# THE JOURNEY

Though many budget airlines now land in Tirana, Albania can also be reached by public transport in two days from the UK, using trains via Paris to Milan, and the next day, a train to Bari and the night ferry to the Albanian port of Durrës. Alternatively, a longer overland route trundles from Paris via Stuttgart, the night train to Zagreb, and onwards by bus to Belgrade, where you hop on the night train to the Montenegrin capital Podgorica. Set your alarm early to enjoy the spectacular views of the kilometre-deep Morača river canyon in the last hour of the trip. Regular buses link Podgorica with Shkodër and Tirana in Albania. Public transport in Tirana consists mainly of minibuses and more comfortable coaches; travel is slow-going, but tickets are affordable. Renting a car, however, will offer significantly more flexibility. Albania's rail system is being reconstructed and is set to open in late 2024, with trains between Tirana, the airport and Durrës.

## DURRËS TO TIRANA

From either the ferry terminal at Durrës or the airport, it's a short ride by bus or taxi to vibrant Tirana, where

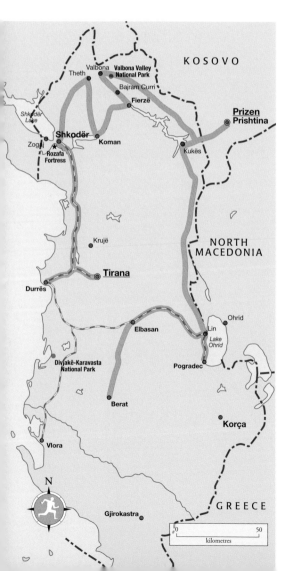

---

**PRACTICAL INFORMATION**

**Distance covered:** 924km

**Recommended journey time:** 15 days+

**Transport details:**

- It is possible to reach Durrës from London by train: travel via Paris to Milan then change for a service to Bari, from where you can catch the night ferry (10hr 45min; from €45) to the Albanian port of Durrës. Alternatively, a longer overland route trundles from Paris via Stuttgart to Zagreb, and onwards by bus to Belgrade, where a night train connects to Podgorica in Montenegro.
- Regular buses link Podgorica with Shkodër and Tirana. Public transport in Tirana consists mainly of minibuses and coaches. Consider renting a car for more flexibility. Albania's rail system is being renovated, with trains between Tirana, the airport and Durrës expected to run from late 2024.
- For public transport in and around Tirana, check schedules and make bookings on www.travel.gjirafa.com.
- The 30km-long Koman–Fierzë ferry journey takes 3hr (www.komanilakeferry.com).

Sinan Pasha Mosque, Prizren

mosques and cathedrals stand next to Ottoman, Italian, and communist architecture painted in bright colours as a symbol of liberation. On the main square, the frescoed Et'hem Bey mosque looms above the statue of national hero Skanderbeg (1405–1468), an Albanian feudal lord and military commander who led a rebellion against the Ottoman Empire during the First Ottoman–Venetian War (1463–1479) until his death.

A little further along the main boulevard, the Pyramid of Tirana was originally a museum dedicated to communist dictator Enver Hoxha, who isolated Albania for four decades until his death in 1985, but has now been converted into a playful multispace venue, including a youth centre. Forty-eight multicoloured cube structures are scattered in, on and around the main Brutalist building like discarded Lego, with steps running up the roof's exterior. Bunk'art 1 and 2, a huge Cold War bunker built for the political elite, has been reimagined as an excellent history and contemporary art museum spread across a string of underground spaces. A visit to the Blloku neighbourhood, ten minutes south of Skanderbeg Square on foot, reveals the modern face of Albania. Once reserved solely for the communist leaders, today the streets are peppered with trendy restaurants, lounges and boutique shops. The city's culinary scene championed the Slow Movement before it became trendy, with a sustainable farm-to-fork philosophy that prioritises local, seasonal ingredients. Tirana Free Tours (www.tiranafreetour. com) offers quality two-hour city walks.

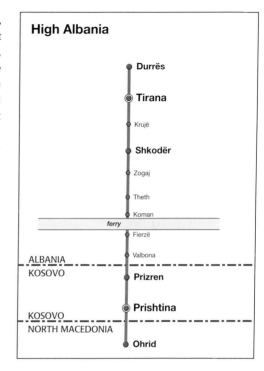

## NORTH TO SHKODËR

It is around two hours by bus to Shkodër, but it's worth taking a detour up the mountainside to the fortress town of Krujë, an hour north of Tirana, where there's an ethnographic museum, a touristy bazaar and an old prayer house of the Bektashi Sufi order, part of the Islamic mystic tradition. Stop off in Fushë-Krujë, a small town clustered at the foot of Mount Krujë, to feast on byrek (cheese or meat pastries) in the local bakery.

Shkodër is a lovely, bike-friendly city near beautiful Lake Shkodër. Through a mix of street scenes, portraits and fledgling photojournalism, the Marubi National Museum of Photography offers an excellent insight into the country's storied past, including its isolation under communist rule. Look out for the first photograph taken in Albania (1858) by Pjetër Marubi.

A ten-minute walk south leads to St Stephen's Catholic Church, which was converted into a sports hall when religion was banned under the communists, and the nearby Franciscan Church is splashed with vivid frescoes that depict the fate of the monks in those dark days. Passing the impressive Rozafa Fortress, the road out of town crosses the Bunë river and eventually reaches the lovely lakeside village of Zogaj, where you can dine on fish and buy kilim carpets from local vendors.

## THE HIGH ROAD TO THETH

From Shkodër, several scenic mountain roads climb up into the heart of the Accursed Mountains, or the Bjeshkët e Nemuna – the 'High Albania' as described by author Edith Durham in her eponymous early-twentieth-century book. This remote region is roamed

by wolves, bears, golden eagles and lynx, sheltered among peaks rising up to 2700 metres. One road twists its way up and over a 1750m-high pass before descending to Albania's Shangri-La, the legendary village of Theth. Cradled in the belly of a valley, this scattered settlement of sturdy stone farmhouses, fruit orchards and a lovely church is encircled by sheer rock walls. Protected under national park status, the surrounding forested and mountainous landscape is threaded with walking trails. It's a fantastic spot for a few days of relaxation, hikes and good food.

Poised on a rock, the Ethnographic Museum displays traditional rooms, artefacts and clothing, while the 400-year-old Lock-in Tower was used to resolve hundreds of family conflicts; the condemned were held here until a solution was negotiated. There are easy hikes to the Syri i Kaltër, or the Blue Eye, a teal-hued pool fed by icy spring waters (a natural swimming spot in summer – if you dare to brave the glacier temperatures), and the 25m-high Grunas waterfall. It's also possible to walk across the mountain pass to Valbona in the next valley within a day.

## THE SCENIC LAKE KOMAN FERRY

One of northern Albania's highlights is the Koman–Fierzë ferry ride, a serene three-hour, 30km cruise along narrow, fjord-like Lake Koman, passing farms and sleepy hamlets tucked into the folds of 1500m-high mountains. Three car ferries shuttle across the lake in summer, with smaller passenger boats stopping off at isolated homesteads – best of which is the half-bus, half-boat Dragobia ferry. Rise early in Shkodër for the winding, two-hour drive or bus journey along the Drin valley and through a 470m-long tunnel to the Koman port, in order to catch a morning ferry. The upper end of the Shalë river, which branches off the lake after around eleven kilometres, is a paradisiacal spot with a pebble beach and a cluster of restaurants.

It's very popular with day-trippers – and best avoided in the high season. A string of sustainable farms along the lake offers stays to visitors seeking authentic encounters with Albanian highland culture.

## CROSSING THE ALBANIA-KOSOVO BORDER

After a short drive from the ferry landing at Fierzë, break up the journey with a stop in the modern mountain town of Bajram Curri for a local lunch and to browse the handicrafts at the excellent Journey to Valbona. It acts as a tourism centre, too, offering information about volunteer work, transport, trips and accommodation. The dramatic Valbona Valley National Park is dotted with charming guesthouses, and is a great base for high-altitude hikes. Local and international environmental organisations have campaigned for years to stop the construction and operation of several illegally built hydroelectric power stations in this stunning valley, but sadly laws and court orders are largely ignored.

From Bajram Curri, it's a short ride to the Kosovo border, where it's well worth making the detour to the magnificent Orthodox monastery at Deçan before heading to Prizren, an attractive town dating back to the Bronze Age. The successive regimes – Roman, Byzantine, Ottoman, Yugoslav, Kosovan – have all left their mark on the city, from hilltop fortresses to churches and mosques, all scattered around the Prizren River. Begin with an exploration of the castle, fortified since at least the Roman period, though much of what remains today is from the Ottoman era. Walk the battlements for fantastic city views, then descend into town to visit the beautifully decorated Sinan Pasha Mosque. Cross the sixteenth-century stone-

Shalë river

arched bridge, and head for the Serbian Orthodox Church of Our Lady of Ljeviš, adorned with magnificent medieval frescoes.

## PUSHING ON TO NORTH MACEDONIA

One option for reaching North Macedonia is to travel via Kosovo's capital, Prishtina, and then across the border to Ohrid. There is, however, a similar-length route along the new highway west to the Albanian coast, which offers travellers a glimpse into Albania's dictatorial past. Turning off the highway at the small town of Reps, it's a twenty-minute drive to the notorious Spaç Prison. This cluster of bare flat blocks, stripped of doors and windows, is where hundreds of political prisoners were held for years, often decades. In 1973, inmates staged a brave, desperate revolt, one of the first instances of resistance to Hoxha's oppressive regime. Prisoners took control of the labour camp for two days and raised an Albanian flag

without the communist star, but they paid the price for it: four leaders of the revolt were executed, and 1400 years of jail time were added to the terms of one hundred prisoners. The camp was abandoned in 1990 and has been deteriorating ever since.

Passing Tirana and Elbasan, the road eventually climbs up to the Qafë Thanë pass near Lake Ohrid, a 360 square-kilometre blue expanse cradled among snow-streaked mountains, and the North Macedonian border. If you're driving, the Albanian lakeside village of Lin is worth a visit for the hilltop ruins of its sixth-century basilica, whose exceptional floor mosaics are occasionally on show.

Bustling in the summer months, Ohrid is one of Europe's oldest human settlements. Its cobbled, history-soaked streets cascade down to the waterfront, and are peppered with exquisite medieval churches – it's said the city once had 365 of them, one for each day of the year. A hilltop fortress peers out

*Byrek*, a meat-filled Albanian pastry

over the glistening waters. A lively weekly fruit and vegetable market is a great place to wander and pick up dried fruits or local honey.

On the lake's southern shores, pebble beaches line the coast all the way to the Albanian border, where the foreboding Sveti Naum monastery sits perched on a bluff (inside are iconostasis dating to 1711 and nineteenth-century frescoes).

## UNESCO-LISTED BERAT
Return across the border to Albania in the direction of Elbasan and then turn south to Berat, a charming UNESCO-protected town with well-preserved white Ottoman buildings tumbling down the hillside, and a Christian quarter across the river. Berat is crowned by an inhabited castle district, where St George's Church shelters an iconography museum with sixteenth-century works by local artist Onufri. In the early evening, don't miss the town's ritual *xhiro*, or promenade, when locals stroll up and down the riverside boulevard.

On the way to the coast, drivers can take a detour to the Divjakë-Karavasta National Park, a wetland area hosting Albania's largest lagoon, often partially hidden beneath a cloud of candyfloss-pink flamingos. The waters are also a feeding ground for Dalmatian (curly) pelicans. The visitor centre has a viewing tower, there are boat trips from the dock on the entrance road, and the beach restaurants specialise in *tave peshku*, fish and eel casserole. The drive direct from Berat to Durrës takes around two hours, so you can spend a pleasant few hours on the seafront boulevard before the ferry back to Italy departs in the late evening.

Theth is sheltered among sheer mountain peaks

# LIKE A LOCAL

## STAY

**Alpeta Agrotourism & Winery** Roshnik; www.alpeta.al. Excellent winery and guesthouse in Roshnik, 12km east of Berat, offering an upmarket agrotourism experience; the farm is known for its wines, olives and figs.

**Bujtina Rupa** Ndreaj, Theth; https://nordalbania.al. The Rupa family home in Theth has comfy rooms and camping spots, and offers communal home-made food.

**Çoçja Boutique Hotel** Rruga Wilson, Shkodër; www.cocja.com. Right in Shkodër's city centre, *Çoçja* is a beautiful oasis of calm, with a remarkable restaurant.

**Hotel Castello** Rruga Marin Barleti, Prizren; www.hotel-castello.com. On the road leading up to Prizren's castle, *Hotel Castello* offer fine views over the Old Town.

**Mangalemi Hotel** Rruga Mihal Komneno, Berat; www.mangalemihotel.com. A welcoming family-run bolthole spread across a string of Ottoman-era buildings in Berat's Old Town; has an excellent restaurant.

**Mrizi i Zanave** Fishtë; www.mrizizanave.al. Off the main road to Shkodër, Albania's most famous *agroturizëm* has fabulous food, elegant rooms and a well-stocked farm shop.

**My Grandparents' House** Ilindenska 47, Ohrid; +389 70 304 797. A charming guesthouse in Ohrid's Old Town; the best rooms have balconies and sea views.

**Neomalsore** Nanbli, Lake Koman; www.neomalsore.com. An old lakeside *kulla* tower house offers an authentic, off-grid *agroturizëm* stay, with simple rooms, tents and stargazing beds on the beach (free, on meal-only basis). Manager Marjana Molla introduces guests to traditional Albanian highland life and offers hikes, tours, gardening and storytelling.

## EAT & DRINK

**Çuçi** Rruga Antipatrea, Berat; +355 69 667 6004. Simple, fresh, affordable meals, including *pilaf* (rice dish), *gjallë* (meat stews) and *tavë kosi* (baked lamb).

**Gostilnica Neim** Goce Delchev 71, Ohrid; +389 70 212 066. Fantastic Balkan grilled dishes, soups and *šopska salada* at a friendly local haunt, whose walls are plastered in motorbike club stickers.

**Pazari i Ri** Sheshi Avni Rustemi, Tirana; www.pazariiri.com. Tirana's bustling 'new bazaar' sells fruit, veg, honey, jam and souvenirs like knitted woollen socks. In a lively area, surrounded by cafés and restaurants.

**Restaurant Kajče** Ilindenska 22, Ohrid; www.restaurantkajche.com. Behind Ohrid's Church of Saint Sophia, this lakefront restaurant treats diners to hearty plates of trout, eel, grilled vegetables and more.

**Shtegu i Gjelbër** Rruga vjetër e Bicaj, Kukës; +355 69 667 9907. En route from Prizren to the coast, this charming restaurant beside Kukës International Airport serves great local dishes, with views of a lake.

**Taverna Shkodrane** Rruga Shiroka-Zogaj, Shiroka; +355 69 225 9646. A wonderful lakeside restaurant near Zogaj, with fish and other local specialities. In low season, call to ask about its famed Sunday concerts.

## SHOP

**Adrion International Books** Sheshi Skanderbeg, Palace of Culture, Tirana; www.adrionltd.com. The country's best bookstore, with guides, maps, history books and translated Albanian literature.

**Artizanes** Rruga Thimi Mitko, Tirana; www.artizanes.al. Over sixty local artists sell their paintings, sculptures, knitwork and ceramics at this shop near the Pazar i Ri.

**Gjino Mjeda Punime në Tezgjah** Shkodra's Blv. Skenderbej; +355 69 340 3992. Beautiful handwoven tablecloths and handkerchiefs can be bought at Gjino Mjeda's shop; call ahead to check opening hours.

**Journey to Valbona** Rruga Sylejman Vokshi, Bajram Curri; www.journeytovalbona.com. This local tourism centre, café and shop sells hiking maps, home-made jam, honey, herbal tea, carpets and knitted socks at fair prices. Book ahead for lunch, to rent kayaks or hire a guide. Also runs the Te Qenit guesthouse.

**Mio Gift Shop** Rruga Mihal Komnena, Berat. Locally crafted goods including ceramics, jewellery and clothes.

**Nebie Qotaj** Zogaj village. Two women-led collectives in Zogaj village weave traditional kilim carpets, and it's often possible to have a look at the production process. Ask for Nebie Qotaj or Ganije Artunda.

Northern lights, Abisko

# NORDIC EXPEDITION
## On board the Polar Express

From Luleå, the Iron Ore Line weaves through spectacular Swedish Lapland: extensive wetlands, vast old-growth forests and crystalline lakes. It skirts past the Kiruna mine, and the Abisko National Park on the slopes of the snowy Scandes. Once in Norway, buses trundle to the rugged Lofotens, where the E10 winds past cascading waterfalls, sandy beaches and colourful, turf-roofed houses. Ferries connect the archipelago with Bodø, from where Norway's longest railway route departs. Windows frame views of Saltfjellet-Svartisen National Park's glaciers and Lomsdal-Visten's rainforests en route to Trondheim, the 'Home of Nordic Flavours'.

# THE JOURNEY

This epic journey begins at Luleå Centralstation at 5am, minutes before the train to Narvik departs in the twilight. As the train pulls away, the first pastel glints of sunrise brushstroke the sky, reflected back in the Lule River's still waters. In Boden, the train makes its initial stop, at the point where the Northern Main Line (Norra stambanan) meets the Iron Ore Line (Malmbanan).

As the train clatters on, the rising sun illuminates a string of crystalline lakes beyond the window and vast wetlands, carpeted in snow come late September. The railway line tracks the meandering path of the Lule River until the waterway veers off into the dense, untouched primeval forests of Muddus National Park, at which point the train crosses the symbolic boundary of the Arctic Circle. Europe's last remaining wilderness, this unspoiled polar region shelters numerous species of arctic flora and fauna, including lynx, bears, wolverines, pine martens, weasels, elk and (in summer) reindeer.

## ACROSS SWEDISH LAPLAND

Muddus, along with the national parks of Stora Sjöfallet, Sarek and Padjelanta and the nature reserves of Stubbá and Sjaunja, is protected under the UNESCO World Heritage Site of Swedish Lapland. The heartland of the Indigenous Sámi, Lapland is characterised by giant swathes of pine and spruce forest, foaming rivers that drain the snow-cloaked fells, and tranquil villages tucked into the folds of lake-dotted hills. You could alight here to hike through glacial valleys and visit Sámi settlements, or in winter, ski the powdery slopes and catch the aurora borealis dancing across the sky.

Polar Express

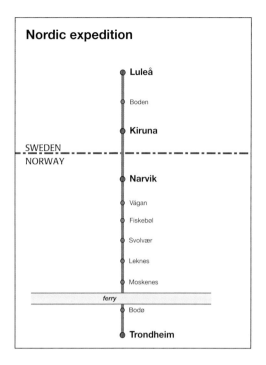

## Nordic expedition

- Luleå
- Boden
- Kiruna

SWEDEN
NORWAY

- Narvik
- Vågan
- Fiskebøl
- Svolvær
- Leknes
- Moskenes

*ferry*

- Bodø
- Trondheim

### PRACTICAL INFORMATION

**Distance covered:** 1642km

**Recommended journey time:** 10 days

**Transport details:**

- Norwegian train operator Vy runs night services from Stockholm to Luleå (12–14hr; from €55; www.vy.se) and onward day services from Luleå to Narvik (8hr; 1–2 daily; from €58). Swedish counterpart Sj operates the Polar Express from Bodø to Trondheim (10hr; 2 daily; from €48; www.sj.no), and a service from Trondheim to Oslo (7hr; 10–12 daily; from €43).

- Ferries connect Moskenes to Bodø (3hr 30min; 1–2 daily; free for foot passengers; www.reisnordland.no).

- Buses run from Narvik to Leknes (5hr 45min; daily). The Nordland Travel Pass offers seven days of unlimited bus travel (€110; www.reisnordland.no). Check bus schedules for the Lofotens at www.reise.reisnordland.no.

As the train approaches Kiruna, Sweden's northernmost town, the landscape grows increasingly austere. There are fewer trees, and a huge black mound looms on the horizon: the world's largest underground iron ore mine – an ugly brooding reminder of Kiruna's prosperity. The train station faces Lake Luossajärvi, and a fifteen-minute stop allows a quick stretch of the legs and a glance at the monument dedicated to the Malmbanan workers who built the Luleå–Narvik line in 1902.

The last stretch of the Iron Ore Line is astonishing, passing through the mighty Scanes, whose snow-capped peaks rise to 2000m, before pushing on towards the vast vermouth-coloured forest surrounding Torneträsk, the peninsula's largest alpine lake.

The train slows down in Abisko National Park, one of the best places to see the northern lights. Opposite the STF Abisko fjällstation, a chairlift climbs 500m up Nuolja mountain (1169m), from where fantastic views unfold over the wilderness below, taking in the 70km-long Torneträsk Lake and the horseshoe-shaped mountaintops of Lapporten; the latter used as landmarks by the Sámi for guiding their reindeer between summer and winter grazing. Tucked away in a corner of the café at the top of the chairlift, the Aurora Sky Station is the place to go to see the northern lights in all their glory; Abisko lies in a rain shadow so the sky is often clear and free from cloud. Experts are on hand to explain the hissing and clicking equipment used to measure the lights.

## CROSSING THE NORWAY BORDER

Once past the Sweden–Norway border, the train rumbles 43km along the northernmost railway of Norway, the Ofoten Line (Ofotbanen), twisting and tunnelling through hostile mountains and rounding the deep-blue Rombaken fjord until it reaches the final station: Narvik, a likeable industrial town. Here, the Fagernesfj ellet cable car glides 656m up the severe Fagernesfjellet, depositing passengers at a café and viewing point overlooking the pewter-hued Otofjord. On a clear day, the landscape glows in the midnight sun (late May to mid-July). Hiking trails delve into the mountains, and from late November to May, skiers and snowboarders descend on the snow-carpeted slopes. This is the best time to see the aurora borealis.

## THE OTHERWORLDLY LOFOTENS

There is no doubt that the #300 bus traces the most beautiful and unique route in Scandinavia (and probably the world). From Narvik's dramatic fjord, it traverses six Lofoten islands by bridge, causeway and tunnel – occasionally boring through the mountains and under the sea. The highway slips through, or skirts close by, all the archipelago's most fascinating villages and towns, many pressed against the shore by the ominous Lofotenveggen (Lofoten Wall), a 160km-long range of cloud-raking mountains.

At first glance, it appears impossible to pass through this rocky fortress but, in fact, the labyrinth of straits, sounds and fjords is peppered with charming fishing villages, in particular Henningsvær, Stamsund, Nusfjord, Reine and Å. The pace of life here drums to a slower beat, calling for unhurried days spent hiking and biking around the stunning coastline in the summer (despite being so far north,

Reine, Lofoten

the weather can be exceptionally mild). On rainy days – frequent in these parts – locals shelter in the *rorbuer* (fishermen's huts), grilling boat-fresh fish over wood-burning stoves and gently wasting time.

## ISLAND-HOPPING ADVENTURE

Lofoten's largest town, Svolvær is draped across a long, tattered peninsula on Austvågøya's southeast coast. It might not be the quaintest of Lofoten's towns, but its harbourfront huddle of red-painted wooden buildings is attractive and it has more places to stay and eat than its siblings. Plus its dramatic landscapes are ripe for exploration: boat trips to the slender Trollfjord, hiking Mount Høgskrova on the idyllic islet of Skrova, mettle-testing climbs to the 'horns' of the 150m-high rocky pinnacle Svolværgeita ('Svolvær Goat').

Another decent base is Leknes, southwest of Austvågøya and home to one of the Lofoten's two airports. It's a humdrum town, redeemed by its location on the spectacular island of Vestvågøy: whose serrated coastline is contoured by a necklace of coves and inlets. You're well placed to explore Stamsund and Ballstad, a pair of pretty fishing villages on the south coast, and the wind-whipped settlements of Unstad, Eggum and Utakleiv strung along the wild northern fringes.

The coastline is laced with unspoiled beaches: among the best is the state-protected Hauklandstrand whose pearly sands ribbon between the grey-green Himmeltinden and Mannen mountains.

On neighbouring Flakstadøya, Ramberg hooks around a sugar-white beach with turquoise waters. The E10 wiggles along the coast, between severe mountains and the ocean, to Moskenesøya. At the tip of a tiny promontory, Reine huddles at the foot of rearing peaks, its red-painted *rorbuer* gleaming in a pure light that's long stoked the imagination of

Børgefjell National Park

Sculpture in Kurin dedicated to the workers who built the Luleå–Narvik line

artists and photographers. It's a great spot for hiking, kayaking and seafood feasts.

From here, embark on boat trips to Vindstad, an abandoned village with just one permanent resident; the Moskenstraumen, a churning maelstrom feared by fisherfolk; and the prehistoric cave paintings at deserted Refsvika. Within fifteen minutes of Reine is Sakrisøy, a rocky speck adrift in the Reinefjord dotted with ochre-hued *rorbuer*. Look out for the wooden racks festooning the harbour that are used to dry migratory cod (skrei) caught in the winter, a tradition that dates back to the Vikings. Learn about the Lofoten's fishing history and former *rorbuer* inhabitants at the Norwegian Fishing Village Museum Å, whose well-preserved nineteenth-century buildings include the old grocery store, post office, fish oil factory, boathouse and bakery – where you can taste freshly baked cinnamon rolls.

## NORWAY'S LONGEST TRAIN JOURNEY

After exploring the oneiric landscapes of the Lofoten islands, it's time to return to the Norwegian mainland. Ferries ply the Vestfjorden from Moskenes to Bodø, a good overnighter for forays into Sjunkhatten National Park or boat trips to Saltstraumen, one of the world's strongest tidal-current maelstroms (reaching up to 10m in diameter and 5m in depth).

Alternatively, hop straight on board the Polar Express – Norway's longest railway – for its ten-hour journey to Trondheim. Beyond the window, the bluish maw of the Svartisen Glacier clings to the mountains in Saltfjellet-Svartisen National Park. The driver will soon announce the approach to the highest point of the journey as the railway line climbs to 680m. The train then crosses the Arctic Circle, traces the emerald Ranaelva to the mighty Ranfjorden before meandering along the River Vefsna to Børgefjell National Park, refuge of the Arctic fox. For much of the year, the last stretch through Trøndelag will be illuminated only by moonlight until you arrive in Trondheim, Norway's third-largest city.

Admire the sculptures adorning the magnificent Nidaros Cathedral; marvel at the colourful houses reflected in the Nid from the Gamle Bybro (Old Town Bridge); and take in fine views of the city and its sweeping fjord from Kristianstenfestning Fortress. Before heading home, dine at one of the excellent restaurants earning Trondheim its culinary clout: it isn't dubbed the 'Home of Nordic Flavours' for no reason.

## LIKE A LOCAL

### STAY

**HI Hostel Bodø** Sjøgata 57, Bodø, 8006; www.hi hostels.com/hostels/hi-bodo. Next to Bodø's train station and within walking distance of the ferry terminal, this comfortable hostel offers spacious rooms, some with a private bathroom. There's a shared kitchen and a common room filled with board games and books. Laundry facilities are available.

**Lofoten Å Hi Hostel** Å, 8392; www.hihostels.com/ hostels/hi-lofoten-a. A welcoming hostel offering dorm beds and a few private rooms with shared bathrooms and a communal kitchen. It is set across two locations: the Hennumgården house, in the centre of Å, and above the Lofoten Stockfish Museum (Tørrfiskmuseum), from where you gaze at the vast pewter-toned sea. Reliable wi-fi.

Abisko National Park

**Lofototen Rorbuer** Jektveien 10, Svolvær; www.lofoten-rorbuer.no. At this long-running Svolvær institution, converted *rorbuer* provide cosy digs; the pick of the bunch overlook the Marinepollen lagoon. A few share a kitchen and bathroom; others have kitchenettes.

## EAT & DRINK

**Antikvariatet** Nedre Baklandet 4, 7014 Trondheim; www.facebook.com/antikvarene. At this Trondheim-based café-bar and cultural venue, you can read over a cup of coffee, taste home-made Norwegian sweets or chat over a local beer. There's also a book swap and regular performances by artists.

**Ramberg Gjestegård** Flakstadveien 361, 8380 Ramberg; www.ramberg-gjestegard.no. In this cosy café, restaurant and guesthouse near Ramberg's heavenly beach, warm your body and soul with a marshmallow-sprinkled hot chocolate while playing board games with like-minded travellers. Or enjoy freshly caught cod or salmon dishes washed down with a pint of Lofotpils, the local beer.

## SHOP

**Anita's Sjømat** Sakrisøy, 8390 Reine; www.sakrisoy.no/seafood. This Reine shop and seafood bar shines a light on local produce, best enjoyed on the outdoor terrace with dizzying mountain views. Feast on dishes like shellfish soup, *tataki* or fish burgers, or buy fresh fish for self-catering stays. Also rents out traditional fishermen's cabins.

**Lofoten Gaver og Brukskunst** Storgata 38, 8370 Leknes. Family-run shop in Leknes selling souvenirs (magnets, cuddly toys, mugs), maps, artisanal crafts and hand-knitted winter clothing.

# ORIENT LOCAL
## A fabled trip from Berlin to Istanbul

In 2025, new life will be breathed into luxury train travel as the iconic Orient Express returns to the tracks – nearly four decades since the original ceased serving Istanbul in 1977. It will carry passengers on a nostalgic journey aboard seventeen original 1920s cars, restored with theatrical flourish by esteemed architect Maxime d'Angeac. For those with an adventurous spirit minus the deep pockets, it's possible to reach Istanbul from Berlin (or even London) entirely by regular railway services, an epic 2000km route that passes through six countries, with stops in Vienna, Budapest, Bucharest and Sofia, before sidling up to the eastern edge of the European continent.

# THE JOURNEY

This first leg of the trip from Berlin to Vienna, on board the red-striped ICE train named Berolina (Latin for Berlin), takes around eight hours. It is easy and comfortable, with power sockets and free wi-fi, plus an on-board bistro serving the likes of goulash and frothy Erdinger beer. The German countryside grows increasingly hilly as the train speeds through Thüringia and Bavaria to pull into the Austrian capital's main station with impressive punctuality at 5.47pm – enough time for a schnitzel dinner and a stroll around its central streets.

To see a less-touristed side to the city, consider bypassing the traditional big-hitting museums and attractions in favour of randomised walks – a pleasant form of slow travel in itself. A daytime stroll around Vienna can throw up plenty of surprises: looming World War II flak towers in Arenbergpark; Otto Wagner's impressive Art Nouveau pavilion at Karlsplatz station; and the main cemetery, home to the graves of Beethoven and Brahms. See what's happening at Improper Walls, an excellent indie art gallery that platforms local and international artists and hosts concerts and other cultural events. Rather than joining the long queues for decadent chocolatey slabs of Sachertorte at the iconic *Café Sacher*, hit the Naschmarkt to feast on local Viennese delicacies such as... hot dogs.

The next day, for a dose of nostalgia, head to the famous Prater amusement park to admire its big

Prater's big wheel, Vienna

Liberty Bridge connects Buda
and Pest across the Danube

## Orient local

```
                      ◉ Berlin
GERMANY
·-·-·-·-·-·-·-·-·-·-·-·-·-·-·-·-·-·-·-·
AUSTRIA
                      ◉ Vienna
AUSTRIA
·-·-·-·-·-·-·-·-·-·-·-·-·-·-·-·-·-·-·-·
HUNGARY
                      ◉ Budapest
HUNGARY
·-·-·-·-·-·-·-·-·-·-·-·-·-·-·-·-·-·-·-·
ROMANIA
                      ◉ Bucharest
ROMANIA
·-·-·-·-·-·-·-·-·-·-·-·-·-·-·-·-·-·-·-·
BULGARIA
                      ◉ Sofia
BULGARIA
·-·-·-·-·-·-·-·-·-·-·-·-·-·-·-·-·-·-·-·
TURKEY
                      ◉ İstanbul
```

### PRACTICAL INFORMATION

**Distance covered:** 2000km

**Recommended journey time:** 3–4 weeks

**Transport details:**

- Daily trains between London and Berlin are operated by Deutsche Bahn, Eurostar and Thalys and bookable on their websites as well as third-party operators such as Trainline. Flights can be booked from most major UK cities via British Airways, easyJet, Ryanair and others.

- This entire route is connected by regular railway services: Deutsche Bahn operates an InterCity Express (ICE) from Berlin to Vienna (8hr; hourly; from £30); Hungarian Railways' EuroCity (EC) train connects Vienna and Budapest (2hr 30min; hourly; from £40); the Dacia Express, operated by CFR Călători/Romanian Railways, runs a night train from Budapest to Bucharest (15hr; also 4 daily trains; from £25 for a regular seat); Bulgarian Railways links Bucharest with Sofia (10hr; 1–2 daily; from £20); and the Sofia-Istanbul Express runs from Sofia to Istanbul (15hr; 1 daily; from £20, can only be booked in person at Sofia train station or in advance via www.discoverbyrail.com).

wheel, kitschy nineteenth-century buildings and the surrounding parkland. Hikers might like to follow the Danube north to pick up a walking trail to the Kahlenberg mountain, passing through vineyards and forests and taking in splendid views.

If time allows, squeeze in a spontaneous trip to Bratislava, just an hour away by train: after walking around the Baroque hilltop castle and charming historic centre, refuel with a classic Slovakian feast – garlic soup in a bread roll, dumplings, sheep's cheese gnocchi – at the old-style *Slovak Pub*.

## VIENNA TO BUDAPEST

Since the train journey from Vienna to Budapest is only two and a half hours, budget-conscious travellers might like to decline the pricier Railjet option (and its free wi-fi, draught beer and business class) in favour of the more basic but comfortable EuroCity (EC) service run by Hungarian Railways. The scenery isn't mind-blowing – unless you like flat, featureless fields and endless wind turbines, that is – but it is exciting to arrive at Budapest's historic and striking Keleti station, surely one of the finest in Europe.

Kick off your exploration of Hungaria's beautiful capital with a riverside walk starting at the Parliament building (Országház) on the Pest-side promenade, skirting past the poignant Shoes on the Danube memorial – a trail of iron footwear paying homage to the Jews executed along this riverbank during World War II – and ending at the Great Market Hall (Nagy Vásárcsarnok), a delightful covered market with food stalls selling the likes of spicy Hungarian sausage. Crossing Liberty Bridge, explore the hillier Buda side of the city, admiring the historic Gellért Thermal Bath, passing through Gellérthegy Jubileumi park, and arriving at Castle Hill (Várnegyed) and the Fisherman's Bastion. After snapping away at the glorious views and chomping on some *kürtőskalács* (chimney cake), drop back down to the river via Buda Castle and its collection of Hungarian masters in the National Gallery.

The next day, stroll the centre and its grand Habsburg buildings, popping spontaneously into small photo galleries (don't miss the tiny but top-notch Robert Capa Contemporary Photography Center named after the late Hungarian-born photographer) and welcoming bookshops, visiting the impressive synagogue in the Jewish quarter and hunting down delicious *lángos* (deep-fried bread topped with cheese, sour cream and garlic sauce). In the afternoon meander the charming pathways, monastery ruins and Art Nouveau water tower of peaceful Margaret Island before heading to the

Alexander Nevsky Cathedral, Sofia

main city park, Városliget. Tour the various buildings – thermal baths, castles, museums – and Heroes' Square before returning to the city centre along elegant Andrássy Avenue. Make time for one last goulash before catching the night train.

## BUDAPEST TO BUCHAREST

There is a daytime train to Bucharest – but that's if a 7am departure on the InterCity Traianus isn't too daunting. The alternative is the sleeper service on board the Dacia Express, which starts its journey in Vienna, picks passengers up in Budapest at 10.45pm, and continues through the night to the Romanian capital. Two-bed compartments are compact but cosy: a sink, coat hangers, climate-control button, bottles of water, a power socket. No wi-fi or on-board restaurant, so pack books and snacks. The gentle rocking of the train easily lulls guests to sleep, though expect an abrupt awakening by Hungarian guards knocking on doors to inspect passports at Lököshaza. A short while later, Romanian officials repeat the checks at Curtici.

Rolling up the window blinds the next morning reveals Transylvanian landscapes – rolling hills and quaint villages, pine forests and Saxon churches, the evocative Carpathian Mountains, often cloaked in snow. This is real slow travel: at some points around 50kph. The Romanian train stations are also diverse, from picturesque Sinaia (which has royal connections) to the communist aesthetic of Braşov, whose concrete towers conceal a medieval Old Town.

The train rolls into Bucharest in the afternoon. A mix of outsized communist structures and rundown, crumbling buildings makes it feel as though you've time-travelled at least three decades into the past. Give yourself a couple of days to immerse yourself in the curiously melancholic atmosphere of this labyrinthine city and its epoch-spanning architecture: the 1888-built Romanian Athenaeum concert hall; the eighteenth-century Stavropoleos Monastery Church; the pretty English-style Cişmigiu Gardens. And, of course, the monstrous 1100-room Palace of Parliament, for which communist leader Ceauşescu demolished one-fifth of the city. Along the way, feast on *scovergi*

Gellért Thermal Bath, Budapest

(fried dough), *mici* (Romanian sausage) and *sarmale* (stuffed cabbage rolls). It may feel forlorn and forgotten in places, but Bucharest leaves a lasting impression.

## BUCHAREST TO SOFIA

The trip from Bucharest to Sofia involves a change at the border station of Ruse and no-frills travel in basic trains. The surroundings are more interesting: the flatlands of northern Bulgaria give way to scenic terrain – including the Iskăr Gorge – on approach to the capital. Sofia is a city of surprises. Its main boulevard, lined with upscale cafés and shops, feels more Parisian than Eastern European – in sharp contrast to Bucharest's tumbledown sprawl and mysterious atmosphere. The sense of space, lightness and fresh air is a welcome respite, as is the view of Vitosha mountain in the distance – a popular hiking

and skiing destination for locals and visitors alike. Closer, the city's two largest green spaces – South Park and Loven Park – are dotted with art pavilions, ponds and cafés and threaded with walking trails.

Devote time to wandering the city centre and surrounding neighbourhoods, stumbling across top-notch street art, cute galleries (don't miss Lyuben Karavelov) and boutiques, and folksy restaurants serving up delicious Shopska salads. The historic bazaar – formerly known as the Zhenski Pazar (Women's Market) – is filled with food stalls serving *mekitsa* (fried dough) and flaky savoury *banitsa* (cheese-filled pastry). Further explorations might reveal the National Palace of Culture, some unexpected Roman-era ruins, the Alexander Nevsky Cathedral, which apparently contains materials brought back from Berlin after World War II, and some Soviet-era monuments. All impressive in their

Palace of Parliament, Bucharest

own way but now, the focus is on boarding the train to our final destination: Istanbul.

## SOFIA TO ISTANBUL

The night train from Sofia to Istanbul is the most complicated part of the trip. Since it's not possible to book online in advance, and there's the risk of trains being sold out, some travellers prefer to pay a local agent like www. discoverbyrail.com to organise a ticket and deliver it to their accommodation the day before travel. The sleeper departs at 6.30pm, with the chance to enjoy a pleasant sundown through the window. Border control is not so pleasant: expect a rude awakening by Bulgarian guards to hop off the train into the freezing night, luggage and all, for passport checks and bags x-rayed. Nonetheless, nothing can dampen the spirits upon arrival in Istanbul in the early hours. You've reached the edge of Europe, with only a small body of water separating the continent from Asia. Revel in Beyoğlu's knot of hillside streets, visit quaint cafés, and cross the bridge to the Hagia Sophia, Topkapı Palace and the Blue Mosque. Share plates of *köfte* and *lahmacun* (flatbread topped with spiced mincemeat), *manti* (lamb-stuffed dumplings) and flaky *börek*. From here, the easiest option is to fly home. However, the immersive option would be to return via one of the many train routes available – if possible, even more slowly.

## LIKE A LOCAL

### STAY

**Hostel №1** ul. Serdika 28, 1000 Sofia. A cheap and simple Sofia hostel with comfortable and safe rooms.

**Stories** Király u. 26, 1061 Budapest; www.stories budapest.com. This funky central boutique can be found in Budapest's hip Király Utca district.

**Suter Palace Heritage Boutique Hotel** Aleea Suter 23–25, Bucharest 040547; www.suterpalace. com. Poised grandly on a hilltop in a restored early twentieth-century villa, this upscale hotel is close to Bucharest's Carol I Park and the National Museum of Romanian History.

## EAT

**Altkat** Rasimpaşa, Karakolhane Cd. 62A, 34716 Kadıköy/Istanbul; www.altkatcoffee.com. Some of Istanbul's finest artisan coffee, pastries and ice creams.

**Caru' cu bere** Stavropoleos 5, Bucharest; www.carucubere.ro. Traditional restaurant in Bucharest with a great selection of Romanian dishes.

**Community Kitchen** Tomtom, 18 Kumbaracı Ykş, 34087 Beyoğlu/Istanbul; +90 538 503 27 36. Friendly and welcoming vegan spot in Beyoğlu offering a plant-based twist on Turkish cuisine, with outdoor seating.

**Great Market Hall** Vámház krt. 1–3, 1093 Budapest; www.budapestmarkethall.com. A nineteenth-century fresh food market tucked inside a carefully restored neo-Gothic hall in Budapest.

**Hadjidraganov's House** Kozloduy St 75, 1202 Sofia; www.kashtite.com/bg. This wood-beamed Sofia restaurant has a fireplace for winter, outdoor seating for summer, and delicious local dishes year-round.

**Rosenstein** Mosonyi u. 3, 1087 Budapest; www.rosenstein.hu. Family-run Budapest restaurant offering an extensive menu of Hungarian dishes, including fish soup and veal goulash.

**Scovergăria Micăi** Calea Victoriei 14, Bucharest 030027; www.scovergaria-micai.ro. A traditional Romanian bakery in Bucharest to try *scovergi* (fried dough) and other local specialities.

## SHOP

**Bey Karaköy** Mumhane Cd. 54, Istanbul; www.facebook.com/BeyKarakoy. Stylish shop in the Turkish capital with urban garments for men.

**Cărturești & Friends** Strada Edgar Quinet 9, Bucharest 030167; www.carturesti.ro. Impressive bookshop in the heart of Bucharest, with several tome-filled levels.

**Galerist** Meşrutiyet Cd. 67, 34430 Beyoğlu/Istanbul; www.galerist.com.tr. Serves as a gateway between Turkish and global artists; has two locations in Istanbul.

**Leila Concept Store** Firuzağa, Boğazkesen Cd. 100A, 34425 Beyoğlu/Istanbul; www.leilaconceptstore.com. Unique and beautiful designs using natural fibres, made by Leila herself.

Istiklal Avenue, Istanbul

Keselo hilltop fortress in Omalo

# HITCHHIKING GEORGIA
## Off-grid in the South Caucasus

On this alluring journey across the breadth of Georgia, you'll hit the road in eclectic Batumi on the shimmering Black Sea coast, traversing the lush slopes of the Gombori Mountains to Telavi's vineyards, before pushing on to the dynamic capital city of Tbilisi. Then, finally, buckle up for the most scenic – and spine-tingling – drive in the country, climbing 3050m to heavenly Tusheti, a remote hamlet-dotted region tucked into the folds of the Greater Caucasus. Hitchhiking across Georgia is relatively easy and commonplace, but more so, it's often a heartwarming and enriching experience too.

Transhumance in rural Georgia

# THE JOURNEY

Hitchhiking can be an enriching experience, deepening an understanding of a different country and its people and culture. A favourite museum or dish, a humorous anecdote or historical titbit – sharing a conversation with a driver can yield surprising insights. Most Georgians believe that visitors are a gift from god, which explains the generosity and hospitality offered to travellers in this South Caucasus country.

Some pointers on etiquette: though many young Georgians are fluent in English, it is good practice to prepare for your journey by learning a handful of essential phrases – *madloba* (thank you), for instance, goes a long way. A few Russian words can also be helpful, but be mindful of the sensitivities

around speaking the language due to Georgia's history and the current Russian-occupied territories. Another appreciated gesture is to pack sweets or small souvenirs from your home country to give as thanks for free rides.

## BREEZY BATUMI

Located between the snow-capped Caucasus Mountains and the Black Sea, Batumi is a cosmopolitan coastal resort with a wide 1884-built corniche wrapping around a pebbly beach. Georgia's second city – the capital of the southwestern Adjara region – is a favoured summer playground for holidaying Georgians. Piece together the border region's layered history through the city's architectural jigsaw: the late Ottoman-style Ortajame Mosque, a neo-Gothic cathedral, an Art Nouveau theatre, a Greek Orthodox church, austere Soviet-era blocks, and the harmonious amalgam of Belle Époque and modern buildings at Europe Square (Evropas Moedani). Wander the charming Old Town before lingering over a coffee at one of the pavement cafés flanking the Venetian-style Batumi Piazza. Catch sunset from the ferris wheel, which offers a decent view of the Alphabet Tower, a 145m-high monument to Georgian script and culture. After dark, visit the mesmerising moving sculpture by Georgian artist Tamar Kvesitadze, *Woman & Man*, or as it's better known, *Ali & Nino* – a nod to the protagonists of Kurban Said's eponymous novel.

When you're ready to move on, head to the fish market on the outskirts of Batumi, and find a spot where drivers can easily see you from a distance and have space to stop without obstructing traffic. You'll likely have to wait a while for a ride, but don't be discouraged: put up your thumb (or sign) and smile, and you'll soon be driving across the relict UNESCO World Heritage Site of Colchic Rainforest and Wetlands. If you're lucky, you'll flag down a driver travelling the full 152km to Kutaisi; otherwise, ask to be dropped off at Magnetiti, Ureki's black sand beach with presumed healing properties, for a short break before hailing another ride.

## PRACTICAL INFORMATION

**Distance covered:** 924km
**Recommended journey time:** 15 days
**Transport details:**

- This hitchhiking trip starts in Batumi and ends in Tbilisi. Allow 15 days for this trip, best taken between spring and summer, as the Abano mountain pass closes from October to May.
- For day-trips, it's easiest to use marshrutkas (shared minibuses); bring lari and pay the driver directly unless you're in a big city, where you must buy tickets in advance at the counter.
- As anywhere, the universal hitchhiking sign is put up your thumb (or sign) and smile; pack sweets or souvenirs to give drivers as thanks for the free ride.

## KUTAISI: CONTROVERSIAL CATHEDRALS AND LEGEND-STEEPED CAVES

Kutaisi, a historic capital of the medieval Kingdom of Georgia, is your base for the next three days. Drop your backpack and wander through the Old Town from Kutaisi State Historical Museum to the effervescent Green Bazaar, one of the largest and liveliest food markets in

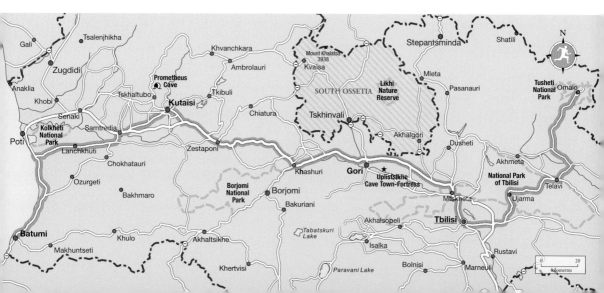

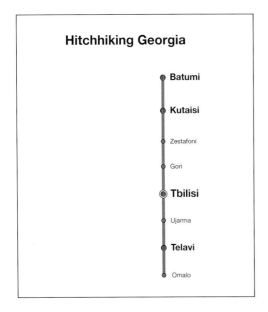

## Hitchhiking Georgia

- Batumi
- Kutaisi
- Zestafoni
- Gori
- ⦿ Tbilisi
- Ujarma
- Telavi
- Omalo

The Colchis Fountain in Kutaisi

Georgia. Pause by two monuments that recall the city's origins: Colchis Fountain, studded with replicas of the gold jewellery unearthed at Vani archaeological site, and the Soviet-era terracotta relief Kolkheti at the entrance of the Kutaisi Central Bazaar. Walk across the Chain Bridge and climb up to the eleventh-century Bagrati Cathedral that looms over the city, whose roof sparked controversy when it was added at the behest of former president Mikheil Saakashvili (the cathedral was stripped of its UNESCO World Heritage Site status for the insensitive restoration). From here, follow the silvery course of the Rioni River as it flows through the Old Town.

If time allows, set off by marshrutka (shared minibus) to Prometheus Cave, a subterranean labyrinth of caverns, tunnels, petrified waterfalls and underground rivers and lakes. According to legend, water droplets seeping down the mountain where Zeus chained Prometheus, one of the titans of Greek myth, have sculpted the stalactites and stalagmites in the gloomy halls of this rocky basilica. On guided tours, multicoloured lights cast psychedelic shadows on the petrified curtains and karst sculptures, and the murmur of the water grows to a low roar; take a boat to navigate the Kumi river running beneath the cave.

When you're ready to continue on to Tbilisi, head to the E60 near the Kutaisi Sports Palace to start hitchhiking. Alternatively, depart in a marshrutka and try to hail a ride in Zestafoni. If the option of a detour to Gori – Stalin's hometown – is on the table, be sure to take a guided tour of the museum complex dedicated to the notorious despot. The ancient rock-hewn Uplistsikhe Cave Town-Fortress, fifteen kilometres away, is one of the oldest settlements in the Caucasus.

## TBILISI, A CAPTIVATING CAPITAL

Straddling the crossroads of Europe and Asia, Tbilisi bears the marks of a complicated history in its architectural medley. Arab, Ottoman, Mongol and Russian imperial forces have all left their cultural imprint on the city. Tbilisi's evocative Old Town is a tangle of narrow streets, fresco-adorned churches and pastel-hued houses punctuated with colourful latticed balconies. Amble through the cobbled lanes

Japanese garden in Batumi

Bathhouses in Tbilisi's Abanotubani district

of the Abanotubani neighbourhood, whose collection of ancient dome-shaped bathhouses have restored Georgians for centuries. Look out for the imposing blue-tiled facade of the Orbeliani Baths, which shelters a string of underground steaming sulphur baths; book a body scrub and massage for silky-smooth skin.

Hop on a cable car up to the fourth-century Narikala Fortress, which is guarded by the 20m-high aluminium sculpture of Mother Georgia, bearing a cup of wine in one hand and a sword in the other – a nod to the country's warm hospitality as well as its stoutness in the face of invaders. Head down to Rike Park, home to a pair of metal exhibition and concert halls designed by Italian architect Massimiliano Fuksas. Return to Old Tbilisi via the Peace Bridge and revive with coffee at one of the snug cafés clustered around Shota Rustaveli Avenue. Don't miss the National Museum of Georgia, the National Gallery, the Botanical Garden and the 50m vertiginous funicular ride to Mtatsminda Park.

As part of the Silk Road, an ancient trading route linking Europe and Asia, Georgia's cuisine incorporates influences from neighbouring countries. Feast on clay-oven-scorched *khachapuri* (bread baked with cheese, herbs and egg), *shkmeruli* (chicken cooked in garlic and cream) and caraway-spiced *khinkali* meat dumplings in local taverns, washed down with local wine. Georgia is one of the oldest viticultural regions on Earth, with around eight thousand years of grape cultivation under its belt. Oenophiles can book a tasting session in one of the city's cavernous wine cellars (try *Vino Underground* near Freedom Square).

If you can spare a day, travel by marshrutka to Georgia's ecclesiastical capital, Mtskheta, around twenty kilometres north of Tbilisi. Even if you aren't religious, it's a spiritual experience climbing to the sixth-century Jvari Monastery and gazing down at the point at which the turquoise waters of the Aragvi River collide with the pearly Mtkvari.

## WINE, GLORIOUS WINE

From Tbilisi, the best way to hail a ride to Telavi, Kakheti's largest town, is to take the metro to Varketili and then a bus to Lilo Bazar to find a good spot to hitchhike. Once ensconced in a car, the route passes the historic fortress-village of Ujarma and then winds upwards, tracing the contours of the Iori river to the point at which it meets the Gombori river. The most picturesque part of the journey is the Gombori Pass, at 1620m, with fine views of the Greater Caucasus mountain range that forms the northern belt of Georgia.

Kakheti, the largest and most famous wine region in Georgia, is a mosaic of vineyards and wineries. Rtveli (harvest season) starts in September and is an extraordinary event: families gather for grape-picking, some following a historic winemaking practice involving *qvevris*, clay amphorae buried underground — today inscribed on the UNESCO list of intangible cultural heritage. Everyone enjoys a well-deserved Georgian feast, known as *supra*. There is no shortage of *kinkhali* dumplings, *mtsvadi* (grilled pork skewers), *nigvziani badrijani* (fried eggplant stuffed with walnut filling) or freshly baked *khachapuri*, and of course plenty of wine and *chacha* (pomace brandy).

## ON THE ROAD TO TUSHETI

When you're ready to press on, try hitchhiking from just outside Telavi railway station. If you can reach Omalo in a single ride, you'll have hit the jackpot. The narrow unpaved dirt track of the Abano — Georgia's most dangerous mountain pass and one of Europe's highest — cuts a treacherous path on its dizzying 2000m-high climb. In fact, it featured in the 2013 BBC documentary *World's Most Dangerous Roads*. But this is the only route to the villages of Tusheti, a remote

Kolkheti ceramic relief in Kutaisi

Svetitskhoveli Cathedral, Mtskheta

shepherding region tucked into the folds of hostile mountains. Since the sixteenth century, shepherds have walked their flocks over 190km down from the Tusheti mountains to the Kakheti lowlands in autumn, where they live until the spring before reversing their tracks and taking their sheep to the summer pastures in the mountains once more.

If you're visiting from June to September, you'll likely pass Georgians travelling along the road from Kakheti to family homes peppered across Tusheti's 49 villages to escape the lowland heat. For the rest of the year, the snow-engulfed pass cuts the region off from the rest of the country (the road closes from mid-October until late May). For those who do venture to Omalo, Tusheti's main village, the reward is pristine nature and unrivalled hospitality. From Upper Omalo, dazzling views take in the Gomtsari and Pirikiti valleys and tiny hamlets studding the mountains. Hike to Keselo to see five hilltop towers built during the 1230s Mongol invasions for locals to seek shelter from raiders. Restored in the twenty-first century, a couple now host museums.

## LIKE A LOCAL

### STAY

**Excellent House** 44 Gelati St, Kutaisi. Nino and her family will welcome you into their excellent hostel where unbeatable views take in Kutaisi and the mountains.

**Karvi Hostel** 69 Parnavaz Mepe St. Decent hostel in a quiet part of Batumi with a lovely inner courtyard.

**Nona's Guest House** 1 Grigol Khandzteli St, Tbilisi. Don't be misled by the uninviting facade: this family-run guesthouse is a home-from-home in Old Tbilisi with a charming inner garden.

## EAT & DRINK

**Agerari Georgian Cuisine** 1 Tsereteli St, Kutaisi; +995 599 08 87 08. This Kutaisi restaurant serves generous plates of traditional Georgian food paired with local wines and beers.

**Barbarestan** D, 132 Davit Aghmashenebeli Ave, Tbilisi 0112; +995 551 12 11 76. Descend the curving iron staircase to this chic family-owned gem in an old brick meat cellar with ageing hooks still studding the ceiling.

**Beer Alkhanaidze** 26 Teimuraz Bagrationi St, Telavi. Taste the freshest and most delicious beer in Telavi (and probably in all Kakheti) at this small local brewery. You can also buy bottles to go.

**Karalashvili Wine Cellar** 19 Vertskhli St, Tbilisi 0105; www.karalashvili.ge. One of Tbilisi's most atmospheric bars to sample a glass (or two) of Georgian wine.

**Legvi Café** Botanikuri St, Tbilisi. Hearty Georgian specialities and Saperavi wine served on an outdoor terrace with fine views of the Abanotubani district.

**Purpur** 1 Abo Tbileli St, Tbilisi 0155; +995 32 247 77 76. A charming Tbilisi restaurant decked out with mismatched tablecloths and vintage lamps.

## SHOP

**Biblusi Gallery** 2 Erekle St, Bakhtrioni St, Telavi. A beautiful bookshop where you enjoy a cup of coffee and tasty cake while reading your latest find.

**Dry Bridge Flea Market** 3 Zviad Gamsakhurdia, Tbilisi. Daily antique market dating to 1950; stalls are piled high with kitsch decorative items, retro appliances, Soviet medals, handmade products and more.

**Gallery 27** N 52 Lado Asatiani St, Tbilisi 0105. An arts and textile gallery selling handmade Georgian crafts.

**Green Bazaar** Kutaisi 4600. Fresh produce at its best. At the largest and liveliest food market in Georgia, pick up seasonal fruits and vegetables, cheeses, herbs, spices, pickles and *churchkhela* (strings of walnuts coated in grape-juice caramel).

The modern Bridge of Peace in Tbilisi

*Raststugor*, wooden shelters for campers

# WILD SWEDEN
## A Scandinavian camping adventure

Few live by the philosophy of *friluftsliv*
('free-loofts-liv') as closely as the
Swedes. The expression roughly
translates as 'open-air living' and
runs deep in Nordic culture like pine
roots. In Sweden you're entitled by
law to walk, camp, cycle, ride or ski
on other people's land, provided you
don't cause damage to crops, forest
plantations or fences; this is known
as *allemansrätten* ('freedom to roam').
Beginning and ending in Stockholm,
this flexible itinerary is proposed to
ignite your inner *friluftsliv* through
a wild camping adventure across
Sweden's national parks, nature
reserves and archipelagos.

Running south from Stockholm through five Swedish counties – Uppsala, Södermanland, Östergötland, Jönköping, Kalmar – this route reveals an ever-shifting landscape of crystalline lakes, dense forests, otherworldly fens and snow-draped mountains, all connected by an excellent public transport network.

However much the capital beckons with contemporary, urban appeal, it's impossible to ignore the call of nature from across the waters. Along the east coast, the Stockholm archipelago is made up of 24,000 islands, islets and rocks, as the mainland slowly splinters into the Baltic Sea. Among the quietest is Grinda, a nature reserve cloaked in pine and deciduous forest, clifftop paths and a coastal trail unfurling along the southeastern headland. Grinda's northern and southern piers are serviced year-round by ferry from Strömkajen, so it is possible to spend a day here, though many stay on and pitch up near the northern

jetty – the only area on the island where camping and starting fires is permitted.

Further afield in the eastern reaches of the archipelago, Svenska Högarna is the largest marine reserve in Sweden, providing resting sites for migratory birds and, come spring, a breeding ground for murre, razorbill and eider. Its cluster of weather-beaten islands and skerries is centred around Storön, a sparsely populated rocky speck that's not on the radar of public ferries (hail a water taxi or rent a boat) and feels like a world away from the capital. With a species-rich seaweed and algae belt wrapping its shoreline, and a thickly wooded interior, this is where ocean and forest collide, pervaded by a salt-tinged pine aroma. Explore the island's contours by boat before falling asleep beneath canvas for a back-to-nature retreat. Northeast of Svenska Högarna is Ängsö National Park, located within the coastal region of Roslagen,

Kayaking the Stockholm archipelago

## PRACTICAL INFORMATION

**Distance covered:** 1100km

**Recommended journey time:** 3 weeks

**Transport details:**

- Deutsche Bahn Intercity-Express connects Brussels and Hamburg (6–7hr; 19 daily; from £70; www.int.bahn.de); an Eurail or Interrail pass saves money on trips that involve multiple train journeys across Europe.
- Sj offers a EuroNight service from Hamburg to Stockholm (12–13hr; 2 daily; from £60; www.sj.se); and daily services from Stockholm to Uppsala (40min–1hr; 15–20 daily; £4); Jönköping to Kalmar (3–4hr; 9–18 daily; from £30); Kalmar to Stockholm (4hr 45min; 9–12 daily; £50); Uppsala to Gysinge Brukshandel (2hr–3hr 30min; 5–12 daily; £9) for Färnebofjärden (40min walk). Vy's trains connect Uppsala and Mariefred Hammarängen (1hr 40min; 12–19 daily; from £15; www.vy.se). Mälartåg trains connect Läggesta and Linköping (2hr 30min; 7–13 daily; from £20; www.malartag.se).
- FlixBus links Stockholm and Uppsala (1hr 20min; 3 daily; from £7; www.flixbus.com); Linköping and Gränna (1hr 5min; 1–3 daily; £5); and Kalmar and Stockholm (6hr 10min; 3–4 daily; £20). Kalmar länstrafik buses connect Kalmar and Ekerum Öland (45min; 13–32 daily; £5; www.kalmarlanstrafik.se).
- Several ferry operators connect the Stockholm archipelago, including Waxholmsbolaget, Strömma and Blidösundsbolaget. For water taxis to Svenska Högarna/Storön (1hr 50min–3hr), visit www.lansstyrelsen.se. To rent kayaks, try Skärgårdens Kanotcenter (www.kanotcenter.com), Långholmen Kajak Uthyrning (www.langholmenkajak.se) or Lek Mer (www.lekmer.nu); for yachts, Hahn Yacht Charter (www.hahnyachtcharter.com) or Charm Charter AB (www.charmcharter.se).
- If you'd rather travel by car, hire an EV at Europcar, a 9min walk from Stockholm Centralstation (from £50 per day; www.europcar.com); which allows cars to be dropped at any of its stations. Download Electromaps App for EV-charging stations.

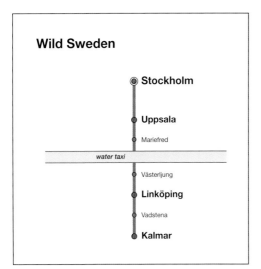

### Wild Sweden

- ◉ Stockholm
- ◉ Uppsala
- ○ Mariefred

*water taxi*

- ○ Västerljung
- ◉ Linköping
- ○ Vadstena
- ◉ Kalmar

where a rich tapestry of wildflowers blankets gently undulating pastures in the warmer months. Spring is the time for wood anemones, followed by elder-flowered orchids that thrive in the temperate climate and paint the landscape yellow and red between April and June. Hemudden, the entryway to the park, leads to Norrviken, where you'll find designated camping areas.

### JOURNEYING TO UPPSALA

Approximately 70km north of Stockholm and well-connected to the capital by road and rail, Uppsala is a vibrant university city with a Gothic cathedral and interesting museums, including the home and gardens of world-renowned botanist Carl von Linné. From here, you can catch a bus to Upplandsleden: a picturesque county-crossing hiking path that meanders 500km

from the bays of Mälardalen in the south to the Dalälven archipelago in the north. Dip in and out of the trail, using any of the 31 access points and picking between a circular or out-and-back route.

On the border of Uppsala County, Färnebofjärden is one of Sweden's more curious national parks, brimming with otherworldly eeriness. Its two hundred islands and islets support 170 of the threatened and endangered plant and animal species from Sweden's Red List, which evaluates risk of national extinction; the feisty yellow-billed ural owl among them. As with other national parks and nature reserves across Sweden, Färnebofjärden is waymarked with signs pointing toward designated areas for camping and lighting fires. Now, with a rise in drought conditions due to climate change, campfire bans are routinely imposed in Färnebofjärden (and elsewhere) through the driest months, when forests are especially flammable.

## ETHEREAL SÖDERMANLAND
Find yourself embraced in the ethereal landscapes of Stendörren Nature Reserve in just under four hours on a combined train and bus journey from Uppsala Centralstation to Mariefred Hammarängen. This maze of islands, inlets and bays, connected by bridges and wooded trails, is best explored at a leisurely pace. Tracing a line through Södermanland County on the southeast coast, the terrain is enormously diverse: coastal meadows, spruce forests, lush pastures, outcrops plastered with reindeer lichen, all ensnared by granite boulders that square up to the Baltic Sea. Pitching a tent here is forbidden but there are wind shelters for overnight stays, and designated fire pits.

Just across the water from Källviks brygga, between Nyköping and Trosa, is beautiful Sävö, an island crisscrossed with coastal nature trails twisting beneath trees. This peaceful destination can be reached by water taxi, boat (www.savogard.se), kayak or canoe, and serves as a good base for exploring the pine-clad Sörmland archipelago such as Långö, Ringsö, Hartsö and Enskär.

## ADVENTURE CAPITAL: ÖSTERGÖTLAND

Around fifty kilometres east of Norrköping, the coastline of Östergötland fragments into some nine thousand rocky outcrops, skerries and forested islands. It's an outdoor adventure playground for hikers, kayakers and wild swimmers (the Baltic Sea is surprisingly warm). You can get here by taking the train from Mariefred to Linköping Centralstation, followed by a bus (www.ostgotatrafiken.se) to Arkösund.

From here, the best way of exploring this corner of the archipelago is to board the Skärgårdslinjen passenger boat, which calls in at half a dozen islands and jetties on its way to end-of-the-line Harstena, before returning to its starting point the same day. Alternatively, you can rent a kayak or canoe (www. skargardskompaniet.se) to delve into the hidden nooks and corners of the especially wild inner St Anna archipelago, pitching a tent for a night or two on whichever deserted speck captures your imagination.

## JÖNKÖPING CULTURE

Hop on the Länstrafiken bus from Gränna hamn to Heda along Lake Vättern, Sweden's deepest and second-largest cold-water lake, and then walk 6km to the Västra Väggar viewpoint in Ekopark Omberg. Hike the park's mountain trails through beech and elm woods, before hunkering down in a wind shelter to a soundtrack of softly hooting owls. The going gets tougher and the scenery increasingly dramatic along the 6km-long Ellen Keys Trail that spirals up to the highest peak, Hjässan at 263m. Further north

Trollskogen, Öland

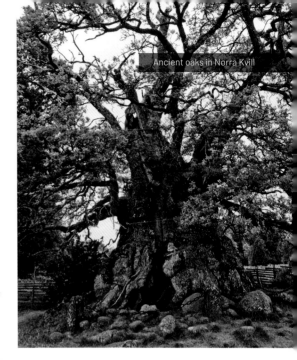
Ancient oaks in Norra Kvill

along the lake's shoreline, a sea of orchids unfurls through the Ombergsliden naturreservat, sweeping from Stocklycke through limestone-rich marshlands and spruce forests. An interesting detour is Tiveden National Park, one of the region's most splendid areas of virgin forest, northwest of Lake Vättern. Camping is permitted for one night only in the Kärringaudden, Metesjön and Mellannäsudden areas. Another worthy diversion is Vadstena, a former royal seat and monastic centre, and whose headline act is its well-preserved sixteenth-century moated castle. A tangle of twisting cobblestone streets, lined with pretty cottages covered in climbing roses, shelters an impressive fourteenth-century abbey, whose existence is the result of the passionate work of Birgitta, Sweden's first female saint.

## ÖLAND

Kalmar, huddled across a cluster of islands at the southeastern fringes of Småland, is an agreeable town with an exquisite fourteenth-century castle, Scandinavia's finest preserved Renaissance palace. From here, a 6km-long road bridge connects to Öland, a splinter-shaped island with pristine beaches, mystical forests, meadows and traditional cottages. Hop on a bike to weave past ruined castles, Bronze and Iron Age burial cairns, old wooden windmills (four hundred pepper the island), runic stones and forts. It's not just a living museum. With an old-fashioned holiday vibe and excellent bathing opportunities, it's a favoured summer hangout of Swedes.

The country's second-largest island has a unique geology: a massive limestone plain known as alvaret unfurls to the south (the rock has long been used to build runic monuments, dry-stone walls and churches); the cragged northern coastline is studded with dramatic *raukar* – stone stacks sculpted by the sea. The northeastern cape (nordöstra udde) is home to the twisted, misshapen pines and oaks of the romantically named trollskogen (trolls' forest).

Set up camp in Lindreservatet, a patchwork of wildflower meadows and boggy marshes, though you can in fact pitch your tent anywhere. Among the island's flora are rare plants such as the delicate rock rose and the wool-butter flower, both native to Southeast Asia. Beyond Öland, Kalmar County envelops the Norra Kvill National Park graced by Rumskulla oak, the largest English oak in Europe with a circumference of around fourteen metres; the equally bewitching Gränsö Naturreservat; Blå Jungfrun ('Blue Maiden'); and Björnnäsets naturreservat in Åkebosjön, a boulder-strewn pine forest steeped in the legend of trolls and Nordic folklore.

## TYRESTA NATIONAL PARK

Allow time for Tyresta National Park in Stockholm County on your return. Its deeply atmospheric walking trails tunnel through one of the largest untouched woodlands in Sweden. Mist-enshrouded lakes punctuated by pines and lichen-covered arboreal skeletons lend an ethereal quality to this primeval forest, especially in autumn, when earthy mushroom aromas compete with the balsamic-like scent of bog myrtle resin. Here, you'll find designated areas to light fires and resting places to champion one final slice of *friluftsliv* before you return home.

# SMALL PRINT

# INDEXES

# CONTRIBUTORS

**Daniel Clarke** is a British-born travel and guidebook writer who, after visiting Portugal numerous times since childhood, decided to finally stay and call the country home in 2018. With a deep love for islands, ferries, trains and more off-beat and in-depth cultural experiences, he's long been obsessed with slow travel and cherishes all the human connections made en route. Follow Daniel on Instagram @danflyingsolo.

**Catherine Edwards** is a journalist and writer who covers European news, languages and travel. Originally from Manchester, she spent six years living in Stockholm and has also lived and worked in Rome, Berlin and Vienna; she speaks French, German, Italian and Swedish. Find Catherine on Instagram @catjredwards.

**David Farley** is a food and travel writer who has travelled extensively in the Balkans. He writes regularly for the *New York Times*, *BBC Travel*, the *Wall Street Journal* and *National Geographic*, among other publications. He's the author of three books, including *An Irreverent Curiosity: In Search of the Strangest Relic in Italy's Oddest Town*, which was made into a documentary by the National Geographic Channel. Farley has lived in San Francisco, Paris, Prague, Rome, and Berlin and currently calls New York City home.

**Tom Ford** is a Salford-born features writer who has lived in London for fifteen years. He most enjoys travelling to African countries and believes you can get to the heart of a destination through eating everything and asking people questions. His work has appeared in *Mundial*, *GQ*, *Vogue*, *Evening Standard*, *Eater London* and more. Follow Tom at @tommerlinford.

An eventful overland journey from London to Beijing in mid-winter sold slow travel to **Gavin Haines**. The West Midlands-born writer has since stepped things down a gear and these days,

travels almost exclusively by rail and bike. He writes mostly about Britain and the cycle-friendly Netherlands, and his work has been published by the BBC, *National Geographic* and *The Telegraph*, among others. Follow Gavin on X (formerly Twitter) at @gavin_haines.

**Laura Hall** is a Copenhagen-based travel, food and culture writer who specialises in uncovering authentic and responsibly led stories about Scandinavia and the Nordics. Her work appears in publications including *BBC Travel*, *Kinfolk*, *The Times*, *Sunday Times* and many more. You can follow her travels via her substack Modern Scandinavian.

Born in the United States, raised in Canada and now based in the UK, **Ellen Himelfarb** has led a life on the move. She's explored Western Africa, lived in China and island-hopped around the Norwegian Sea, but her time in Western Estonia felt as far-flung as any. Her writing appears regularly in British broadsheet newspapers and magazines, including *National Geographic Traveller (UK)* – as well as the Canadian press. Find Ellen online @ellenhimelfarb.

**Paula Hotti** is a Finnish travel journalist and author with a penchant for train journeys and road trips. She spent more than six years not flying and still prefers slow travel over quick trips. Her work has appeared in publications like *Lonely Planet*, *Sunday Times*, *DK Eyewitness*, and many more. Follow Paula on Instagram at @retrotravels.

**Gemma Lake** is a UK-born, England-based travel writer and PhD student of contemporary women's travel writing. She has travelled throughout Europe, most recently in the north where she developed a strong connection with the nature of Scandinavia. Follow Gemma on X (formerly Twitter) at @gemroxlake.

Teacher-turned-travel-writer **Doug Loynes** broke into journalism after winning a *National Geographic* writing competition in 2020. Since then, he has shared stories from all seven continents for titles including *BBC Wildlife*, *Wanderlust* and *National Geographic Traveller*. Follow him on Instagram at @Instdougramm.

**Imogen Malpas** is a London-based journalist whose work has appeared in *The Guardian*, *Atmos*, *DJ Mag*, *Clash* and many others. Having lived across four continents, she's passionate about introducing readers to unexpected wonders in well-travelled locations. She's the founder of Club SOL, a collective helping people to connect to their roots through culture, community and creativity. Follow her work on Instagram at @clubsol.

**Justin McDonnell** is a London-based travel and culture writer. He lived in Croatia for several years, working as the editor of *Time Out*, throwing himself headfirst into Balkan life and experiencing all the incredible joys Croatia has to offer. His work has appeared in publications like *Thrillist*, *Time Out*, *Atlas Obscura*, *Lonely Planet* and many more. Follow Justin on X (formerly Twitter) @justinmcdonnel.

**Kieran Meeke** lives in Ireland's Kerry, and Granada in Spain. He is a keen hiker and cyclist who enjoys exploring the mountains of both countries. Born in Northern Ireland, he has worked in media in Belfast, Maputo, Dublin, London, and Amsterdam. As a travel writer, his favourite country is "the next one". Follow him on Instagram @kieran_meeke.

**Emerson Mendoza Ayala** is a travel and investigative journalist from Spain who specialises in environmental research on the Iberian Peninsula, particularly sustainability and culture. He has slow-travelled Europe by land and sea, from the Mediterranean to the Black, Baltic and Norwegian seas. Follow Emerson on Instagram @emetheglobetrotter.

**Tom Peeters** is a Belgian-born writer who specialises in (slow) travel, the outdoors, and nature conservation. In the dark winter of 2016, a writing residency brought him for the first time to rural Finland, where he learned to appreciate sahti (farmhouse ale) and sauna. He has since returned multiple times, always travelling by train, bus or hitchhiking. Read more of Tom's work on www.volcanolove.org or follow him on Instagram at @tomas_paradise.

**Joanna Reeves** is a Sussex-based travel writer and Rough Guides editor who has updated several Rough Guides for destinations she is passionate about, including Skye and the Outer Hebrides, Porto and Reykjavík. She came up with the original concept for this brand-new *Rough Guide to Slow Travel in Europe*, having long had an interest in train travel and sustainability, and has worked on the book from commission to completion.

**Eleanor Ross** is an adventure travel writer living in Scotland. She has spent many summers cycling and travelling through the Arctic and the world's colder places. Her work has been published in publications from *The Guardian* to *BBC Travel*, through to *National Geographic Traveller* and *Newsweek*. Follow Ellie @ellie_ross_outdoors_.

**Sarah Ryan** is a Sheffield-based freelance writer who regularly pens features on nature, wildlife and UK travel. She's had work published in *Trail Magazine*, *Country Walking*, *The Guardian*, *Wanderlust*, *Trail Running* and *BBC Countryfile*. As a qualified mountain leader, she's spent over a decade roaming the high and wild places of England, Scotland and Wales and this spring completed the 400km Cape Wrath Trail.

**Pavan Shamdasani** was born in Dubai, raised in Hong Kong and has lived in New York, London, Florence, Ho Chi Minh City and, now, Budapest. He has written on travel, culture and lifestyle for *TIME*, BBC, CNN, *The Economist*, *Fodor's* and more. He has also contributed to guidebooks on his favourite cities, and is currently working on a book-length history of his favourite Hong Kong video game.

**Paul Sullivan** is a British freelance writer, editor and author, living in Berlin since 2008. He has written and updated over a dozen guidebooks for Rough Guides, *Wallpaper*, DK, *National Geographic* and others, and his work regularly appears in *The Guardian*, *Telegraph Travel*, *Sunday Times Travel* and *Matador Network*. He also runs sustainable portal www.slowtravelberlin.com. Find him on Twitter or Instagram @slowberlin.

Travel writer, editor and tour guide **Jeroen van Marle** grew up in England, studied geography in the Netherlands, learnt Romanian, and hitchhiked everywhere between Sofia and St Petersburg, bribing a Russian consul with cognac for a fast-track visa. He started his writing career with the InYourPocket.com city guide to Bucharest in the 1990s, moving 28 times between eight countries across three continents since then. Particularly fond of Albania, Jeroen wrote guidebooks to Tirana, Shkodra, Gjirokastra and Korça, and even took his new bride on a 4WD honeymoon trip across the country. He has worked on multiple Rough Guides titles, including the *Rough Guide to the 100 Best Places on Earth*. He tweets at @jeroenvanmarle.

**Peter Watson** is a travel writer and founder of outdoor travel blog *Atlas & Boots*. A keen trekker and climber, he can usually be found on the trails of the Greater Ranges of Asia. He's visited over one hundred countries and all seven continents. He is currently focused on climbing the seven summits – the highest mountain on every continent. Follow him at @atlasandboots.

# ACKNOWLEDGEMENTS

**Catherine Edwards** would like to thank the Rough Guides team and the people (and pastries) of Sweden. Special thanks to Jade, Lara and Sam, and most of all my partner Jason, for all the adventures.

**Tom Ford** would like to thank his father, Fred, for introducing him to the bothies of Scotland and the wild nature of the Highlands almost three decades ago, and for instilling his obsessive need to walk the path less travelled. He would also like to thank the people of Cape Wrath for the privileged insight into their lifestyle and for their generous cooperation in the making of this feature.

**Gavin Haines** would like to give special mention to his wife Imogen, who completed the journey he wrote about in this book while carrying their son Zach. He could not do his work without her support. Gavin is also grateful to the visionary Dutch for crisscrossing their land with cycle lanes before it was fashionable. He'd also like to give thanks to Rough Guides editor Jo Reeves for the commission, and his family and friends for their support.

**Laura Hall** would like to thank Súsanna Sørensen at Visit Faroe Islands for all her help, every sheep that stepped into the path of her car as she toured the archipelago, the weather gods for shining on her, and her family for being accepting and supportive of her insatiable wanderlust.

**Paula Hotti** would like to thank Eurail for providing global passes for her train trips around Europe. She also extends her gratitude to the Rough Guides team, especially editor Jo Reeves, and the keen rail travellers' communities who are always quick and eager to help with practicalities.

**Gemma Lake** would like to thank the people of Sweden for preserving the beauty of this country and giving people around the world the right to roam freely in its green spaces. She extends thanks to the highly talented and welcoming team at Rough Guides, in particular editor Jo Reeves who has worked tirelessly to pull this environment-oriented title together.

**Doug Loynes** owes his interest in Romanian culture and history to the Roma children he taught in his hometown of Manchester, whose playful spirit and boundless enthusiasm belie the persecution their people have faced – and continue to face – at home and across Europe.

**Kieran Meeke** thanks the wonderful people of the Kingdom of Kerry for exceeding every cliché about Irish hospitality. Their warmth is matched all along Ireland's west coast by people who have a deserved pride in the beauty of their landscapes, towns and villages. *Go raibh míle maith agat* (Thank you very much).

**Imogen Malpas**: thanks to the fantastic Jo Reeves, whose diligent work has been invaluable in bringing this guide to life, as well as to the hosts of featured locations in this guide who responded to my doubtless tiring questioning with warmth and generosity.

**Justin McDonnell** would like to thank the awesome team at Rough Guides, especially the lovely editor Jo Reeves. Thank you also to Morgan, Ronan, Elvis, Holly, Beth, Flami and Jack – you supported me through a turbulent year and helped me get back on the road again. Thanks also to my fellow travel writers PJ Cresswell and Jonathan Bousfield; I learned from the best.

**Joanna Reeves** would lile to thank all of the writers who have contributed to this brand-new *Rough Guide to Slow Travel* with their inspiring ideas, original writing and shared passion for sustainable travel. Thanks also to Tom and Piotr for working on the imagery and creating a beautiful backdrop for our words, to Siobhan for her eagle-eye proofreading, Katie for her patience with the cartography, and Rebeka for her production prowess. Finally, thanks to Brooke Harrison-Davies and the team at Gosh PR for pulling together such an incredible slow journey through Austria's Wachau Valley and to VisitScotland for all their help and advice.

**Eleanor Ross** thanks Laura Laatikainen for sharing the Finnish Lake District with her and letting her stay in her family cabin, and also to the team at Rough Guides for the brilliant editing and ideas. Thanks also to Rory M and Mabel for keeping the fort warm back home.

**Tom Peeters** would like to thank all his Finnish friends who have invited him to saunas, on hikes, for coffee with *pulla* (cardamom bread) or to barbecues. Special shout-out to Janne, whose *mökki* (cottage) in Virrat offered a great break during this Arctic odyssey. Thanks also to the people who make the trains run and all the ever-friendly bus drivers up north. And to Lief, Ronny, Kim and Anete.

**Pavan Shamdasani**: Thanks to the Romanian and Moldovan railways for keeping a Soviet relic alive, intentionally or otherwise. Thanks to the folks at Rough Guides (honestly my favourite guidebooks) and editor Joanna Reeves. And thanks to Europe for being so much more than most tourists realise.

**Jeroen van Marle** would like to thank Elton at Albanian Trip, Roza at Nord Albania, and Catherine at Journey to Valbona for their insights and their invaluable contributions to promoting sustainable travel in Albania.

# PHOTO CREDITS

(**Key:** T-top; C-centre; B-bottom; L-left; R-right)

**Abacatus Farmhouse - Tavira** 205
**Beca's Kitchen** 65
**Belgrade Urban Distillery** 37
**Clay Gilliland/Flickr** 63
**DominguezVieira/Nau Palatina** 202
**Eco Resort & Winery Cermeniza** 36
**Gwenael AKIRA Helmsdal Carre/Heima í Stovu** 16
**Heckmann Dirk/imageBROKER/Shutterstock** 206
**Hotel Soča** 88
**Juho Kuva/Visit Finland** 210
**Kealy's Seafood Bar** 133
**Kuanza** 142
**Mackay's Rooms** 43
**Mariana Lopes/Azul Singular** 143
**Pilguse estate** 26
**Piotr Kala** 4CB, 170, 173
**Rasmus Malmstrøm/Mikkeller** 17
**Shutterstock** 4T, 4TC, 4B, 8, 10, 12, 15, 18, 20, 23, 24, 25, 27, 28, 30, 33, 34, 35, 38, 40, 46, 47, 50, 53, 55, 56, 58, 60, 64, 66, 68, 70, 73, 75, 76, 79, 80, 82, 84, 87, 89, 90, 92, 95, 96, 97, 98, 100, 103, 105, 106, 107, 108, 109, 110, 112, 115, 116, 117, 118, 120, 122, 124, 127, 128, 129, 130, 131, 134, 136, 138, 139, 140, 141, 144, 147, 148, 151, 152, 153, 154, 157, 159, 160, 161, 162, 164, 166, 168, 169, 174, 177, 179, 180, 181, 182, 184, 186, 187, 189, 190, 191, 192, 194, 197, 198, 199, 201, 203, 208, 212, 215, 216, 217, 218, 220, 223, 224, 225, 226, 227, 228, 229, 230, 233, 234, 236, 237, 238, 239, 240, 242, 244, 247, 248, 249, 250, 251, 252, 254, 256, 258, 259, 260, 261, 262, 264, 267, 268, 269, 270, 271, 272, 274, 277, 278, 279
**Toni Zorić** 44, 49
**Traditional Dream Factory** 204
**Werney Beyer Consulting** 74

**Cover** View over the Atlantic Ocean Road (Atlanterhavsveien) in Norway **Giedrius Akelis/Shutterstock**

# INDEX